Military Power and Popular Protest

Military Power and Popular Protest

The U.S. Navy in Vieques, Puerto Rico

Katherine T. McCaffrey

Rutgers University Press

New Brunswick, New Jersey, and London

Library of Congress Cataloging-in-Publication Data

McCaffrey, Katherine T., 1966–
    Military power and popular protest : the U.S. Navy in Vieques, Puerto Rico
/ Katherine T. McCaffrey.
        p. cm.
    Includes bibliographical references and index.
    ISBN 0-8135-3090-3 (cloth : alk. paper) — ISBN 0-8135-3091-1
(pbk. : alk. paper)
        1. Vieques Island (P.R.)—History—20th century. 2. Protest movements—
    Puerto Rico—Vieques Island—History—20th century. 3. United States.
    Navy—Target practice—History—20th century. 4. Civil-military relations—
    Puerto Rico—Vieques Island—History—20th century. 5. Government,
    Resistance to—Puerto Rico—Vieques Island—History—20th century. I. Title.

F1981.V5 M33 2002
972.95'9—dc21

                                                                            2001048838

British Cataloging-in-Publication data for this book is available from the British
Library.

Manufactured in the United States of America

For Howard and our children, Benjamin and Julia

Contents

Preface

When I first traveled to the Puerto Rican island of Vieques in the summer of 1991, the U.S. Navy, at war with squatters, had secured the contested boundaries of its western perimeter with tall cyclone fences, rimmed with coils of razor wire. Behind navy fences stood a majestic old Ceiba tree. The Ceiba recalls the forest that once covered Vieques before sugar cane fields and navy bulldozers cut across the terrain. Its massive, buttressed root system has anchored this huge tree against the fury of countless tropical storms. The Ceiba came to symbolize for me the beauty and resilience of the people who struggle to live on this island.

Ten years later the fences that delimited the Ceiba were torn down. In response to a widespread popular movement, the navy relinquished one-third of its landholdings in Vieques. Under an agreement reached by U.S. president Bill Clinton and Puerto Rican governor Pedro Rosselló, eight thousand acres of land under military jurisdiction returned to civilian authorities in June 2001. The reversion of land suggested how dramatically the course of Vieques's history had changed in one decade.

I first came to Vieques with the support of an Alexander C. Naclerio Award from the City University of New York Graduate School for research in housing and urban studies and a graduate research fellowship from Intercambio, the City University of New York–University of Puerto Rico exchange program. Because I was interested in squatting as a social movement in Puerto Rico, a number of colleagues had suggested I look at Vieques. Just two years earlier, in 1989, two hundred families on the island had seized eight hundred acres of land under the jurisdiction of the U.S. Navy and built an organized settlement that was ultimately wiped out later that year by Hurricane Hugo. I was intrigued by the boldness of the action and by the fact that the disputed land was controlled by the navy. I soon learned that this battle was only one chapter of a much longer story.

In the summer of 1992 I conducted documentary research on Vieques at the Centro de Estudios Puertorriqueños, Hunter College; the New York Public Library; and the Library of Congress, again with the support of an Intercambio graduate research fellowship. I was interested in gaining a historical and contextual sense of Vieques both in relation to Puerto Rico and in relation to other military bases. I learned about the grassroots mobilization that had erupted in opposition to the navy in the late 1970s, championed by island fishermen.

In October 1993 I returned to Vieques to spend a year conducting fieldwork with a doctoral dissertation research grant from the Intercambio program. The core of my project was ethnographic research. From October 1993 to September 1994, I lived with a local woman on the island. I observed and participated in daily activities and events. I formally interviewed over one hundred residents and conversed informally with many others. I conducted additional documentary research at the Archivo Histórico, Fuerte Conde de Mirasol, in Vieques; La Colección Puertorriqueña, at the University of Puerto Rico; the documentation center of the Proyecto Caribeño de Justicia y Paz; and the files of the Misión Industrial in Puerto Rico.

Several basic concerns guided my work. The first was an interest in understanding the local political, economic, and cultural context that had been such a fertile ground for protest and discontent. The second was an interest in analyzing the antimilitary movement of the 1970s that was a key expression of the discord. Finally, I was interested in understanding the current status of the conflict and its implications for future action.

When I returned to New York, I conducted additional research on the role of U.S.-based support groups in sustaining the antinavy movement in Vieques. With the continued support of the Intercambio program, I interviewed U.S.-based activists in New York, Washington, D.C., and Philadelphia on their involvement in solidarity work and their perceptions of the movement in Vieques. This research became the basis of an article (McCaffrey 1998) and sharpened my understanding of both the politics of the local movement and the solidarity network.

I returned to Vieques in the summers of 1995, 1997, 1999, and 2000. During these shorter visits I conducted additional interviews and attended political meetings, rallies, demonstrations, and other events. I visited the encampments on the bombing range and attended vigils and church meetings.

Over the years I have found that people are curious to know how this *gringa* ended up in Vieques. Quite a few people there suspected that my dark-haired husband must be Puerto Rican (he is not); why else would an *americana* be interested in their lives? My interest in Vieques stems not from my own ethnic background, but from my sense that the story of this small island speaks to vital historical and contemporary political realities: Puerto Rico's enduring colonial status, the power of the U.S. military, and the relationship of the military to civil society are topics that demand attention.

From a personal standpoint, it has been remarkable to witness this dramatic popular mobilization unfold. When I first stepped off the ferry in 1991, I would never have guessed that this quiet, rural island would become a pilgrimage spot for leading New York politicians and that the Rev. Al Sharpton would one day languish in federal prison for his role in supporting Vieques's struggle. Since 1999 Viequenses have dramatically presented their grievances to a world audience. This book presents a historical account of this popular mobilization. It is motivated, ultimately, by the hope that one day soon islanders will achieve a long overdue measure of justice.

This account emerges from a decade's acquaintance with the island's struggles and a long-term relationship with island residents. I have watched people who accepted the status quo emerge as daily participants in picket lines and prayer vigils. I have seen local activists metamorphose into international celebrities. In this light, it seems awkward to use pseudonyms when quoting individuals I interviewed. This work, however, draws on data that extends back to the early nineties, when people were not as bold and eager to be identified. I promised individuals anonymity then, and have elected to abide by that commitment by using pseudonyms throughout the book, except where drawing from the historical record. Likewise, I have used pseudonyms to preserve the anonymity of navy officials who were generous with their time and spoke with candor, but did not want their comments to be construed as official. I trust that the people of Vieques who have struggled for a future for their island will find themselves in these pages.

Acknowledgments

This book is the result of many years of work, and along the way I have accumulated many debts. I could not have conducted my research without the vital support of the Intercambio program at Hunter College. I am extremely grateful to the staff, to Frank Bonilla, and especially to Antonio Lauria for his support and encouragement from the beginning. My thanks go also to my editor, David Myers, at Rutgers University Press for his enthusiasm for my work and his careful guidance in bringing this project to fruition.

In Vieques, I thank Robert Rabin for his generosity, hospitality, and friendship. Bob found me a place to live, introduced me to many people, and guided me through the Archivo Histórico de Vieques. He has answered many questions and given me inestimable help. I am grateful as well to his partner, Nilda Medina, for her warmth and generosity.

Matilde Rivera Belardo was the bedrock of my Vieques experience. She shared with me her deep love of the island, its seasons and colors and rhythms. The day I arrived in her home off the ferry from Puerto Rico she had a pot of chicken soup waiting for me, a sure tonic for a queasy stomach. When I apologized that I was a vegetarian and couldn't eat the meal she had thoughtfully prepared, she took my quirks in stride. For the next year she prepared and shared with me rice and beans, noting that a vegetarian diet was probably good for her as well. With these meals, Matilde communicated a warmth and a generosity of spirit that still move me and connect me to Vieques. I am very thankful for her friendship and the sustenance she provided while I lived with her. I express my appreciation as well to her brothers and sisters, especially Raúl, Isolina, and Nery, for keeping me on my toes and teaching me so much about Vieques.

My gratitude goes also to Mario Solís, who not only helped me considerably with my research but filled my knapsack with mangoes and coconuts from his yard. Mario, his wife, Nilda Suárez, and their children, Mario Hijo, Edwin, and Alexia, became dear friends. Their home is among my children's favorite places on the island. My deepest thanks to Mario and his family for all their help, kindness, and generosity.

Many Viequenses spent hours with me discussing their life histories, their analysis of local politics, and their feelings about the military. I am particularly grateful to Charlie Connelly, Ismael Guadalupe, Daniel Medina, Myrna Pagán, José Rivera, Rafael Rivera Castaño, and the late Lula Tirado for the time they took to talk with me and for their encouragement of my research. Thanks also to Jenny Benítez, José Brignoni, Ernesto Calzada, Judith Conde, José García, Pablo Hernández, the late Nana Ortiz de Castaño, Manuel Otero, Rubén Reyes, Carlos Rivera, Emilia Santiago, Juan Silva, the late Mary Simmons, Miriam Sobá, Radamés Tirado, Carlos Vélez, Carlos Ventura, and Carlos and Leidi Zenón. I am further indebted to all of the members of the Comité pro Rescate y Desarrollo de Vieques, the Navy League, the Vieques Conservation and Historic Trust, the Naval Sea Cadets, and the students at the Germán Rieckehoff High School who shared with me their opinions and ideas.

I am saddened that a number of Viequenses who spoke to me and helped me have fallen ill or died of cancer. Among them I remember Elías García, Esaul Sánchez, Lula Tirado, and Vero Ventura as individuals with a great love for Vieques and a commitment to seeing it whole.

In Puerto Rico, I thank Judith Berkan, Liliana Cotto, Humberto García, Neftalí García, and especially Juan Giusti for sharing with me their opinions and insight. Juan was particularly generous with his time and friendship and pushed me to take my analysis to a deeper level.

I am also appreciative of those institutions and staff in Puerto Rico that assisted me with my research. The Colección Puertorriqueña of the University of Puerto Rico, the Proyecto Caribeño de Justicia y Paz, the Misión Industríal, Servicios Científico y Técnico, the Vieques Catholic Church, and, most important, the Archivo Histórico de Vieques all provided critical resources and assistance.

In the States I am grateful for the help of the staff at the Centro de Estudios Puertorriqueños at Hunter College, and particularly Ramon Bosque for his time. Thanks also to the staff at the Center for Defense Information in Washington, D.C., for their guidance and to Admirals Eugene Carroll and John Shanahan for kindly fielding my questions. I am eternally grateful to Kathleen Murphy at the Maplewood Memorial Library for her attentiveness in tracking down numerous books for me, as well as to the rest of the staff for helping me find quiet corners in the library in which to work.

In New York, I would like to thank Ida Susser, Marc Edelman, the late Delmos Jones, and the late William Roseberry for the vital guidance and encouragement they gave me in the early stages of this project. I also thank my friends and colleagues at the City University of New York— Cristiana Bastos, Arlene Dávila, Jonathan Hearn, Yvonne Lassalle, Maureen O'Dougherty, and Ara Wilson—for insightful criticism of earlier versions of the manuscript. Special thanks must go to Anthony Marcus and Charles Menzies, who have always supported my work. I am indebted as well to Alcira Forero for the hours she worked with me, sharpening my translations of interviews conducted in Spanish.

The manuscript benefited from the careful reading and criticism of a number of colleagues to whom I am deeply grateful. César Ayala, Flavio Cumpiano, Marc Edelman, Olga Jiménez de Wagenheim, Luis Martínez Fernández, Charles Menzies, Dennis Sherman, Kal Wagenheim, and an anonymous reader all provided invaluable comments and advice. Special thanks to César Ayala and Kal Wagenheim for sharing with me what they know about Vieques and Puerto Rican politics.

My final thanks go to my family for their constant encouragement. My parents, Tim and Jane McCaffrey, and my in-laws, Jerry and Sheila Fischer, have provided many years of emotional and material support. Special thanks to my mother for rescuing me when my childcare crashed in the final stages of the book's completion. My brothers, aunts, uncles, and grandparents were always supportive and interested in my research. My aunt Martha Schwope provided inestimable help, thoroughly copyediting and cutting the manuscript to size. Thanks also to Christine Haselwarter and Kerstin Sachs, who traveled to Vieques with me and lovingly tended my children while I worked.

My husband, Howard Fischer, deserves much credit, not only for juggling his own responsibilities at work with full-time weekend care for our children but for midnight shifts as the invaluable "chapter doctor." All the berry-picking escapades, movies, canoe trips, and visits to the local bowling alley with our children have given me much needed quiet, but left him in a state of chronic exhaustion. This book is lovingly dedicated to him and to our children, Benjamin and Julia, that they might learn about the struggle for social justice.

Acronyms and Spanish Terms

agregado	Squatter on private land, landless tenant
arepas	Savory fried biscuits
central	Sugar-processing complex, including mill and land
colono	Independent sugar grower
independentista	Supporter of Puerto Rican independence
jíbaro	Subsistence-producing peasant, a national symbol
PIP	Partido Independentista Puertorriqueño (also known as the pro-independence party)
PNP	Partido Nuevo Progresista (also known as the prostatehood party)
PPD	Partido Popular Democrático (also known as the pro-Commonwealth party)
PSP	Partido Socialista Puertorriqueño (Puerto Rican Socialist Party)
patronales	Patron saint festival
pípiolo	Member of the PIP
plena	A form of folk music with African roots that often comments on and satirizes contemporary events.
popular	Member of the PPD
ROTC	Reserve Officer Training Corps
ROTHR	Relocatable-Over-The-Horizon-Radar
VCHT	Vieques Conservation and Historic Trust

Military Power and Popular Protest

Introduction

The marshals came in the early morning darkness, wearing bullet-proof vests and black helmets, heavily armed with automatic weaponry. They handcuffed teachers, fishermen, housewives, politicians, artists, and Catholic priests. For more than a year, demonstrators had lived in tents and little wooden houses on the bombing range. They blocked the gates to the navy base with church pews and held nightly prayer vigils by candlelight. They covered the chain-link fence to the base with white ribbons, a petition for peace and an end to the bombing. They set up makeshift kitchens under burlap tarps and dished out rice and beans for hundreds of visitors who came to support the effort. For more than a year, demonstrators halted military maneuvers on this small, inhabited island, blocking the planet's most powerful armed forces.

Zoraída López, a sixty-year-old island resident, was one of those taken into custody that morning. She recalled the moment when the SWAT teams descended upon elderly demonstrators who had been camped out through the night at the entrance to the base: "We were a group of mature people who were willing, anxious, to make a real international statement about the feeling of the people, *ni una bomba más* [not one more bomb], and we'll be elegant about it, we will be clear. I didn't go out there to be arrested; I went out there to be with the people. . . . All of a sudden they came down with bulletproof vests, gas masks, plastic shields at their faces and *armed to the teeth*. And we were out there singing religious hymns together, 'God is watching over us.' This was a question of human dignity."

In the summer of 2000, a wall of armed Puerto Rican policemen in bulletproof vests guarded the entrance to the base. They were large and muscular, wearing black glasses and iron expressions. The chain-link fence demarcating the base's entrance had been moved forward fifty feet to the edge of the street. The protest camp had relocated across the street from the base, a shell of the vibrant city that was dismantled earlier that May morning. But every Saturday night the protest still came to life in a lively picket outside the gates to Camp García. Women with curlers in their hair and old men with canes circled and danced a musical picket to the beat of *plena*, chanting "*que se vaya la marina*," we want the navy out of Vieques.

This book tells the story of a grassroots movement against the U.S. Navy's live-bombing exercises on a small Puerto Rican island municipality. Although Vieques Island is the site of one of the navy's key military installations in the Western Hemisphere, it is simultaneously the home of nearly ten thousand American citizens. The navy asserts that the Vieques installation plays a crucial role in naval training and national defense. The civilian community of Vieques argues that the military control of land and live-fire exercises have caused severe ecological destruction, cancer and other health problems, and overwhelming social and economic crises.

This community struggle is also a more fundamental story of power and resistance, of ordinary people in conflict with global forces. The story of Vieques is one of a people struggling to maintain a viable community where they can work, live, and raise children. This most basic story is at the heart of a more complicated tale involving the strategic requirements of the most powerful military in the world and the colonial relationship between the United States and Puerto Rico.

Vieques has thus proved one of the most intractable conflicts between the U.S. military and a civilian host community. Despite a series of compromises reached by leading navy, U.S., and Puerto Rican officials, the protest against the naval presence in Vieques continues. The historical roots and progression of this conflict reveal why a resolution remains so elusive.

The Naval Presence on Vieques

The central contradiction of the story is that a small rural community of roughly ten thousand people is situated on the same island the U.S. Navy uses for a bombing range. Vieques is an island municipality of the Commonwealth of Puerto Rico, a nonsovereign territory of the United States. Its residents are U.S. citizens who serve in the U.S. armed forces and can be drafted to fight in times of war, but who have neither political representation in Congress nor the right to vote for president. Military strategy and colonial politics have turned Viequenses' home into a surreal battlefield, an inhabited island doubling as an international theater of war.

In Vieques, the navy rehearses amphibious landing exercises, parachute drops, and submarine maneuvers. It conducts artillery and small arms firing, naval gunfire support, and missile shoots. The navy bombs the island from air, land, and sea. Vieques is the navy's declared "university of the sea," a small island target range situated next to 195,000 square miles of ocean and airspace controlled by the military for so-called integrated training scenarios. Vieques, the navy claims, provides a unique venue for the realistic training of U.S. troops, one of the few places where different naval units on the East Coast can come together to prepare for combat.

Furthermore, the navy argues that Vieques is crucial not only to the battle readiness of its Atlantic Fleet but to the training of U.S., NATO, South American, and Caribbean allied forces. Thousands of U.S. and allied troops invade Vieques during large-scale maneuvers, or "war games." Since 1992 alone, the U.S. military has rehearsed interventions in the Balkans, Haiti, Iraq, and Somalia in Vieques. The training of military forces on Vieques, the navy asserts, is essential to protect U.S. interests, meet national security commitments, and ensure the readiness and safety of military personnel. The navy argues that the island is crucial to national defense.[1]

The Civilian Presence in Vieques

The navy notes that Vieques is only one of a number of civilian communities living side by side with the military. The geography of the situation, however, makes this case unique (see map 1). Vieques is a fifty-one-square-mile island, roughly twice the size of Manhattan, where residents live wedged between an ammunition depot and a maneuver area. The navy has taken control of two-thirds of island land, squeezing a civilian residential community into its center. Residents frequently refer to Vieques as a ham sandwich and see themselves as lunchmeat between thick slices of bread.[2]

In Vieques, schoolchildren in starched uniforms laugh and play at recess while automatic-weapons fire echoes in the town plaza. People go about their daily routines as helicopters cut across the horizon and warships prowl the coastline. The rhythm of everyday life is punctuated by the thunder of bombs.

Although the navy maintains no formal jurisdiction over the civilian sector, in reality it controls the fate of the entire island. The navy controls the majority of the land, water, and air surrounding Vieques. It controls nautical routes, flight paths, aquifers, and zoning laws in civilian territory. For decades the navy held title to the resettlement tracts in the civilian sector, where the majority of the island's population lived under constant threat of eviction.

The navy has long maintained ambivalence toward island residents. It has regarded the socioeconomic development of the island as a threat to naval

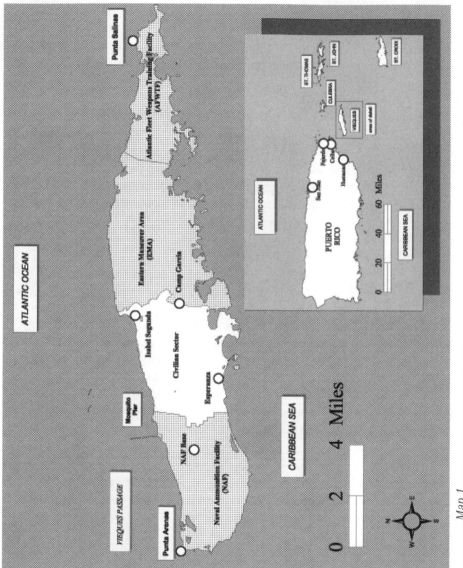

Map 1
Vieques, Puerto Rico

operations and actively thwarted development plans in the civilian sector. In the 1960s, the navy secretly planned to remove civilians from Vieques and relocate them elsewhere. A presidential order prevented the navy from evicting residents, but left unresolved the underlying tension between military interests and the human needs of the community. For decades, people in Vieques have lived helter-skelter and uncertain while the navy carefully orchestrated the movement of thousands of troops, the testing of weapons, the business of war.

Recent Conflict

During the 1990s the long-running dispute between the navy and the community continued to simmer. This "cold peace" finally ended near the decade's conclusion. In April 1999 a navy jet on a training mission mistakenly dropped its load of five-hundred-pound bombs not on the intended target range but on the military observation post one mile away. The explosions injured one guard and killed a civilian employee of the base, David Sanes Rodríguez.

Outrage over the death of Sanes reignited the decades-long conflict. Protestors occupied a military target range littered with live ordnance and built little wooden houses on hills pierced with missiles. They slept in hammocks strung from the barrel of a battered tank and ferried food back and forth in small, weathered fishing boats. They staked Puerto Rican flags in the muddy craters left by bombs and covered an entire hillside with white crosses, naming the hill Monte David (Mount David), after David Sanes. The white crosses symbolized all those Viequenses who have died of cancer—poisoned, people here believe, by air, land, and water contaminated by decades of bombing.

The death of Sanes spurred a wider mobilization that led tens of thousands of Puerto Ricans to march in the streets of San Juan, Puerto Rico's capital city, demanding a halt to military training exercises in Vieques. Puerto Ricans across the United States organized rallies and marches to stop the bombing of Vieques. The nonviolent resistance movement has drawn the support of prominent Puerto Rican celebrities, artists, and U.S. politicians as well as Nobel Peace Prize winners Rigoberta Menchú and the Dalai Lama. Vieques has been the focus of international solidarity efforts from Seoul, Korea, to Okinawa, Japan, to India and Europe. Hundreds of protestors have been arrested for acts of civil disobedience on the island. Prominent U.S. political figures such as Congressman Luis Gutiérrez, environmental lawyer Robert Kennedy, Jr., and New York political activist Rev. Al Sharpton have been jailed for trespassing on federal land during demonstrations on Vieques. Protest temporarily halted all military activity at this central training facility for over a year and continues to disrupt naval training exercises.

A Colonial Dilemma

Protest against the navy in Vieques has focused international attention on the contradiction posed by U.S. advocacy for global democracy and human rights and the U.S. Navy's apparent subordination of a community of
American citizens with no voice in the U.S. federal government. "This is part
racism, and in part environmental racism," argues Ivan Meléndez, a forty-year-
old fisherman and antinavy activist. "The navy is doing things here that it would
never do in the States. Leaving its garbage here, destroying our environment.
Getting paid by other countries to leave its garbage here."

While the navy is quick to argue the necessity of Vieques to national defense, Meléndez's comments highlight an aspect of Vieques's subordination
that the navy is less quick to acknowledge. Vieques makes good economic
sense for the military. Although in many countries the U.S. military pays rent
or "permission cost" for access to land, the navy pays no fees to Puerto Rico
for the base in Vieques.[3] Neither does it pay taxes or contribute financially in
any way to this municipality that has been impoverished by the expropriation
of two-thirds of its land and the strangling of its entire economic base. On the
contrary, the municipality acts as a source of revenue for the U.S. military. The
navy rents out Vieques to foreign militaries to bomb, earning by its own estimates $80 million per year.[4]

"I think if this were happening in Manhattan, or if it were happening in
Martha's Vineyard, certainly the delegations from those states would make
certain that this would not continue," says former Puerto Rican governor Pedro
Rosselló.[5] Statehood proponents in Puerto Rico note that political pressure
forced the navy to close its live bombing range in Kaho'olawe, Hawaii, an un-
inhabited island in a U.S. state, while protestors and politicians have been unable to leverage a similar deal for the inhabited island of Vieques, a U.S.
possession. The navy responds that Vieques is only one of fifty-seven military
training sites in the United States using live or inert ordnance, and that the
burden borne by Vieques citizens is no different from that of other American
citizens in locations with full congressional representation (U.S. Navy 1999).

It is clear, however, that a different set of standards governs military activity in Vieques and exercises in the mainland United States. In 1997 the Environmental Protection Agency ordered a halt to live and dummy artillery
shelling at the Massachusetts Military Reservation on Cape Cod when evidence
showed that explosive fallout was contaminating the water supply.[6] Yet for years
environmental officials have recognized the contamination of Vieques's coastal
waters and drinking supply as a result of the navy bombing, and no comparable action has been taken.[7]

The restructuring of the U.S. military in the aftermath of the cold war has stimulated a wave of base closures and new scrutiny of the material effects of the U.S. military on its surrounding communities. Scientists have discovered significant environmental contamination caused by the most routine military activity, raising troubling questions about both the extent of contamination at firing ranges like the one in Vieques and the scope of a cleanup. Here thousands of tons of unexploded ordnance have accumulated over decades, with staggering implications for the environment and the health and safety of the civilian population.

It is not only the extent of bombing that poses problems in Vieques, but also the nature of military testing practices. The navy itself, in a controversial web page, advertised the availability of the Vieques target range to foreign navies, to fire "most non-conventional weapons inventory" and to provide "airspace, surface, and subsurface water space for developmental and operational testing of new and existing weapons systems." The term "nonconventional weapons" typically refers to nuclear, biological, and chemical weapons.[8] What constitutes a "developmental" or "new" weapons system is an open question.

The inference from military advertisements that the U.S. Navy and its allies are testing nonconventional and new weapons systems on an island inhabited by nearly ten thousand human beings raises the eerie specter of the past. It recalls the trauma unleashed by nuclear testing in Nevada in the 1950s, where clouds of atomic dust traveled hundreds of miles to contaminate dispersed farming communities, where moon-faced children bore testament to the dangers of human design.[9] It evokes the memory of the fireball four miles wide that vaporized an entire island in the Bikini Atoll and the rain of white ash that poisoned islanders already made nomads by strategic design.[10] Recent revelations that the navy fired depleted uranium munitions on the Vieques range in violation of federal law and navy policy raise additional concerns about the contamination behind military fences. What is the impact on the surrounding civilian population of this type of new weapons testing? How is it that the navy carries out these activities in the face of opposition and protest from a resident population of American citizens?

Questions of National Sovereignty

The conflict in Vieques ultimately raises issues of national sovereignty. Who will control the land and for what purposes? Who exercises supreme authority over Vieques Island? Vieques's position as an inhabited bombing range is fundamentally an expression of Puerto Rico's position as a U.S. colony, lacking political power, representation, and voice over its own destiny; Vieques demonstrates the subordinate position of Puerto Rican citizens within the U.S. polity. This underlying question of national sovereignty is the most contested issue in Puerto Rico.

After more than one hundred years of colonialism, Puerto Rico's political status is still unresolved, and its residents are deeply divided over their vision for the island's future. Recent plebiscites have demonstrated that an overwhelming majority of Puerto Ricans favor continued political and economic association with the United States, through either statehood or a modified form of the current Commonwealth status.

Although the movement for political sovereignty is weak, Puerto Ricans have strong feelings of a common Puerto Rican national identity. Most Puerto Ricans regard themselves as a territorially distinct national entity, defined by a common culture, language, land, and history (Dávila 1997; Duany 2000; Morris 1995). This schism between national and political identity turns Vieques's clash with the U.S. military into an expression of the divided loyalties and ambivalence at the heart of the colonial state.

In a political context where national identity is contested and ambiguous and is informed by competing pulls of cultural and political identity, criticism of the U.S. Navy is highly controversial. Because the navy stands as the most potent symbol of U.S. political power and influence in Puerto Rico, protest against the military is seen as part of the anticolonial movement. The dilemma in Vieques is that the navy is not only a symbol of political power but also a very real actor that has caused the community material harm.

The protest movement is framed by this tension. Viequenses object to the military presence on material grounds, citing restrictions on economic opportunity, denial of access to natural resources, destruction of the environment, and degradation of public health. Merely raising these grievances becomes a highly charged political act. The U.S. Navy interprets objections to military operations, however specific, as ideologically motivated and as a threat to national defense. The Commonwealth government avoids confrontations that could jeopardize its relationship with the United States, particularly as they affect ongoing debates about potential statehood or a modified form of association. Activists from Vieques and Puerto Rico who are concerned specifically about military actions become embroiled in debates over sovereignty. Many residents from Vieques itself are reluctant to confront the navy, yet are fiercely attached to their island and determined to stay. This book considers how activists struggle to build a grassroots movement that asserts a basic set of claims within this tangled web of power.

Interpreting Antimilitary Protest

Although Vieques's underlying conflict is fundamentally rooted in Puerto Rico's status as a U.S. colony, protestors have consistently framed their grievances in a way that consciously sidesteps the politically sensitive issues of sovereignty and independence. Much recent analysis of conflict around military bases assumes that nationalist ideology is a central motivating factor beneath expressions of discontent (Smith 2000). What the recent mobilization in Vieques makes clear is that material harm caused by the military—the destruction of the ecology, the health effects of weapons testing, the stifling of the economy, the navy's dislocation of and antagonism toward civilians—is the basis of protest.

Overseas American military installations are often hotly contested. From Madrid to Okinawa, from Greece to South Korea, antimilitary protestors have opposed the U.S. military. U.S. foreign policy analysts are concerned that overseas bases act as lightning rods for anti-American sentiment, threatening U.S. political and military hegemony abroad (Blaker 1990; Smith 2000). Indeed, the U.S. Navy has repeatedly asserted the centrality of the Vieques installation to the training and support of the Atlantic Fleet and has regarded protest and agitation on the island as a threat to its operations in the Western Hemisphere.

Antimilitary protest is often misunderstood when analysts overlook local material conditions and focus excessively on broad political forces and ideologies. Many foreign analysts see military installations as symbols of U.S. interests and power and neglect their major impact on local environments, economies, and social relations. Analysts often emphasize the role national elites play in rallying nationalist sentiment in an effort to solidify a tenuous grasp on power. Conflict is frequently interpreted as stemming from nationalist sentiment, triggered by the emotional affront of a foreign presence on the land.[11] This framework obscures both the more basic set of local complaints that are often the driving force of conflict and the regional, class, and ethnic dimensions of conflict that complicate political solutions.

The presence of overseas bases is often a bone of contention not only between the United States and foreign states but between local communities and national politicians.[12] Bases are frequently established on the political margins of national territory, on lands occupied by ethnic or cultural minorities or otherwise disadvantaged populations. For example, U.S. military bases in the Philippines were established on land reserved for Filipino indigenous peoples known as "Negritos," who ended up combing military trash to survive when evicted from their land and whose rights were never central to Filipino nationalist campaigns against the U.S. military presence (Simbulan 1983). Okinawa, a peripheral prefecture of Japan, site of one of the bloodiest battles of World War II, absorbed the large majority of U.S. military facilities and personnel, acting as a buffer for the rest of Japan. These groups have their own experience with the military that diverges from that of national elites.

The navy has consistently portrayed the struggle in Vieques as an anti-American agitation, led by outside extremists.[13] Such a portrayal evokes images of street protests against the U.S. military and lanced effigies of Uncle Sam on fire, which do not resonate with the political context in Vieques. Despite highly confrontational tactics and dramatic imagery, the Vieques struggle has been characterized by its political moderation. In the 1970s many leading local activists were proponents of Puerto Rican statehood. The current movement has broad support from diverse sectors of the community, including prominent religious leaders. Vieques is not a bastion of nationalist ideologues or radical separatists, but a community of American citizens, the majority of whom support continued political and economic association with the United States. Many residents have lived in the United States or have family members living there. They have served in the armed forces or have relatives in the service. They support the U.S. government and even the navy itself—somewhere else.

Despite widespread popular support from many sectors of Puerto Rican society, including Governor Sila Calderón, Vieques's struggle with the navy to date has been consistently abandoned by the Puerto Rican government. This abandonment was expressed very clearly in the 1970s, when Puerto Rican governor Rafael Hernández Colón negotiated with the navy to transfer military bombing practices to Vieques from the adjacent Puerto Rican island municipality of Culebra. Again in 2000, then Puerto Rican governor Pedro Rosselló reversed his position of avowed opposition to any bombing and signed a compromise agreement consenting to ongoing bombing. These political events are reminders that Vieques's struggle cannot be understood in purely national terms, because the interests of the community differ from those of Puerto Rico. Vieques residents often express a feeling of subjugation to Puerto Rico, referring to themselves as the "colony of a colony."

The Material Basis of Discontent

Conflict in Vieques has its foundation in the material conditions of everyday life. Vieques is the poorest municipality in Puerto Rico, with 73 percent of the population living below the poverty line. It has among the highest rates of unemployment, with almost half the adult population without work (U.S. Census 1990). It has among the highest infant mortality rates in Puerto Rico and a growing rate of cancer and other health problems that residents believe are caused by weapons testing.[14] This socioeconomic crisis is the result of the military presence on the island and is at the heart of civilian grievances against the navy.

Vieques's plight challenges many common assumptions North Americans hold about the economic contributions of military bases.[15] In the United States, attitudes about bases have been shaped by the expansion of the armed forces during and after World War II. For many communities in the United States, proximity to bases or military industries brought affluence through armament and other military contract industries, increased demand for housing and fa- cilities, and services supplied to soldiers. Bases came to be regarded as eco- nomic motors that spurred local economies (Lotchin 1984; Markusen et al. 1991; Sorenson 1998). Consequently, local politicians often struggle to main- tain military installations within their districts, and base closings generate popu- lar outcry.[16]

Military wartime expansion, however, also created dislocation and hardship for numerous communities across the globe. Vieques stands as an example of the underside of this expansion. The navy usurped land, water, air, and ma- rine resources and caused environmental degradation. It evicted the majority of residents from the land and relocated them to resettlement tracts without addressing questions about their future. It interfered with the island's economic development, which it viewed as a threat to military operations. Vieques did not benefit from economic progress or affluence; its legacy from the military occupation has been stagnation and poverty.

The Geography of Military Control

Vieques is officially part of the Roosevelt Roads Naval Station, cen- tered near Ceiba, Puerto Rico, which the navy asserts is a major economic force in eastern Puerto Rico. But few if any of those benefits are experienced in Vieques. In Puerto Rico, the base supports a resident population of three thou- sand military personnel and their families and offers a variety of amenities and services. Vieques, however, is separated from eastern Puerto Rico by six miles of sea. The base, the PX, the sailors, and military families are across the wa- ter. Vieques hosts only a skeleton crew. Once envisioned as an integral part of a major naval station, Vieques became more useful to the navy as an empty piece of land on which to rehearse maneuvers, store weapons, and test bombs.

Residents have long complained that the navy consumes much of the island's land and productive potential, yet offers them few work or economic benefits in return. The land the navy possesses in Vieques, roughly twenty-three thousand acres, makes Roosevelt Roads, in physical size, the largest military installation in the world. Most of the Vieques installation, however, is miles and miles of rolling, scrub-covered hills and empty beaches. On the western side of the island, dozens of magazines are cut into the rock and horses graze quiet fields. On the eastern side, empty barracks and old sugar cane warehouses sit in tangled acres of spiky mesquite, guarded by a pack of feral dogs. Until recently, the borders between navy and civilian territories were defined by a series of roadblocks and wooden gates, and a security guard slumped in a chair. Vieques, which the navy contends is its strategic keystone and crown jewel in the Caribbean, appears as an abandoned no-man's land.

Approximately thirty sailors are housed in rudimentary barracks in Vieques for a one-year, unaccompanied tour of hardship duty. Another sixty "Seabees" (derived from the abbreviation C.B., for construction brigade) commute daily to Vieques, where they spend most of their time bulldozing earth and breaking rock. Although thousands of troops invade the island during maneuvers, they return to Puerto Rico to spend their money at the end of the day. Occasionally in Vieques one might see a sailor sipping a beer at a bar in the civilian sector or swimming at a beach on military land.

Contrary to popular notions of the military as an economic provider, there are few, if any, local industries in Vieques that are sustained by the presence of this meager handful of troops. The Department of Defense hires twenty-two residents as public works employees. Another handful of individuals is contracted to cut grass, work in the kitchen, or clean the barracks. In response to protest in the late 1970s and in an effort to build a supportive constituency, the navy hired approximately seventy Viequense security guards through a civilian agency to patrol the base. These jobs do not address the economic crisis on the island, where unemployment rates are among the highest in Puerto Rico.

One of the ironies of the military's presence on the island is that it has shaped the physical landscape in the civilian sector as serene, quiet, and slow paced. The lack of economic development means that unlike in San Juan, there are no high-rise hotels or casinos in Vieques. There are no strip malls, chain stores, or Burger Kings. It means that unlike St. Thomas, whose busy port docks enormous cruise ships teeming with thousands of tourists, Vieques's harbor is filled with small fishing boats, and the high point of the day is the coming and going of the passenger ferry. Horses and cows graze along the side of the road, and the day breaks with the cacophony of hundreds of roosters. The views of the water are unobstructed, and wherever you look over the horizon there is brilliant blue-green sea. Flame trees rage orange on the hills and towering coconut palms stand on empty beaches with sugar-white sand.

Vieques's slow pace, rural charm, and physical beauty intensify residents' attachment to it. Although many Viequenses leave the island to look for work, education, and opportunity, they return to the island in their golden years, buying public taxis with money earned in northern factories or building dream houses of cement and erecting large satellite dishes. Some maintain plots of land with half-built homes, preserving a stake in the island for when they return.

Underneath the surface beauty is tension and chaos. The island has developed without a plan. Large swaths of brush-covered land are grazed by a few cattle while families live piled up on top of one another in densely settled neighborhoods. Houses are half built, half painted, half paid for, the legacy of living without title (Rivera Torres and Torres 1996). They sprout like mushrooms on the hills with little consideration for the delivery of municipal services like electricity and water. Roads follow the houses in a twisting, winding maze. Vieques is an island awash with the empty shells of abandoned factories that have closed shop for more profitable shores. An exclusive luxury resort is dubiously planned between an airport and sewage treatment plant on land originally intended for agricultural rehabilitation. Federal grants are seized like apples from a tree for piecemeal construction projects; the laying of cement is presented as a panacea for joblessness and poverty.

While for decades residents clamored for access to land and economic development, since the late 1980s concern has focused on the health effects of the military presence. A 1988 study documented high concentrations of explosives in the drinking water, presumably an airborne by-product of weapons testing.[17] The Puerto Rican Department of Health documents a rising cancer rate.[18] Local studies point to toxic levels of heavy metals in residents' hair.[19] Such concerns have taken center stage in residents' opposition to the military presence.

The Military and Civil Society

The community struggle between Vieques and the navy ultimately raises important questions about the relationship between the military and civil society. A central tenet of liberal democracy is the subordination of military power to civilian authority. With the end of the cold war, U.S. analysts have become increasingly concerned about the deterioration of civilian authority over the military (Avant 1998; Burk 1998; Desch 1998; Dunlap 1992; Kohn 1994; Weigley 1993). Vieques's protest against the navy brings this issue to the fore.

The struggle to halt live bombing exercises on this small island inhabited by U.S. citizens has gained widespread popular support not only in Puerto Rico but throughout mainstream U.S. society and the international community.[20]

Despite the Clinton administration's expressions of sympathy for the plight of Vieques islanders, however, the president failed to issue an executive order halting live bombing exercises on the island.[21] Instead he proposed a referendum that was overtly favorably to military interests. Clinton's failure to back a popular demand of civil society is indicative of his administration's inability to exert civilian authority over the military.[22]

The Clinton failure is only one chapter in a longer history of civilian inability to direct the navy. In 1974 the Nixon administration ordered the navy's exit from Culebra, Puerto Rico, and the Senate Appropriations Committee allocated $12 million for the navy to relocate its bombing exercises to an uninhabited island off of Puerto Rico's west coast. With no apparent authorization, the navy took the money and relocated its firing practices to Vieques (U.S. House 1994: 5). In 1981 a special Armed Services Committee panel concluded that the navy should find an alternate bombing site to Vieques, to no effect (U.S. House 1981). In 1983 Puerto Rican governor Carlos Romero Barceló signed a memorandum of understanding with the navy, in which the military agreed among other things to improve the local economy. The navy did not comply with the terms of the agreement (U.S. House 1994: 9).

The navy's general approach to the civilian population of Vieques has been one of arrogance and inflexibility, and this attitude is a central reason for the development and continuity of protest. The issue is not limited to Vieques; recent international incidents suggest a growing problem for the military. The Okinawa rape case, the killing of skiers in Italy, and the sinking of a Japanese fishing boat raise serious questions about military training and attitudes toward the civilian society it is supposed to serve.[23]

Vieques poses additional concerns about the overall compatibility of military practices with civilian existence. Military theorists have argued that a sense of separateness is crucial to the creation and maintenance of a distinct military identity. For the young trainee, the isolation from the civilian world, the uniform, the learning of a distinctive language, are all part of making a warrior (Sorenson 1998: 10). Indeed, as we shall see, the navy has attempted to solve tensions in Vieques by eliminating civilians from the island altogether. With the cold war's end, however, analysts increasingly question the entire practice of stationing large numbers of troops in enclaves on foreign territory. Some ask whether the whole model of military-civilian relations is cut from an outdated mold (Smith 2000). Indeed, it appears that the changing nature of warfare demands an increasing use of troops in humanitarian and peacekeeping missions, requiring a fundamental change in the relationship between the military and civilian society.[24] U.S. military personnel on peacekeeping missions have been accused of threatening and assaulting civilians in Kosovo, and a U.S. soldier was convicted of the rape and murder of an eleven-year-old Kosovo Albanian girl. These incidents present major concerns about the essential capability of armed forces trained for combat and warfare to interact with civilians in times of peace.[25]

As Vieques demonstrates, these problems with civilian populations are not merely side issues of "public relations." They are central concerns that affect the very nature of military operations. Protest in Vieques has not only drawn unwelcome negative publicity to the navy. Demonstrators have also shut down training operations for over a year at the facility the navy proclaimed to be its crown jewel.

Overview

The trajectory of this book is historical, analyzing the roots of Vieques's modern dilemma in its position as a strategic colony and satellite to Puerto Rico. It considers the origins of the conflict and the vicissitudes of protest since the military usurpation of the island in the 1940s. The current Vieques movement is one episode in a much longer story of tension and confrontation. In particular, the book considers the relationship between the current mobilization and a strident popular movement in the late 1970s. A central interest is the way protestors have framed their grievances to avoid charged debates over Puerto Rican sovereignty.

Chapter One presents Vieques's history within the broader context of Puerto Rican colonial history, from the era of Spanish to U.S. hegemony. It explores the roots of current tensions and the fundamental contradiction between strategic goals and civilian life on the island.

Chapter Two describes the response of residents to the military usurpation of island land and its transformation from a rural sugar cane island into a military theater of war. Of central importance is the specific nature of Viequenses' response to tensions and conflict with the military. Their resistance has been marked not by nationalist or anti-American sloganeering but by a heightened sense of cultural identity and attachment to the island. The chapter examines local class relations to understand this response.

Chapter Three looks at the grassroots mobilization that erupted in Vieques in the late 1970s and the constellation of factors that converged to propel local fishermen to the leadership of the antinavy movement. It considers the importance of this framework for sustaining the movement within a charged colonial context and the way broader political tensions ultimately led to its demise.

Chapter Four examines the interlude between the Fishermen's War and the antinavy mobilization of 1999. The Fishermen's War ended when the navy signed an agreement promising to improve the local economy and environment. The navy's failure to live up to these promises caused considerable bitterness and disillusionment among islanders. Residents became wary of involving themselves in further controversy with the navy. Cultural identification with the island strengthened, however, increasing the potential for future mobilization.

Chapter Five examines the politics and ideology of a new group and its struggle to build a grassroots movement to close the base. The navy's resistance to compromise created the conditions for renewed protest. The chapter considers how a struggle over a radar installation laid the groundwork for the current protest movement. The radar mobilization, by tapping into residents' anxiety about cancer rates on the island and deep-seated perceptions of genocide, focused local identity politics on environmental and health concerns.

Chapter Six considers the most recent transformation of Vieques's long struggle. This movement's structure and cultural framework have provided a space for the emergence of new actors and wider civic participation. Vieques's popular movement has emerged as a potent political force that has effectively challenged naval hegemony and changed Puerto Rico's political relationship with the United States.

Chapter Seven examines the implications and future of Vieques's struggle in light of current discussions to close the range. Of central importance is the cleanup of the range and the designation of land use in order to guarantee Viequenses a future on the island.

One

A Strategic Colony on the Margins of the Empire

A nineteenth-century Spanish fort sits perched over Vieques's capital and principal town, Isabel Segunda. A massive wall of brick cuts into a quiet hillside, brushed by high grasses and grazing horses. From the summit, the fort affords clear views of eastern Puerto Rico, six miles across turquoise sea. A row of cannons defends the vistas.

Yet while the fort suggests the strategic importance of Vieques to the Spanish, its construction was almost an afterthought, a last-ditch effort to secure a crumbling empire. Spain first laid claim to the island in the 1500s, but for centuries it languished as a disputed no-man's land contested by the Spanish, English, and Danes. It was not until 1843 that Queen Isabel II built a fort to protect Spain's claim.

Vieques developed on the margins of the Spanish and American colonial empires. For the past five hundred years, international power relations and foreign domination have shaped the island's history. Military interests have been paramount. Because Vieques's history is integrally linked to that of Puerto Rico, the chapter nests this discussion within an overview of Puerto Rico's colonial history.

Spanish Colonial Roots

In the sixteenth century Spain emerged as the preeminent European power. Its expansion into the New World, firmly backed by the Catholic church, threatened the existing balance of power in Europe. The Caribbean became

17

the entry point into the Spanish empire and the site of intense clashes between rival European powers.

Puerto Rico played a vital role in securing Spain's access to its New World colonies, defending the path of the Spanish fleet and guarding the entrance of the Caribbean from incursions by its European enemies. To fend off repeated invasions by the French, English, and Dutch, the Spanish heavily fortified the Puerto Rican coastal city of San Juan.

Although Spain introduced sugar and slavery into the New World, its Caribbean colonies were late to develop the plantation complexes that enriched France, England, and Holland. Puerto Rico developed instead as a military colony. Spanish colonial policy inhibited the island's economic development. While the French colony Santo Domingo became one of the leading world producers of sugar, and the Danish colony St. Thomas developed as a thriving commercial center, Puerto Rico's economy was tied directly to several mercantilist houses in Spain and trading was prohibited with the United States and the non-Hispanic Caribbean. The military operation in Puerto Rico was subsidized by taxes levied on Mexico. Smuggling and small-scale subsistence cultivation became the main strategies through which settlers survived and kept the colony afloat (Morales Carrión 1971: 10). Puerto Rico developed as a strategic colony, and Vieques was its satellite.

Christopher Columbus had spotted Vieques Island on his second voyage to the Americas in 1493, but it was not until several decades later that Spain's attention focused on this island off Puerto Rico's eastern coast. In 1514 two Taino chieftains from Vieques launched repeated raids on Spanish settlements in Loíza, Puerto Rico, killing a local chieftain and her Spanish husband.[1] These raids alerted Spain to the risks of a hostile settlement so close to Puerto Rico. The governor of Puerto Rico, Cristóbal Mendoza, launched a counterattack, razing all Taino settlements on Vieques, massacring most of the Tainos, and selling the rest as slaves in Santo Domingo. These raids put an end to permanent settlement of Vieques by the Tainos, and ended the most immediate security threat to Spain. In 1524 Spain proclaimed dominion over Vieques (Brau 1912: 235-239; Rouse 1952: 554-555).

Despite declaring its sovereignty, Spain failed to establish any settlement on the island that would fortify its claim. Vieques was an extreme expression of Spain's emphasis on military over economic concerns in the Caribbean. Spain's main interest in Vieques was that it remain empty of any settlement that might threaten Spanish hegemony. Historical accounts generally describe Vieques as abandoned and overrun with wild cattle until the mid-nineteenth century. Spain used the island as a hunting preserve until danger from Carib raids caused authorities to ban access to the island (Rouse 1952: 555).

But although the island was not formally settled, it was never completely unoccupied. The records refer to "Indians," who were probably refugees from the neighboring islands. Teófilo Le Guillou, the first governor of Vieques, wrote in his autobiography: "From the year 1493 when it was discovered by Admiral Columbus, to 1828, Vieques was inhabited by Carib Indians, freebooters, pirates, deserters, evildoers, thieves, privateers, and smugglers" (quoted in Rivera Martínez 1963: 50). The island's proximity to Puerto Rico and lack of internal development made it an ideal hideaway for smugglers. In 1699 the infamous pirate William Kidd used Vieques as a staging ground to plunder ships off the Puerto Rican coast (Morales Carrión 1971: 56). Vieques may also have served as a major stepping stone for escaped slaves from the Leeward Islands who sought refuge in Puerto Rico (Gaspar 1985: 205–206; Morales Carrión 1971: 62–63).

From the mid-seventeenth to the mid-nineteenth century, England and Spain, and to a lesser degree Denmark, clashed over Vieques. With no Spanish settlement to bolster Spain's claim, the island's geographical position, within ten miles of the east coast of Puerto Rico and thirty miles of the Virgin Islands of St. Thomas and St. Croix, fostered political disputes. Spain claimed Vieques as a dependency of Puerto Rico, and England, which called Vieques "Crab Island," declared Vieques to be one of the Virgin Islands. Denmark made tentative claims to Vieques, but never pursued them with attempts at colonial settlements or military conquest (Dookhan 1973: 2).

England wanted to colonize Vieques, viewing it as "the best of all the Virgins, if not better than them altogether" (Morales Carrión 1971: 49). In 1617 an Englishman, John Pinard, led a group to Vieques to carry out contraband activities. The governor of Puerto Rico quickly summoned forces to evict them (Brau 1912: 5). England's attempts later focused on establishing permanent settlements, which would be crucial in substantiating its claims to the territory. In 1672 the Spanish discovered a mixed settlement of approximately three hundred English and French colonists living on Vieques, who, under the orders of the English governor of Antigua, were constructing a fort. The Spanish sent an armada to raze the fort, burn houses and farms, and remove the colonists. In 1688 the Spanish razed another English settlement on Vieques and sold their captives as slaves in Santo Domingo (Brau 1912: 5–6; Dookhan 1973: 4–5; Rivera Martínez 1963: 14–15).

Despite the fear of Spanish reprisal, English colonists continued attempts to settle Vieques throughout the eighteenth century. Colonists were attracted to the island's resources. Unlike a number of the neighboring Leeward Islands, Vieques possessed its own water source. It was rich in wood and had fertile soils regarded as suitable for sugar cane cultivation. Vieques also had strategic advantages. Its shores provided harbor for ships sailing between the Leeward Islands and Jamaica, and its coasts offered clear views of the movements of Spanish ships (Dookhan 1973: 2–4; Morales Carrión 1971: 49–50). It was precisely this strategic advantage that the Spanish found so threatening, and thus Spain continually razed English settlements on Vieques.

Not until the nineteenth century did Spain attempt to settle the island that it had defended for so long against English interests. The first Spanish settlement in Vieques, established in 1815, was raided and expelled by the English. In 1829 the Spanish attempted more vigorously to colonize the island. The governor of Puerto Rico, Miguel de La Torre, sent three hundred colonists to Vieques under the leadership of Francisco Roselló. Forty-five of these settlers were organized into a colonial militia by a former French naval officer, Teófilo Le Guillou, who was determined to rout all pirates and parties hostile to the rule of Spain.

With the construction of a fort authorized by the queen of Spain in 1843, Spain finally committed the military resources necessary to establish the success and growth of a colony and its control over Vieques. Le Guillou became the commandant of Vieques after Roselló's death, and the town was officially founded in 1843 as part of Puerto Rico. After three hundred years of dispute, Vieques was formally settled, formally declared Spanish, formally associated with Puerto Rico. In less than six decades it would fall to the Americans.

Vieques was founded at a turning point in Spanish colonialism. By the early nineteenth century, Spain was losing its grip on its New World empire. The struggle for independence unseated Spanish colonial governments from Mexico to Chile. By 1820 only Cuba and Puerto Rico remained under Spanish power. In 1815 the Spanish crown issued the Cédula de Gracias, a royal decree that reversed Spain's suffocating commercial policies temporarily until 1830. This attempt to keep Cuba and Puerto Rico loyal came at a time when much of Spain's Latin American empire was at war against it. The Cédula de Gracias promoted foreign commerce and liberalized immigration policy. Immigrants came to Puerto Rico from Louisiana, Haiti, the Caribbean, Europe, and the Americas, attracted by land grants or propelled by slave revolts and civil unrest in the non-Hispanic Caribbean and the faltering Spanish empire (Knight 1990; Morales Carrión 1971; Dietz 1986).

Nineteenth-century Vieques society developed within this context. Its economy was based almost exclusively on sugar cane. Vieques's planter class was composed mainly of immigrants from other Caribbean isles, notably French planters who fled to Vieques with their slaves in the wake of slave uprisings in Martinique and Guadeloupe. At the outset, its work force was heavily slave based. The founding of the municipality coincided with the peak years of slavery in Puerto Rico, 1834–1846, when slaves made up 11 percent of the total population (Scarano 1984: 135). But slave society in the Caribbean was crumbling. England had already abolished slavery in 1834 and pressed Spain to agree to an accord outlawing the slave trade. Planters were forced to find alternate sources of labor.

In Puerto Rico planters turned to the island's interior, adopting a series of coercive laws to compel the white peasantry to work. In Vieques, however, planters relied on black contract laborers from neighboring British isles. Although formally "freed" from slavery, these workers ended up toiling side by side with slaves in the sugar cane fields. Contract labor was little more than a disguised form of slavery.

The import of foreign laborers was only a passing experiment in Puerto Rico, but contract labor shaped the character of society in Vieques. The island was nearly deserted in the 1870s when planters extended cane and cotton cultivation. Within several years, Vieques's population grew to three thousand, most of whom were foreigners. In 1872 the British consulate claimed that 90 percent of Vieques residents were British laborers working under contract (Ramos Mattei 1989: 134). Harsh and exploitative working conditions fueled revolts in 1864 and 1874. By late 1880s, however, the stream of contract laborers dwindled. Puerto Rico's sugar industry was in crisis, crippled by falling sugar prices, antiquated production technique, and lack of capital investment (Ramos Mattei 1985).

The American Mediterranean

Vieques's twentieth-century history is inextricably linked to the rise of U.S. imperialism and naval expansion. Its fall into the U.S. Navy's web of power is part of the larger story of Puerto Rico's colonial relationship with the United States and the way that relationship has been shaped by military concerns.

Puerto Rico attracted the attention of U.S. military strategists in the late nineteenth century during a period of aggressive American imperial expansion. The center of the U.S. vision of national glory was the construction of an isthmian canal in Central America. The Caribbean was considered to be the American Mediterranean. Puerto Rico, long a military bastion of the Spanish, took on new significance for American military strategists concerned with securing the entry to a canal.

Alfred Thayer Mahan's *Influence of Sea Power upon History* articulated a vision of U.S. national power and greatness linked to a program of conquest and control, an image that was later described in Frederick Jackson Turner's "frontier thesis" (Dietz 1986: 80). The United States' destiny, Mahan argued, rested upon expanding foreign commerce. Control over an isthmian canal was the key to strategic and commercial domination of the hemisphere. A canal in Central America would give U.S. Atlantic states equal access with Europe to Far East markets. In order for the canal to be secure, it required a strong navy and a network of bases and coaling stations to support the military. Colonies, therefore, were a key part of Mahan's formula, acting as necessary stepping stones to protect and fuel ships and gain access to enormous markets in Latin America and Asia. Supremacy over the Caribbean was crucial (Sprout and Sprout 1939).

Mahan's theories were not new. Britain had embraced such a military policy for at least two hundred years. This time, however, these views were articulated at a critical moment in U.S. history by an outspoken advocate—Theodore Roosevelt, the assistant secretary of the navy under President William McKinley (Sprout and Sprout 1939). Roosevelt promoted Mahan's program of naval expansion and argued for Spain's expulsion from the Caribbean. "Until we definitely turn Spain out of those islands (and if I had my way it would be done tomorrow)," Roosevelt wrote, "we will always be menaced by trouble down there" (quoted in Morales Carrión 1983: 134). This vision propelled the United States into a war against Spain in 1898 and changed the course of Puerto Rican history.

At the turn of the twentieth century, U.S. strategic interests were predominantly focused not on Puerto Rico but on Cuba. The island had long been viewed as central to U.S. interests and the defense of an isthmian canal. In 1825 the United States blocked the Cuban movement for independence, concerned that a sovereign and free Cuba would threaten the institution of slavery in the U.S. South (Foner 1972: xvi). Cuba had waged one unsuccessful war for independence (1868–1878) and now, at the start of a new century, rebel forces revolted against Spain. The United States intervened in Cuba's war of independence to evict Spain from the Caribbean and to have a voice over the affairs of an independent Cuba. The United States easily defeated its weaker rival and snatched up the remaining Spanish colonies—Puerto Rico, the Philippines, and the Mariana Islands—in a bid for commercial domination. The war with Spain launched the United States as a world power and found Puerto Rico "the hapless victim of an explosive U.S. drive to assert military and naval hegemony in the Caribbean" (Cabán 1999: 15). The United States claimed Puerto Rico as "indemnity" for the war and thus effectively eliminated the Spanish presence in the Caribbean. The U.S. Navy took control of Puerto Rico, declaring martial law and establishing military bases in San Juan and Culebra. Vieques was initially not of interest to the navy. Early surveys recommended closing its military installation (Estades Font 1988).

Colonial Citizens: Puerto Ricans under the Eagle

When U.S. troops landed on the shores of Guánica in July 1898, Puerto Rico's autonomous government was only five months old. Spain, under the threat of war with the United States, had only months earlier conceded a measure of political freedom to Puerto Rico after years of struggle. Puerto Rico gained full representation in the Spanish parliament, the right to negotiate commercial treaties with foreign nations, and control over trade and tariffs. The island's government was run by an appointed governor and a bicameral legislature that controlled internal affairs (Jiménez de Wagenheim 1998; Morales Carrión 1986). The autonomous government, however, the pinnacle of the Creole elite's long dream of self-government, would convene only one legislative session before Puerto Rico fell to the United States. No Puerto Ricans were consulted about the transfer of power from Spain to the United States. No Puerto Ricans participated in negotiations about the island's future. The U.S. colonization put an abrupt end to the movement toward autonomy and left as a question mark the political status of islanders.

The U.S. invasion of Puerto Rico met little resistance. The war had produced hunger and hardship and feelings of abandonment by Spain. Many sugar planters saw a possibility for greater freedom under the U.S. flag. Liberal intellectuals were captivated by promises of freedom and democracy after so many years of oppressive Spanish rule. Many among the working classes saw U.S. rule as preferable to the domination of the Spanish. They hoped that living standards would improve under the extension of U.S. labor laws and practices, such as the right to organize unions and strike (Dietz 1986; Quintero Rivera 1980; Scarano 1993).[2]

The U.S. invasion exploded latent anti-Spanish sentiment and class conflict in the countryside. The working class, revolting against brutal working conditions, torched plantations and robbed and murdered plantation owners (Cabán 1999; F. Picó 1987). In this volatile climate, the military government initially won popular support through a program of public works and relief measures, modest measures that contrasted with the legacy of Spanish neglect (Cabán 1999: 81). Few in Puerto Rico, however, expected that the island would remain a colony, and many welcomed the idea that it would eventually become a state (Dietz 1986: 83–84).

Early enthusiasm began to sour. Puerto Ricans expected a resolution of their political status, anticipating that a democratic government would replace military rule. Already the ambiguity of Puerto Rico's political position had had a negative effect on the island's economy, as it lost favored trade status with Cuba and Spain, yet had no privileged access to U.S. markets. Instead the Foraker Act of 1900, which acted as the island's first constitution, enshrined Puerto

Rico's political position as a U.S. colony while laying the groundwork for the massive penetration of the island's economy by U.S. capital.

The Foraker Act defined Puerto Rico as an "unincorporated territory" and granted residents "Puerto Rican citizenship," an undefined, derivative form of U.S. citizenship. Initially intended as a temporary measure, the Foraker Act remained in effect until 1917. Although the act formally shifted control from military to civilian rule, U.S. military concerns continued to dominate. The island fell under the jurisdiction of the Department of War until 1934, and the Puerto Rican governorship in practice became a retirement package for U.S. military officials. The island's political structure was subordinated to U.S. power and interests, while no clear colonial policy was established that might define the island's future. The Puerto Rican economy was restructured to serve U.S. corporate interests.

The United States modernized the island's infrastructure, dramatically improving roads, irrigation, and ports. It instituted a program of public health to address poor sanitation, widespread disease, and anemia. It introduced a system of education, part of an "Americanizing" mission that emphasized "patriotism" and use of the English language. U.S. investors poured capital into the island's sugar industry, modernizing machinery and expanding output (Cabán 1999).

These improvements were more successful in increasing productivity than in reducing popular misery. Land ownership remained concentrated, while living conditions, which were deplorable under the Spanish, remained the same or worse. The ascendancy of U.S. sugar undermined the Puerto Rican coffee industry and the power of local sugar growers. By 1920 half of the island's sugar production had fallen into the hands of four U.S. corporations (Clark 1930: 643), while most Puerto Ricans lived in poverty.

World War I focused the United States on the strategic importance of the Caribbean and the vital role of Puerto Rico in regional security. German warships menaced the U.S. Atlantic Coast, and Germany invited Mexico to form a military alliance against the United States. To strengthen its influence amid these growing tensions, the United States purchased the Virgin Islands from Denmark in 1917 for $25 million. This same year, just weeks before it entered the European conflict, the United States modified Puerto Rico's colonial government through the Jones Act. The act provided for a popularly elected bicameral legislature and extended U.S. citizenship to islanders to shore up their loyalty (Wagenheim and Jiménez de Wagenheim 1994: 123). Although Puerto Ricans had pressed for years for citizenship, this was not conferred until it meshed with U.S. strategic objectives. "A fact was emerging in the long and patient Puerto Rican struggle to achieve self-determination," notes Arturo Morales Carrión: "The administration and Congress could only pay real attention when the issues ceased to be internal and were related to the U.S. national security and its Caribbean hegemony" (1983: 199). Although the Jones Act increased good will in Puerto Rico, it left the island's colonial political structure largely intact and did nothing to mitigate the island's growing economic crisis spurred by the rise of monopoly capitalism.

Crisis of the 1930s

In the 1920s the Brookings Institution documented conditions of appalling poverty throughout Puerto Rico. "It is a country," the research team wrote, "where the masses depend for their right for a place to live, to raise a garden or to keep a cow, a pig, a goat, or a chicken upon the goodwill of the landowner upon whose property the little single-partitioned hut happens to be built" (Clark 1930: 13). Most people lived in cramped worker barracks, in shacks made of boards and galvanized iron, or in thatched hovels made from debris—stray pieces of boards and boxes, patched with "straightened oil cans, odd pieces of bark and board, ancient strips of zinc" (ibid.). As much as 90 percent of the rural population suffered from hookworm, due to lack of shoes and poor sanitation. Tuberculosis was epidemic in urban areas (Clark 1930: 57–67).

The misery of the twenties turned disastrous by the 1930s. In 1928 and 1932 two hurricanes ravaged the island, nearly wiping out the coffee industry. When the world market crashed, Puerto Rico reached a nadir. The island became "the poor house of the Caribbean" (Carr 1984: 57).

Vieques stood as one of the most severe expressions of Puerto Rico's plight. Its economy showed the effects of sugar cane monoculture. By the 1930s, 95 percent of the rural population, or two-thirds of the total population of 10,582, was landless, while two sugar corporations consumed 71 percent of island land. Only two other Puerto Rican municipalities, Santa Isabel, dominated by the Aguirre Sugar Company, and Guánica, dominated by the South Puerto Rico Sugar Company, had sharper inequalities of land ownership (Ayala 2001).

The island's sugar industry was in crisis. Although Vieques had been dominated by sugar cane production since its founding, its output had never reached the levels of the major *centrales*, or sugar-processing complexes, on the main island of Puerto Rico.[3] Vieques supported four *centrales* at the turn of the century that had merged into two by the 1920s. One of those *centrales*, the Central Vieques, owned by the United Porto Rico Sugar Company (one of four large U.S. corporations that dominated the Puerto Rican sugar industry), closed its mill in 1927.[4] Vieques's remaining *central*, Playa Grande, struggled to stay afloat in the face of intense economic pressure before declaring bankruptcy in 1939.

According to the 1935 Special Agricultural Census, Vieques had the most dramatic rate of male unemployment in all of Puerto Rico, with 64.4 percent of its male labor force formally unemployed.[5] The island hemorrhaged its population to St. Croix, which like Vieques had an economy based on sugar cane. In 1927, the same year that the Central Vieques shut down, U.S. immigration laws were applied to St. Croix, leading planters to look to Puerto Rico rather than the British Virgin Islands to recruit agricultural laborers. Vieques's economic crisis made the island a fertile recruiting ground.[6] Thousands of workers traveled to St. Croix, many bringing their families and permanently settling on the island (Senior 1947). The exodus of Viequenses to St. Croix was so great that a 1939 *El Mundo* headline declared, "The Island of Vieques is being deserted: families migrate by the hundreds to St. Croix hoping to escape the horrible situation of misery there [in Vieques]."[7] It was a measure of the desperation of life in Vieques that islanders moved to St. Croix, which at the time was also suffering an economic downturn. "Puerto Rican migration to an island in such a depressed condition," wrote Clarence Senior, "would seem like 'jumping out of the frying pan into the fire'" (1947: 1).

Those who remained in Vieques lived on the brink of starvation. A 1933 study estimated that the island's population subsisted on less than seven cents per day per person (Wagenheim and Jiménez de Wagenheim 1994: 167). In 1937 the Puerto Rican government sent an agricultural team to address the mounting crisis. The team reported: "The tragedy of Vieques Island is analogous to the tragedy of Puerto Rico, only much more serious. Thirty-three thousand acres of land are hoarded, for the most part, by two large sugar corporations. Eleven thousand inhabitants are living on what little remains of the land. A very rich island, with every kind of fruit, fish, and livestock is impeded from developing its full agricultural and industrial potential. The per capita income scarcely reaches the ridiculous level of $22" (Jesús Castro 1937: 14).

Vieques's harsh living conditions epitomized the crisis that faced Puerto Rico thirty years after the United States took control. Anger and frustration over the island's social conditions and the failure of dominant political organizations and parties to speak to widespread misery spawned radical political activity.

The thirties saw a growing militancy of labor unions and the rise of the Nationalist Party, headed by Pedro Albizu Campos. The Nationalists articulated a fiery, anticolonial message, demanding immediate independence for Puerto

Rico. They had limited electoral success, but they tapped into a groundswell of popular discontent and defined a more confrontational political style.

Washington recognized that Puerto Rico's plight demanded remediation. Federal control of the island shifted in 1934 from the War Department to the Department of the Interior. Federal relief programs were expanded to address the island's economic crisis.

Still, tensions remained high. In October 1935 police shot five Nationalist Party members driving to a demonstration at the University of Puerto Rico, Río Piedras; they were allegedly carrying explosives. Four were killed, and the surviving member was later acquitted of all charges. Albizu pronounced that for every Nationalist who was killed, a North American would die (Carr 1984). Four months later in February 1936, in retaliation for the Río Piedras shootings, two young Nationalist Party members assassinated the North American Insular chief of police, Colonel Francis Riggs. The Nationalists were apprehended and shot dead while in police custody.

The Riggs assassination polarized U.S.–Puerto Rico relations. In Puerto Rico, the two Nationalists were seen as martyrs. But in the United States, the assassination of the chief of police appalled the public (Wagenheim and Jiménez de Wagenheim 1994: 180). Insular authorities waged a crackdown on the Nationalists. Albizu and other Nationalist Party leaders were sentenced to six years in federal prison after being convicted of sedition and conspiracy to overthrow the U.S. government. When in 1937 the Nationalists organized a parade in Ponce on Palm Sunday, the Insular police, acting on orders from the governor, attempted to block marchers before opening fire on the crowd, killing twenty and injuring more than one hundred others.

In Washington, Maryland senator Millard Tydings, a close friend of Colonel Riggs, lashed out at rising discontent with a bill granting immediate Puerto Rican independence. The bill proposed independence in terms that were overtly favorable to the United States and extremely punitive to Puerto Rico; it linked political independence to nearly certain economic disaster (Dietz 1986: 169–170). The Tydings bill fractured political alignments in Puerto Rico. The Partido Popular Democrático (PPD), headed by the charismatic Luis Muñoz Marín, emerged in the late thirties out of a split in the Liberal Party. Although Muñoz had once been outspoken in favor of Puerto Rican independence, he shifted course in an increasingly contentious and violent political context. The PPD set aside the status issue to focus on Puerto Rico's overwhelming poverty and misery. The *populares* (PPD followers) espoused a populist message of "bread, land, liberty," putting issues of social and economic justice before issues of sovereignty. They were less confrontational than the Nationalists. Unlike Albizu, who derided the *yanqui* imperialists, Muñoz adopted more diplomatic rhetoric, lamenting the unfortunate, misguided approach of the United States toward Puerto Rico. The *populares* channeled the fiery sentiment of the Nationalists into a potent, yet less strident populist platform. Muñoz was able to build support and gain power within a colonial context only by shifting his political program away from an emphasis on sovereignty, an important precedent for the politics of protest in Vieques.

By the 1940s, the United States had to face the increasingly volatile situation in Puerto Rico. The world was at war and Puerto Rico's stability was crucial to U.S. strategic interests in the region.

Defending the American Lake

The rise of German fascism in Europe raised American anxiety about the security of the Caribbean region and the Panama Canal. The United States had been wary of the German presence in the Caribbean ever since the Anglo-German blockade of Venezuela in 1902. There were rumors of German plots to foment revolution in Brazil, Uruguay, and Argentina, and of German interest in Samaná Bay in the Dominican Republic (Langley 1989: 147–149; Stetson and Fairchild 1960: 6). German submarines were active in the Caribbean. U.S. strategists were uncertain of German motives, and feared that Germany might be interested in naval sites in the region.

U.S. military strategists saw the heightened importance of strengthening existing American military installations in the Caribbean and around the Panama Canal Zone and securing new bases in the event that European conflict spilled into this "American Lake." The clash between British and German warships off the coast of Brazil in 1939 suggested that the region was not immune to conflict. Although the United States possessed bases in Puerto Rico and Cuba, the outbreak of war in Europe raised concerns about the security of French, British, and Dutch colonies ringing the southern entrance to the Panama Canal (Langley 1989: 152). Furthermore, if the Germans managed to capture the British and French navies, they would pose a real threat to the Western Hemisphere.

The fall of France in 1940 greatly heightened these concerns. Britain blockaded Martinique and landed troops in Aruba to protect its oil supply. The United States prepared forces to defend the Brazilian coast and occupy key British, French, Dutch, and Danish colonies in the Caribbean and Latin America (Morales Carrión 1983: 248).

The U.S. presence in the Caribbean was dramatically increased through the Anglo-American destroyer-base agreement of September 1940. The United States had previously limited access to base facilities in Bermuda, St. Lucia, and Trinidad, but it now extended its access to these areas and acquired additional access to facilities in Jamaica and British Guiana. This was a crucial element in bolstering the air defense of the region (Stetson and Fairchild 1960). In addition, the United States expanded its marine air base in St. Thomas and started construction on a submarine base.[8] Puerto Rico emerged as an essential component of U.S. military strategy.

Puerto Rico in the War

In the context of this regional threat, U.S. policy makers needed to address Puerto Rico's political and economic vulnerability immediately. Surrounded by German submarines, Puerto Rico was isolated and paralyzed. There were severe food and oil shortages and the population was on the brink of starvation. Sugar corporations compounded the war's hardship by refusing to cede any acres of sugar land for food cultivation, even in these drastic circumstances (Dietz 1986: 202). The bloody confrontations with the Nationalists defined the political tenor.

Rexford Tugwell, a New Deal economist appointed by Franklin D. Roosevelt as the governor of Puerto Rico in September 1941, recognized the importance of quelling an increasingly volatile situation. Tugwell's appointment to Puerto Rico represented the first significant break with the string of military governors who had dominated island politics since the U.S. invasion. But Tugwell's liberal reformism was informed by his recognition of vital strategic concerns. "Puerto Rico was central," Tugwell noted. "Bases there were, in a strict sense, strategic and essential. Puerto Rico therefore had to be maintained as a controlled and, if possible, friendly base. As wartime governor, this was my first responsibility" (quoted in Wagenheim and Jiménez de Wagenheim 1994: 187). Tugwell understood that creating a stable economic climate was key to maintaining U.S. control over the island. "If we had bases in the Caribbean, and especially air bases," Tugwell wrote, "had we not a real and immediate interest in the tranquillity, even loyalty of its people? How could we build a chain of fortresses on thickly settled islands which were hostile?" (Tugwell 1976: 69). Tugwell's administration initiated a dramatic process of economic restructuring and political liberalization designed to ensure the stability of the island.

The second major change in Puerto Rico was the expansion of the U.S. military presence. In 1939 Congress authorized $30 million to build large air and naval bases on the island to defend the Panama Canal (Wagenheim and Jiménez de Wagenheim 1994: 185). The army conceived of Puerto Rico, together with Florida and Panama, as forming a defensive air triangle that would guard the eastern approaches to the Caribbean and act as a stepping stone to South

American air bases (Stetson and Fairchild 1960: 13). The military leased large tracts of land across Puerto Rico, dislocating thousands of people and checkering the island with bases.[9] Workers moved tons of earth to fill mucky swamp in San Juan Harbor, building a naval air station (Langley 1985b). The most dramatic buildup was on Puerto Rico's eastern shores. Declaring a national emergency, the navy expropriated 6,680 acres of land in Ensenada Honda, on Puerto Rico's east coast, and 21,020 acres of Vieques, two-thirds of that island's land. Here the navy planned to build its most important operating base in the Caribbean.

The Making of a Caribbean Pearl Harbor

The Roosevelt Roads Naval Station was planned to rival Pearl Harbor in scale and significance. The base would stretch across the Vieques Sound to connect Ensenada Honda and Vieques. Roosevelt Roads would provide anchorage, docking, repair facilities, fuel, and supply sources for 60 percent of the Atlantic Fleet. Furthermore, with the threat of a German invasion of Great Britain looming, naval planners saw the base as a potential point of supply, repair, and refuge for the entire British Fleet. The plan was to excavate tons of rock from Vieques in order to build a sea wall between the island and a new home port in Ensenada Honda. Huge magazines would be cut into the hills of Vieques, and a marine camp established on the neighboring island of Culebra (Langley 1985a: 271–275; Tugwell 1976: 68).

Vieques's stark social inequality and overwhelming poverty facilitated the military takeover. The concentration of the land in the hands of two sugar corporations and a few wealthy farming families eased the transfer of two-thirds of the island from private to military control. The landless majority that lived on the expropriated acres had little political clout with which to counter the U.S. Navy, and were summarily removed from their homes.

Although decades later the mayor of Vieques would lambaste the Puerto Rican government for handing over Vieques to win the goodwill of the U.S. Navy, it seems that the insular government had little choice.[10] The United States government put strong pressure on its Caribbean and Latin American allies to unite behind it in the common cause of regional security (Langley 1989). In Puerto Rico, there was widespread popular support for the war against fascism. The *populares* of the PPD, who had emerged as the dominant political force on the island by the 1940s, adopted a platform supporting the democratic cause in the hemisphere, asserting that "neither independence nor statehood nor social justice could be achieved if democracy perished on the American continent" (Morales Carrión 1983: 249). Even leftist groups set aside grievances against the United States to devote their struggle to the war against fascism

(Quintero Rivera 1976: 230). Over thirty-six thousand Puerto Rican men were drafted, and another twenty-three thousand volunteered to guard the Caribbean and to join armed forces in the Pacific, North Africa, and Europe (Morales Carrión 1983: 257). In such a political climate, few rallied against the expropriation of land in Vieques for the war effort.

Thousands of people were dislocated from their homes in Vieques. Most lived as *agregados*, tenant laborers on sugar cane plantations. Navy officials went from shack to shack, issuing eviction orders translated by an overseer from the sugar *central*. Soon after military officials returned to load families onto the backs of trucks and began bulldozing their plots. Families brought with them whatever few belongings they had, and maybe some pieces of wood from their dismantled shacks. They were deposited in razed cane fields the navy declared "resettlement tracts."

The navy's focus was preparing for war and building a base, not the fate of the thousands of homeless. Still, the massive construction project filled people with hope. In 1941, when the navy arrived in Vieques, the island was on the brink of disaster. Hunger and poverty, already endemic, were intensified by wartime food shortages and rising unemployment. This socioeconomic crisis shaped people's understanding of and response to the military usurpation of the island. Many hoped that the opportunity to work would mitigate their upheaval.

Base construction proceeded at breakneck speed. The navy cut dozens of magazines into the Vieques hills to store ammunition. Thousands of Puerto Rican men worked around the clock breaking rock for the massive stone and cement breakwater that would connect Vieques to Puerto Rico through the rough waters of the Vieques Passage. Many more Puerto Rican women and men found work fishing, cooking, and washing for the laborers. A *San Juan Star* article recounts the frantic pace of construction in the early forties: "In late 1940 and early 1941, the German air blitz over London and Coventry intensified the construction to make Ensenada Honda and Vieques another Pearl Harbor Naval Base. So great was the pressure to advance the pier a few more yards every day towards Puerto Rico that, except for saving the driver, any truck that slipped or tumbled off the pier would not be salvaged but left to be entombed under tons of stone and cement, and eventually become a part of the pier."[11] Justo Pastor Ruíz, the Episcopal pastor of Vieques in the 1940s, described the optimism of the time: "The town swam in gold for a while during these years. Rents increased three and four times in value and people bought good clothes and treated them with little care and liquor was consumed without end. There were those who tried to wash the floor with beer and who bought a $35 suit on Saturday and on Monday wore it to work and spoiled it within two hours. The base is here and gives more, they said" (Ruíz 1947: 206).

The construction of the base stopped almost as quickly as it had begun. Military priorities shifted to the Pacific when the United States entered the war, and the navy scaled back its original plans. The devastating destruction at Pearl Harbor challenged the wisdom of concentrating a fleet at one massive installation (Tugwell 1976: 68). The construction of the breakwater from Puerto Rico to Vieques was suspended, and work on Roosevelt Roads slowed because of the shortage of supplies.

By the time Roosevelt Roads was completed in 1943, it was only a shadow of the original vision. Though German submarines were active in the Caribbean and indeed sank hundreds of ships, the Caribbean never evolved into the theater of war strategists anticipated. The only battle in the Caribbean took place in February 1942, when German submarines attacked oil installations in Dutch Aruba (Langley 1989: 162). By 1943 naval planners concluded that a major naval base in Puerto Rico was unnecessary. Roosevelt Roads was placed on maintenance status at the conclusion of World War II (Langley 1985a: 272–273).

The abrupt halt of construction had a devastating effect on Vieques's economy. Without the military project, there was no work left on the island. The navy's expropriations of land had effectively liquidated the sugar cane industry. Playa Grande's *central*, the last operating mill in Vieques, was dismantled and sold. Most sugar cane lands had become military property, either part of the base or the resettlement tracts where tenants were relocated. Though some small- and medium-sized independent farms remained, the farmers had no mill to which they could sell their harvest, nor did they have access to transportation to ship their cane to the mainland to be ground. In the summer of 1943 there were marches in town in which Viequenses raised black flags and clamored for work and attention to their suffering (Ruíz 1947: 203). The economic boom that many Viequenses had hoped for did not come to pass:

> This flood of cash—this golden illusion—never compensated for the many setbacks caused by the Naval base. The most fertile and rich land was expropriated by the Navy and the neighborhoods of Tapón, Mosquito, and Llave disappeared. All the inhabitants and small landowners disappeared and left to form new neighborhoods in Moscú and Montesanto. Families that had a little house, cows, a horse and farmland came to have nothing but a makeshift house, a fistful of coins and the sky above them. Those who had their subsistence plots or who lived happily as tenants among farmland and fruit trees today live piled up and lack even air to breathe. (Ruíz 1947: 206)

Under pressure from the Puerto Rican government, in 1944 the navy leased some of the property to the Insular government for the agricultural rehabilitation of Vieques. Early programs initiated by the Puerto Rican Agricultural Company (PRACO), such as a pineapple-processing factory and cattle raising, met with success. Within three years, however, the navy would reevaluate Vieques and find new strategic purposes for the island in a shifting geopolitical context.

Puerto Rico in the Postwar Period

Puerto Rico's economic structure and political constitution changed significantly in the years after the war. In less than two decades, through Operation Bootstrap, a state-sponsored development plan, the island shifted from a predominantly rural society with an agricultural base to a predominantly urban society with a manufacturing-based economy. The early years of Puerto Rico's economic transformation saw remarkable economic growth and improved living conditions. These improvements were not without cost, however. Operation Bootstrap relied on the mass migration of the labor force, greater trade dependency on the United States, and institutionalized unemployment for a large sector of the work force (Baver 1993; Dietz 1986; History Task Force 1979).

In 1948 Puerto Ricans for the first time elected their own governor, Luis Muñoz Marín. Muñoz inherited the unresolved problem of Puerto Rican political status. In the postwar years, President Harry Truman wanted a resolution of Puerto Rico's colonial status that would satisfy the new UN charter. Muñoz, who had once favored independence, increasingly focused on economic reform and saw independence as an impediment to Puerto Rican progress. Muñoz and the PPD promoted instead a new "Commonwealth" status for the island that was ratified by a plebiscite in 1952.

The Commonwealth political arrangement provided for enough internal autonomy to satisfy the UN in 1953 that the territory had been decolonized. But under the Commonwealth arrangement, ultimate decisions about Puerto Rican self-determination were made not by the islanders, but by the U.S. Congress. Puerto Ricans continued to hold U.S. citizenship, but had no representation in federal government. They paid no federal taxes, but were subject to the military draft. Foreign policy matters were in the hands of the United States. Nowhere was the contradiction between internal autonomy and external control over "foreign policy" so vividly expressed as in Vieques, where "national security" directly impinged upon the community's internal affairs.

Puerto Rico's political status and economic policies were inseparable from broader U.S. geopolitical interests. As Ivonne Acosta (1989) demonstrates, Puerto Rico's reformed political status and capitalist development program went hand in hand with U.S. efforts to confront communism. Operation Bootstrap was seen as Puerto Rico's "democratic manifesto," issued one hundred years after the *Communist Manifesto*. Its Commonwealth status, ratified by plebiscite, was an answer to both Puerto Rican agitation for independence and accusations of U.S. colonialism.

The ascendancy of this model was also contingent upon the suppression of dissent. Puerto Rico's gag law (*la ley de la mordaza*) made it a crime to advocate the overthrow of the island's government. The ambiguity of the law enabled Puerto Rican officials to squelch and imprison Nationalist Party members, often on ideological grounds, without clear evidence of violent activity. The suppression of the Nationalists paved the way for the ratification of the Commonwealth. Thus the very foundation of this so-called democratic showcase was laid with strongly antidemocratic tendencies (see Acosta 1989).

The Commonwealth was in part a creation of the cold war. The U.S. military regarded Puerto Rico as central to U.S. security in the region, and World War II had expanded the military presence on the island. In the next decades, Puerto Rico would become increasingly positioned as a capitalist alternative to communist Cuba. Vieques became hostage to rising tensions.

Military Consolidation

Long after the menace of German submarines disappeared, long after the war was over and the troops went home, the U.S. Navy remained in Vieques. Vieques epitomized the Puerto Rican government's struggle to advance Puerto Rican interests in the face of the power of the navy. The U.S. military presence in Puerto Rico had grown dramatically during the war. The Puerto Rican government pressed the military to return the land it had taken for wartime purposes, but the military adamantly claimed an ongoing need. This struggle over military-controlled land became a key irritant in U.S.–Puerto Rican relations. Nowhere was the conflict more pronounced than in Vieques.[12]

From the earliest days of the military presence on Vieques, it was clear that the navy had given little consideration to civilian needs. There was no reasonable resettlement policy to guide the evictions. Once families were transported to the opposite side of the island, they were dumped in razed cane fields that the navy had just expropriated. Residents were assigned plots without title to the land and were not allowed to transfer lots. They were warned that they would be evicted if the navy wanted to reclaim the land (U.S. House 1981: 3).

The lack of title to the land had multiple damaging effects. It was impossible to secure loans to build decent homes; residents were left languishing in squalid conditions, without a clear sense of what the future would hold. The lack of property rights left unanswered issues of inheritance, raising questions as to whether an individual's child would hold any rights to the house or land on which he or she was raised. It is possible that the navy saw residents as a valuable labor force during the frantic construction of the pier. But circumstances changed in 1947.

In 1947 the navy drew up new strategic plans for Vieques. The navy redesignated Roosevelt Roads as a naval operating base for use as a training installation and fuel depot (Langley 1985a: 273). Vieques would be converted into a training site, to be used for firing practice and amphibious landings by tens of thousands of sailors and marines. The navy revoked its lease of agricultural land to the Puerto Rican government, throwing into disarray governmental efforts to spur the local economy (R. Picó 1950: 217). Because this new vision of the base required more land, the navy planned to expropriate over four thousand acres from eastern Vieques, displacing 130 families.[13]

The second round of expropriations would wedge Vieques's population between an ammunition depot and maneuver area. Puerto Rican officials were outraged at the navy's interference in their efforts to salvage the island's crippled economy. Rafael Picó, a member of a planning committee, wrote in an internal memo:

> The first real effort to rehabilitate the people of Vieques was progressing in a highly satisfactory manner, with their cooperation and support, and with the cooperation of Navy officials *until* Admiral Barbey came to Puerto Rico. He has refused to cooperate with the established Insular agencies, humiliated their representatives whenever possible, caused them to lose money and in particular, has made every effort to wreck the Insular program of the rehabilitation on Vieques.
>
> Admiral Barbey should be recalled immediately and the Navy lands should be released for the development of their fullest potentialities. The people of Puerto Rico and Vieques are too poor to give up 28,000 acres of land in order that the Navy use it one month a year for maneuvers. (quoted in Rodríguez Beruff 2001)

The Department of the Interior and the Insular government conducted closed-door meetings to address alternatives to squeezing the civilian residential community between the two installations. The Department of the Interior proposed resettling the population in St. Croix, just as the U.S. military had usurped Bikini Island the prior year and deposited its inhabitants on a distant atoll (Delgado Cintrón 1996; Dibblin 1988; Kiste 1974; Weisgall 1994).

The Puerto Rican government managed to block the eviction of Viequenses from the island, but the naval expropriations prevailed. Wary of the spectacle of dislocated families dumped on the street, the Puerto Rican government agreed to build housing in a new resettlement tract. The only concession the

Puerto Rican government won from the navy was that the military would provide materials for this new construction. Another minor provision permitted continued cattle grazing on the western area of the military property used for ammunition storage. Since naval maneuvers would include launching live bombs, the rest of the island was too dangerous for civilian entry. The navy justified its plans by pointing to a "changed international situation"—what it perceived to be the threat of communist infiltration of the world.[14]

With three-quarters of its land usurped, Vieques found its quality of life severely debased and its economy crippled. Residents were sandwiched between an ammunition depot and a vast maneuver area. The municipality lost its tax base. Residents on the arid tropical island lost access to major aquifers on military-controlled land. Although only six miles lay between Puerto Rico and Vieques, ferries were now forced to travel a circuitous twenty-two-mile route in rough waters to avoid the navy danger zone. The military dismissed islanders' worries, arguing that the spending of troops would offset any economic problems. This prediction did not come to pass.

Although the navy argued that the military installations in Vieques would provide work and opportunity to islanders, they brought instead ongoing unemployment and poverty. The number of troops permanently stationed on the island was not large enough to promote the development of a service economy. Vieques was used primarily for ammunition storage and maneuvers, and secondarily as a marine base (1959–1978). Thousands of troops would pour onto the island in the 1950s and 1960s, but their visits were so sporadic and brief that they could not sustain the local economy. Despite initial enthusiasm for the construction of the base, by the time the breakwater project was terminated in the mid-forties it was clear that the installations had only exacerbated poverty, joblessness, and economic insecurity.

Vieques: A Cold War Hostage

"The communist threat is everywhere and can be expected to continue indefinitely; it is particularly near your homes since the recent communist thrust into Cuba," commented Captain Hunt, assistant chief of staff for operations of the Tenth Naval District and Caribbean Sea Frontier, speaking at a Navy League Luncheon at the Caribe Hilton in San Juan in 1961.[15] Although the United States was officially at peace, Vieques became a hostage of the cold war. Despite growing social tensions and repeated calls for the navy to return land, the military remained entrenched on the island. After the Korean War, U.S. rivalry with the Soviet Union intensified. The Soviets tested the guided missile, giving the United States new impetus to compete for technological superiority. Roosevelt Roads assumed new strategic significance as a place to test missiles, and Vieques was a perfect bull's eye (Langley 1985a). The Cuban Revolution of 1959 jolted the U.S. military, which feared the rise of communism in a crucial strategic position in the region. That year, the navy activated a marine base on Vieques, Camp García. With the fear of a "communist menace" in Latin America, the island took on increasing importance as a staging ground for interventions, as in, for example, Guatemala (1954) and the Dominican Republic (1965). When the Bay of Pigs failed in 1961, surviving forces gathered in Vieques.

While the navy was planning the war against communism, Puerto Rican planners attempted to resuscitate the island's ailing economy. In 1955 the Commonwealth Economic Development Administration created a ten-year plan for stimulating tourism, community development, and industry in Vieques. The program depended on efficient air transportation to the island, and the government sought access to navy airfields. Civilian flights regularly use military airports in the United States without conflict, but the navy refused to allow civilian flights access to its airport in Vieques.[16]

The Puerto Rican government persisted with its plan, however, focusing on tourist development. In spite of the military's control of so much of the island and its extensive training operations, Vieques had beautiful beaches on its southern coast. Planners hoped to attract a resort.

In 1960 the Puerto Rican government secured a commitment from Frederick Woolworth's Woolnor Corporation to build a multimillion-dollar resort on Commonwealth lands on the south coast of Vieques. The proposed resort would act as an anchor to local development and feature a hundred-bed hotel, a marina, and a golf course. This was the most significant proposal to address Vieques's economic woes in years, and there was hope that the project would stimulate the failing economy.

The navy was bluntly antagonistic to the project. Tourism, it argued, was incompatible with large-scale amphibious training activities. Naval planes and helicopters would fly at low altitudes directly above the hotel, creating conflicts over noise. Civilian boats would have to be restricted during amphibious landing practices. The increase in civilian air traffic would affect the mine-laying operations off the shores of Roosevelt Roads.

Vieques had assumed increasing importance to the navy in light of the changed political climate in Cuba. Vieques, the navy argued, was its "last frontier" for training in the Atlantic, the optimum location "in which all operational training, both guided missile and conventional, could be conducted under realistic, tactical conditions."[17] The navy would not accept a resort in the civilian sector that might compromise its operations. A spokesman commented: "The U.S. government has spent more than $100 million in developing Vieques and

Roosevelt Roads. We're not going to throw away such an investment so that Vieques should be converted into a Mecca for tourism."[18]

The navy squelched the resort. The success of the project hinged on adequate air transportation to shuttle tourists between Vieques and Puerto Rico. The navy controlled the airspace over the island. The Commonwealth government petitioned the Federal Aviation Administration for air rights over the western portion of Vieques, so that commercial flights could land in Vieques. While conceding the vital importance of national defense, the Commonwealth government argued that security was not an issue in this case. It urged the FAA to allow commercial flights to land in Vieques, arguing, "It is our belief that a prosperous community of small and free enterprise in that island will be to the credit and best interest of the United States and Puerto Rico."[19] The navy, however, refused to cede air rights over Vieques. The navy granted that it would continue to allow a limited corridor of passage for essential surface and air transportation for residents, but refused to expand air access to commercial flights. To make their intentions to control Vieques clear, navy officials told the Woolnor Corporation that any resort it constructed risked expropriation by the navy in future. After spending $1 million on plans for the resort, Woolnor pulled out of Vieques.

Vieques, which had already surrendered more than three-quarters of its land, effectively lost control over the civilian sector as well. The military neither allowed civilians to develop a viable economic base nor provided any economic benefits to compensate for the liquidation of Vieques's economy. "Of the millions spent on maneuvers," the mayor declared, "Vieques does not get anything. Not a single civilian works at the base as they do in Aguadilla and Roosevelt Roads, where hundreds of Puerto Rican fathers earn their daily bread."[20]

The controversy over the Woolnor project revealed that the navy increasingly saw the conflict between the military and the civilians in polarized terms. The economic development of the tourist sector was seen not merely as an inconvenience but as a threat that would ultimately force the navy off the island. "It is inevitable," a marine major declared, "that resulting conflicts would only operate to limit the scope or degree of our training, and ultimately, because of numerous limitations imposed, would force the Marine Corps to abandon Vieques entirely."[21] In light of growing tension, the navy resolved to end the simmering dispute once and for all.

In 1961 the navy drafted secret plans to remove the entire civilian population of 8,000 from the island of Vieques. No one would remain. Even the dead would be dug up and removed from their graves. The 570 residents of the neighboring island of Culebra would also be removed to provide a "suitable impact area for the rapidly increasing missile training" (Fernández 1996: 203). The plan would allow the navy to expand the base with access unfettered by civilians. The expansion of the base was crucial, the navy argued, because the United States required a place to test its missiles and train covert forces.

Secretary of Defense Robert McNamara sent word of the "real estate negotiations" to Governor Luis Muñoz Marín. The plan included incentives for Puerto Rico. In exchange for Vieques's land, the navy would return land it had expropriated from the government during the war and sell back to Puerto Rico land it had acquired from private owners. Under intense pressure from the navy, Muñoz agreed that if this were "really, absolutely and unequivocally necessary for the security of the United States" he would consent to the plan (Fernández 1996: 202).

Muñoz, however, was also a consummate politician who perceived the political implications of a case the navy saw mainly in military terms. While the navy moved forward with its plans, Vieques's mayor continued to agitate for the navy to return the expropriated land. It became clear that the political climate was different from 1941, when the navy seized Vieques in the shadow of the war. Viequenses would not go quietly from the island.

Muñoz recognized the public relations significance of Vieques in a political climate dominated by cold war tensions. The United States was politically invested in Puerto Rico as a model of democracy and progress in the Caribbean. The United States had argued before the United Nations that Puerto Rico's colonial status had been resolved with the conferral of Commonwealth status. The proposed expropriation of the rest of Vieques Island and the eviction of its residents, however, suggested the continued domination of the U.S. military, and called into question the nature of Puerto Rico's political association with the United States. The liquidation of two Puerto Rican municipalities in the face of opposition from residents would only be marshaled as evidence by the Cubans, Soviets, and sympathetic Latin American neighbors of continued U.S. imperialism and interventionism in the region. Although the navy had removed the population of Bikini with little outcry, the politics here were different.[22] All the effort the United States invested in promoting its relationship with Puerto Rico and touting the island's economic miracle could be jeopardized by such a callous show of force.

Muñoz wrote to President John F. Kennedy to apprise him of the serious political implications of the navy's plan. Kennedy intervened and ordered a halt to the seizure of the island. Vieques residents were to remain.[23]

Any true victory was elusive, however. The navy proceeded with its tactical operations, bombing an island inhabited by eight thousand people. Kennedy's intervention saved Vieques from the plight of the Bikini islanders, who wandered homeless for decades. It did not resolve the underlying conflict between residents and the navy, which was considering new tactics for complete island domination.

In 1964 the navy inadvertently leaked the news that it intended to acquire a strip of land along Vieques's south coast to unite its two bases. Vieques mayor Antonio Rivera learned that the U.S. Armed Services Committee had authorized this plan and the navy expected Congress to fund it. The implications of the project, which blandly proposed to acquire real estate to unite the two bases, were not lost on the mayor. The four thousand acres the navy planned to expropriate constituted half the civilian sector and the only beaches that were not under navy jurisdiction. The acres held the remaining pier where sugar was shipped to Puerto Rico. They held the only remaining aquifers that supplied water to the civilian sector. The expropriation would uproot two hundred families and reduce the civilian sector of Vieques to a narrow, U-shaped strip of land. Thirty thousand of Vieques's thirty-three thousand acres would be in the hands of the navy. The acquisition of land here, the navy declared, would "further block hotel development and permit marine vertical assault forces greater freedom of action."[24]

The navy was essentially maneuvering toward the same goals it had in 1961. Any community left on the island after the next round of expropriations would be unsustainable. All hope for the island's future lay in some sort of tourist development, yet the navy planned to take every island beach. It was doubtful that any other economic player would emerge to take the place of tourism. "As long as this fear of future expropriations exists," wrote one reporter, "no industry will locate its factory in Vieques, no tourist company is going to construct hotels, nor will any farmer invest what is necessary to obtain the maximum yield of the land."[25]

Although the 1961 plan has been classified, the 1964 effort to expropriate the south coast of Vieques became public and stirred great controversy. Recognizing that naval expropriations would squeeze them completely off the island, people in Vieques organized in opposition to the plan. Mayor Rivera declared the plan the "savage assassination of the life of a people" and headed a Citizens' Committee for the Defense of Vieques, composed of thirty citizens who included businessmen, cane farmers whose lands were directly threatened, the Methodist minister, and the superintendent of schools. In an epoch of land reform, when Puerto Rico struggled to eliminate rural poverty and squalor, Rivera declared that the navy was trying to make *agregados* out of Puerto Ricans living on island. The expropriations would "condemn Vieques to death and lead us out of our homes. . . . The philosophy of the '*agregado*,'" he said, "is incompatible with the dignity of an American citizen. We repeat our willingness, as good American citizens, to contribute to our national defense, but we also demand justice for Vieques."[26] The Citizens' Committee met in San Juan with Governor Muñoz and urged him to intervene. Rivera said the Committee would take its case to the streets of Washington, if necessary.

Muñoz's public response was muted. He supported the Committee members' legal rights as American citizens to resolve a situation they felt was unjust. He noted that the Department of Defense should have all the land that was strictly necessary for national defense, because the defense of the nation was a priority. He conceded, however, that any land not strictly necessary should be returned as soon as possible for the use of civilians. Puerto Rico had a large population with few natural resources, he noted, and no piece of land should be left unused that might help Puerto Rico attain a higher standard of living.[27] Such a public statement vaguely supported Rivera's cause while deferring to military judgment.

The Puerto Rican press denounced Muñoz's apparent indifference.[28] Reporters pressured Puerto Rico's resident commissioner, Antonio Fernos Isern, who sat as a nonvoting member on the House Armed Services Committee, to reveal whether he consented to the navy's proposal or whether he attempted to intervene on Vieques's behalf. "I'm not in a position to acquiesce or not acquiesce," he responded.[29]

Rivera vowed to travel to Washington to take his case directly to President Lyndon Johnson. Vieques bootblacks chipped in pennies to pay for the trip. The local Catholic church took up a collection from parishioners to fund the journey. Only the mayor seemed determined to save Vieques.

Muñoz was not as indifferent as he seemed, however. The situation put him in a difficult position. He had already written to Kennedy about the political implications of further navy expropriations, but he was also committed to maintaining a show of patriotic support for a military he had no real power to contest. As the Puerto Rican resident commissioner had noted, Puerto Rico had no voice, no power in the federal government. Muñoz reminded Johnson of the political ramifications of the case and of Kennedy's critical commitment. In light of Cuba, the United States needed the security of stability in Puerto Rico. When Rivera arrived in Washington, he was welcomed and told that the navy had already resolved not to take the land.

Protesting the Navy

Rivera returned to Vieques triumphant, with a pledge from the navy not to expropriate additional land. Vieques's victory made the headlines of the Puerto Rican newspapers. The Citizens' Committee's lawyer, José Arrarás, said, "This was one of the finest examples of living, working democracy in action. It should serve as an example to other communities of what can be done when partisan differences are set aside for a noble cause."[30] Rivera established himself as a hero who worked tirelessly for Vieques and who successfully challenged the navy in the pursuit of justice for the community. The committee that he headed stood as the first organized effort in Vieques to confront the military. His popular success relied on the careful position he staked between the assertion of local needs and declarations of loyalty to the United States, a framework important in the development of subsequent movements as well.

Rivera was not a radical. He maintained cordial relations with navy officials in Vieques and frequently attended maneuvers as a spectator. He made it clear that there was no place for communist or anti-American ideology in his Citizens' Committee.[31] He was, above all, a *popular*. The *populares* had ascended to power by staking an ideological position not far from that of the Nationalists. Although *populares* were vehemently anticolonial, they shied away from expressions of anti-Americanism. They were proreform, but not anticapitalist (Dietz 1986: 180). The subtle distinctions in ideology were crucial. The Nationalists were gunned down in the streets; the PPD ascended to power.

Rivera traveled to Washington professing loyalty as a citizen. At the same time, he denounced the navy's plans as contributing to the "annihilation of a community." Despite widespread support for Vieques's cause, Rivera's fierce rhetoric and defense of the local provoked consternation within a cold war context where Puerto Rican patriotism was continually scrutinized.[32]

Rivera's struggle illuminated the tensions within Puerto Rican society between feelings of loyalty to the United States, on the one hand, and a strong sense of local identity and belonging, on the other. The navy's intransigence heightened Viequenses' sense of community and peoplehood, which developed explicitly in relationship to the struggle to remain on the island. The framework Viequenses adopted to express their grievances could not be nationalistic, given the political sensibilities of the populace and the broader cold war context. But the continual pressure the navy placed on the population fostered a resilient cultural identity grounded in the local and in the defense of community.

Two

*I was born here. I was raised here and I raised nine children
here, two of whom I have given to the navy. They are not
throwing me out of here alive.*
—Eugenio Vélez, 1964

Cultural Identity in Vieques

How did residents respond to the military usurpation of Vieques? What was it like to live on an island that was simultaneously a rural residential community and an international theater of war? What was the effect of the naval presence on the life of the people as a whole?

The navy's control of land, air, and water resources on Vieques set up fundamental obstacles to stable civilian life. Use of the island as an ammunition depot and a site for war games inhibited the development of a service economy that might compensate for the loss of three-quarters of island land. Unemployment remained high and out-migration continued. Troops on pass, drinking, carousing, and harassing women, created significant conflict. Underlying this tension was the threat that the navy would usurp the entire island and evict the civilian population.

Yet political and economic conditions militated against the development of nationalist or anti-American sentiment. U.S. overseas military bases are commonly regarded as lightning rods for nationalist ferment, and the affront of a foreign presence is often assumed to threaten local life ways and inspire ideologically based protest. In Vieques, however, residents were ambivalent in their attitudes toward military personnel and the navy as a whole.

At the same time, Viequense cultural identity emerged as an important reaction to the military presence. Discontent with the navy and anxiety about the island's future spawned a fierce sense of attachment to Vieques and a determination to stay. It produced a sense of peoplehood that was specifically identified with the island.

In Puerto Rico, writes Jorge Duany (2000: 8), issues of identity "acquire a sense of urgency seldom found in well-established nation states that do not have to justify their existence or fight for their survival." Nowhere is this struggle more vivid than in Vieques, where people struggled to remain on the island and eke out a living despite military efforts to remove them. In a context in which expressions of anti-Americanism were deemed subversive, people's visceral, emotional response to the travails of the military occupation was channeled into the defense of the local.

Fishermen, in particular, expressed this local identity and cultural resistance to the navy. In the late 1930s, the PPD had ascended to power on a program of agrarian reform, celebrating the image of the *jíbaro*, the highland subsistence-dwelling peasant, as a central component of Puerto Rican identity (Carr 1984: 115; Giusti Cordero 1996: 58). As Arlene Dávila (1997) describes, once the PPD gained control of the Commonwealth government, the party explicitly promoted a nostalgia for the island's rural past. The *jíbaro*, the peasant past, became extolled in music, art, and cultural programs. Ironically, Dávila notes, this official romanticization occurred while the government itself undertook economic policies that eliminated the island's rural base.

In Vieques, the cultural and symbolic importance of fishing emerged within this broader context, but was not propagated from above, by government officials or cultural elites. Rather, fishing developed as an organic expression of cultural identity from the grassroots and spoke to the community's particular struggle to coexist with the United States. Fishing emerged as a key cultural assertion with its roots in *agrego* social relations. An exploration of these relations illuminates the way in which people who were so powerless formed such a strong sense of entitlement to the island.

The Expropriations: Nationalism and Class Experience

In 1948, shortly after he was released from federal prison, Nationalist Party leader Pedro Albizu Campos denounced the recent military expropriations of land on Vieques Island as the "vivisection of the Puerto Rican nation."[1] Despite Albizu's condemnations, the usurpation sparked little nationalist resentment in Vieques. People's experience of the expropriations was profound and significant, but the response it evoked was not anticolonial or anti-American.

Local antinavy activists and Puerto Rican nationalists have continually emphasized the military expropriation of Vieques Island in chronicling the history of injustice perpetrated against the people there. Some have looked for the seeds of rebellion in people's experience of eviction. Indeed, a number of local activists attribute their political radicalization to their experience of eviction in the 1940s. Others have emphasized Viequenses' victimization at the hands of the military. Statehood proponents have suggested that Viequenses' compliance with eviction proceedings offers evidence of supreme patriotism and sacrifice to the nation.[2]

All discussion of the expropriations in Vieques is charged, and memory of the past is often colored by understandings of the present. Still, people's recollections offer a window into their political sensibilities and attitude toward the military.

One of the most important elements of the expropriations experience is the way in which people have internalized it. When people talk about the expropriations in Vieques, they speak of *themselves* as having been expropriated. Technically, the navy expropriated Vieques's land. Yet in Vieques, residents say "me expropriaron," or "they expropriated me." Phrased in these terms, the act of usurping property is identified as a viscerally felt personal experience and a deep-seated grievance. At the same time, the use of the passive voice expresses people's feelings of victimization and powerlessness in the face of forces beyond their control.

Interviews with residents evicted in the 1940s revealed a marked ambivalence about the experience. By the 1930s there was growing discontent with colonialism throughout Puerto Rico, but Puerto Ricans believed that their future was linked to continued association with the United States. When wartime shortages crippled Puerto Rico, Vieques's population was on the brink of starvation. It was common to hear people associate the navy's arrival with food and recollect sailors' casual acts of generosity, a testament to the state of destitution in which most people lived in 1941. For example, sixty-two-year-old Dolores Torres, whose family was evicted from the Playa Grande estate, remembered, "When they came, there was a lot of movement, a lot of work because they were constructing the base and all. They brought in trucks of coffee and apples. People benefited. They [sailors] were throwing coins in the air. Children would collect them and bring them to their mothers." In the same way that many working-class people in Puerto Rico had been hopeful that the U.S. invasion of 1898 would bring about an improved standard of living, Viequenses in 1941 were hopeful that the base would lift them out of poverty.[3]

The class structure of Vieques Island militated against the development of anti-American sentiment. On the eve of the military's arrival in 1941, 95 percent of the rural population was landless, most living as *agregados* on property owned by two sugar companies. A fundamental element of people's understanding of the military expropriations was their class experience of the sugar era.

Agrego *Relations*

Puerto Rico's economy from the mid-1800s to the 1940s was dominated by coffee and sugar plantations, which relied initially on slave and then on "free" labor to work in the fields. Plantation society was originally founded on slave labor, and at its essence was based on forced labor and exploitation. One critical tension in Puerto Rico, and indeed in the Caribbean as a whole, stemmed from workers' struggle for freedom and autonomy. Access to the land became the crucial factor that allowed workers to escape from slavery or the drudgery of plantation labor (Mintz 1985). Wherever they had access to land, working people withdrew from commercial agriculture and tried to survive on subsistence production.

Puerto Rico's mountainous interior long served as a refuge to those seeking autonomy from the Insular civil and military authorities. At the beginning of the nineteenth century, a large part of Puerto Rico's population lived in the interior and engaged in subsistence farming on unattended crown land (Mintz 1989: 88). When the sugar industry expanded, the mountain region acted as a barrier against the encroachment of cane and became a source of refuge for working people (Scarano 1984: 6). As Laird Bergad (1983) demonstrates, the expansion of commercial agriculture in nineteenth-century Puerto Rico relied not only on coercing labor (the heart of the infamous *libreta* system) but also on dislocating people from the land.[4] *Agrego* relations came to embody the tension between coercion and autonomy.

Bergad describes *agregados* as "service tenants who exchanged usufruct rights to small parcels of land for various labor obligations" (1983: 88). Technically, *agregados* were landless: they lived without title on someone else's property. *Agregados*, however, lived at the intersection between peasant and proletarian social relations. They lived on the land without owning it; they moved between wage labor and subsistence production.

The term *agregado* derives from the Spanish verb *agregar*, "to attach." *Agrego* relations encompassed a range of social relations that varied regionally and historically. In eighteenth-century Puerto Rico, Mintz describes *agregados* as settlers who attached themselves to colonists already cultivating highland land, either offering their labor or farming on a share basis (1989: 88). In late nineteenth-century Cuba, César Ayala describes *agregados* as a central part of the sugar cane labor force, who received plots of land for food production on the condition that they work in the cane for wages during the harvest (1999: 158).

Agregados have traditionally been regarded as the most exploited sector of the Puerto Rican working class, because they had no formal rights to the land and lived at the whim of the landowner. But Bergad argues that among landless laborers, the use rights *agregados* staked to the land were central to their survival and autonomy. *Agrego* relations were crucial to avoiding complete disenfranchisement and exploitation by the landowner (Bergad 1983: 89). Worse than the plight of the *agregado* was that of the *jornalero*, the landless wage worker who lived in barracks and migrated from town to town in search of work.

In Vieques, the sugar industry operated through a combination of *agregado* and *jornalero* labor. Workers migrated seasonally to Vieques from eastern Puerto Rico and lived in barracks on sugar company land. Others lived in shacks, either on the landholdings of the big estates or on *colono* land, smaller farms belonging to independent cane farmers. *Agrego* relations encompassed access not only to small plots for subsistence crops but to the lagoons and mangroves to fish, to the coastal areas to collect shellfish, coconuts, and fruit, and to the woods to collect wood for charcoal making.

Agrego relations shaped the worldview of people in Vieques on the eve of the navy's arrival. On the one hand, *agrego* relations signified disenfranchisement and powerlessness. *Agregados* were subject to political repression and control.[5] On the other hand, to describe *agregados* as landless obscures the intimate relationship residents forged with the local ecology. In Vieques, *agregados* not only had access to subsistence plots on parcels of land allotted by the *central* but also had access to the fertile coastal areas that eluded the control of the sugar plantations.

The complexity of *agrego* relations fundamentally affected Viequenses' response to the military occupation. Because they lived in positions of relative powerlessness and subjugation, people did not initially respond in nationalist terms. At the same time, *agrego* relations help explain a sense of entitlement and attachment residents feel to the land, a connection that might be obscured if residents were understood simply as "landless."

The use rights *agregados* derived from land should not be romanticized: Vieques's rural population was on the edge of starvation when the navy arrived. Neither, however, should the relationship residents forged with landowners over rights to the local ecology be dismissed, because it greatly influenced the way residents understood the navy's usurpation.

The Evictions

Leonardo Gómez and Nilda Figueroa, an elderly couple who live in the Montesanto resettlement tract, were *agregados* when the navy arrived. Their memories reveal an ambivalence toward the military that many working-class Viequenses share.

Don Leonardo was born on the Playa Grande estate in Vieques in 1911. His family lived in a wooden shack on sugar company land. His father worked in the *central*, grinding cane. Doña Nilda was born in 1921 in Puerto Negro, on the opposite side of Vieques. Her family lived on the estate of Miguel Simons, one of the island's wealthy farmers. When asked about his life as a youth, don Leonardo was not at all nostalgic. "When I was young I was a worker," he stated. "A cane worker. I cut cane. I weeded and planted cane. I only worked a bit in the *central*. Two nights. I started working at sixteen or seventeen, the age boys worked in these times." Don Leonardo remembered that he earned twelve dollars a week. "We worked from 7 to 4. Eight hours . . . in the fields the sun was fire."

Don Leonardo's memories of the past were stark. "In 1930, '31, almost no one could eat. . . . Life was not very good." He recalled that during the dead time, the months that stretched between planting and harvest, it was a struggle to find food. In order to survive, people would fish or collect mangoes. Some work could be found on the Esperanza estate (Central Vieques), owned by a big U.S. sugar corporation. "They paid fifty cents for half a day's work, one dollar per day," he recalled. "How many hours for a half a dollar!" doña Nilda interrupted. "A dollar a day! A half a dollar for four hours, five hours! That's what they paid! A man worked and had to buy from a store. One dollar for a family to eat!" Doña Nilda remembered that while men were working in the sugar cane, women found work "washing and ironing for the rich."

In 1941 the navy expropriated the land that don Leonardo lived on and transferred his family to a military resettlement tract in the Barrio Montesanto. "They threw us on a truck and brought us to Montesanto. No one could return. No one helped me. The navy did not help me," he recalled. When asked if his family had been compensated for the home that they lost, he responded, "They did not give us any money." The shack he had been living in was bulldozed and the family was given the wood pieces to build a new home on an assigned lot.

The transition was difficult. Families lost animals and subsistence crops that provided a hedge against future hard times. Doña Nilda and her family were evicted from their home in the second wave of military expropriations, in 1947. "I also was living as an *agregado* when the navy came," doña Nilda explained. "The land we lived on the owners of the land gave us to live on. But we didn't receive money [when the land was expropriated]. I had chickens, pigs, all of this I had to let go. I had to let the animals go because in Tortuguero there was no place to raise animals. As *agregados* we could raise them on the land." "How did you learn of your eviction?" I asked doña Nilda. "The owner of the land told us," she responded. "Because we were *agregados* they just told us to leave."

After he was evicted from his home on Playa Grande, don Leonardo found work on the base, constructing the pier. The work was constant for about two years. After that, like many Viequenses, he traveled to St. Croix to find employment. Doña Nilda found work in Vieques, washing and ironing for the sailors. The pay was good, she recalled, $3.50 per dozen shirts. She could wash and iron four or five dozen a day, earning as much as $17.50 per day. "When there was a maneuver, when the troops of gringos came, there was a lot [of work]. They came to my house with their clothes."

Describing their quality of life before and after the navy came, doña Nilda said, "It was better because they were helping." Don Leonardo was confused. "Who?" he asked. "Them, the Americans," she retorted. "Well, they [the land owners] paid for the land," she explained. "They paid," she stressed. She could offer no specific way the navy had helped Vieques, however. Instead, she blamed the Puerto Rican government for isolating and betraying them, an opinion commonly heard in Vieques. "Not a cent went to us, it went to the governor over there [in Puerto Rico]," she argued. "The government sold the *central* here and the people who were working in the cane went without work. They lived as they could, fishing and so forth."

The feeling that Viequenses are pawns in negotiations of power between the Commonwealth of Puerto Rico and the U.S. military echoes the feelings of powerlessness people reveal as they describe their lives as *agregados*, living at the whim of the plantation owner. This feeling of separateness and subjugation is a fundamental element of local identity.

When asked if his quality of life in Vieques was better or worse since the navy came, don Leonardo answered, "Better, because we have food stamps and social security now. There's no work. I collect social security." He distinguished between the navy's influence on the island and the effect of federal transfer payments such as social security and food stamps that have been crucial in subsidizing the Puerto Rican economy.[6] Frequently, however, residents associated the arrival of the navy with the end of rural squalor. The dramatic social and economic change Puerto Rico experienced with the Operation Bootstrap model of export-oriented development is often attributed to the navy, the major expression of state power on Vieques Island.

Thus some residents argued that the expropriations were positive because they ushered in a new era and ended the feudalistic sugar era. Clara Serrano, an eighty-five-year-old retired schoolteacher and the daughter of a wealthy sugar cane farmer, was one such proponent. Doña Clara has strong links to the local PPD political machine and is an avid proponent of Puerto Rico's "commonwealth association" with the United States. She lived through the upheavals of the forties and defended the navy against charges that it callously evicted Viequenses from their dwellings. In fact, she argued, most Viequenses were not really "expropriated" from their homes:

> The people lived in homes that the *central* provided for them. That means that when they expropriated the *centrales*, they didn't expropriate the people; they had nothing there. All of the houses belonged to the *central*. . . . They expropriated only the owner. But when they expropriated everyone had to go, because all of the houses were within the *central*. But they were so good, those Americans. To each one who lived there, they gave a house to live . . . to each one they gave an acre of land. When were these people going to have houses? When they came to take land, they expropriated nothing from them, nothing. When the navy came, the poor made out better than the rich!

Doña Clara's analysis turned on her interpretation of the word "expropriate." She argued that the rich were the ones who lost when the navy came; they were the ones who were "expropriated." The poor, she believed, benefited from the navy and hence support the military: "Don't talk bad about the navy in Montesanto [one of the resettlement tracts]. Everyone there supports the navy. There are some, yes, who are against the navy, who remember, alas, when we were thrown out of there we suffered. But [the navy] gave them a house, gave them land. The truth is that they are ungrateful. I tell you, I have never seen so many cars in Vieques before. Before, there were almost no cars here. And nowadays, if you need a lady to clean your house, she comes driving an automobile. A car. Yes, that's right."

Doña Clara's defense of the navy reflected her class position and her political identity. Her family rose to political prominence during the military's tenure on the island. Although her land was not expropriated, she sympathized with landowners who lost their property. She believed that the land is the rightful heritage of the rich and resented any implication that the working classes had a claim as well. Like many Viequenses, she also associated the military presence with the dramatic social and economic change Puerto Rico experienced after World War II. She defended the navy's presence in Vieques with the same vigor with which she defended Puerto Rico's political relationship with the United States. She was essentially in favor of the status quo, and she held the common view that criticism of the navy was fundamentally anti-American.

Doña Clara seemed to overstate the enthusiasm of the working-class response to the navy. *Agregado* families often perceived a double-sided nature to the military takeover. The bulldozer, the dismantled home, the razed cane field signified dislocation, usurpation, and loss. Yet the arrival of the military also gave hope to the desperately poor for a new era with work and a secure future.

Still, residents tended to highlight their sense of victimization and trauma. Carlos Zenón, a fisherman leader of the antinavy struggle, described his family's eviction:

> I was four years old when the expropriations began. . . . I remember the day we received the notice giving us 24 hours to move because we were being expropriated. My parents were divorced and I lived with my mother, a brother and a sister. At first my mother could not believe that after living her entire life there, they could suddenly tell her to leave. . . . She did not know where to go or what to do with the house. Our house was made of wood and zinc, rather small for us but comfortable. She decided not to believe what was happening and to remain. But the following day they returned and told her that they had warned her.
>
> They told my mother that she had to leave immediately. She asked to where. She explained that she had three small children and no means of transportation. They simply gave her a form indicating that in the barrio Santa María a small lot of land had been set aside for her. The form had on it Santa María and four numbers indicating the four corners of the lot. Nothing more. Some people say that the expropriated were given tents. Well, those relocated to Santa María did not receive anything. They told her to leave because they were going to tear down the house that instant. They had brought a bulldozer with them. At the moment I remember thinking that it was a huge toy. I had never seen anything like it. I was extremely happy with the bulldozer until I saw the fear on my mother's face and the way she was hurriedly putting things together to take with us. She thought they were going to tear the house down on top of us. At that time there was a fear of federal authorities that does not exist today. I remember vividly that many Puerto Ricans, including Viequenses, believed that the penalty for a violation of federal law was imprisonment in Atlanta. . . . My mother, I am sure was thinking just that. She quickly put some dishes, our possessions, and whatever she could, including something with which to heat up food or milk for us in a blanket. She tied it up and left with the three of us. I remember looking back and being fascinated as the bulldozer tore down our home. My mother, on the other hand, was crying, not knowing where to go. (Zenón 1982)

Zenón's narrative describes both his mother's fear and her refusal to passively comply with orders to vacate the land. Indeed, his mother denied her eviction notice until the navy arrived at her house with a bulldozer. Such foot dragging, however, did not translate into active resistance. Radamés Tirado, who served as mayor of Vieques between 1976 and 1980, was evicted with his family from land belonging to the Playa Grande sugar *central*. He explained his parents' response to orders to vacate the land: "In this time period, people lived in a state of ignorance. Most people understood that a navy order was something they had to obey. Most understood it this way. Most people in this time period did not go to school, did not have any academic preparation." Viequenses did not rally against the navy in the 1940s, or have a sense of their collective identity or power to resist.

Gender Dimensions of the Military Presence

By the 1950s Vieques emerged as a vital area for naval training exercises. Over the course of the 1950s and 1960s, tens of thousands of sailors invaded it on maneuver. At times almost one hundred thousand sailors converged on the small rural island.[7] When training exercises were completed, sailors on pass poured into town. Conflict was inevitable.

In her pathbreaking work, Cynthia Enloe (1990, 2000) has argued for the central role that ideas about masculinity and femininity play in international politics and, in particular, in the functioning of the military. Military bases, Enloe suggests, may slip unnoticed into the daily life of the surrounding community as long as they insinuate themselves into preexisting understandings about male and female roles and behavior. "If the fit between local and foreign men and local and foreign women breaks down," she notes, "the base may lose its protective cover. It may become the target of nationalist resentment that could subvert the very structure of a military alliance" (1990: 67).

A number of international incidents, such as the abduction and rape of a twelve-year-old girl in Okinawa, Japan, by U.S. servicemen (Enloe 2000; Johnson 1999) and the murder of a prostitute in South Korea by a U.S. soldier (Moon 1997), have spiraled into significant antimilitary demonstrations. Such sexually charged conflicts seem to confirm Enloe's thesis. Yet in Vieques, while the military presence did challenge existing relations of gender and sexuality and provoke conflict between sailors and Viequense men, conflict did not escalate into the kind of nationalist uprising that Enloe predicts.

When the navy first arrived, most people in Vieques anticipated that the base would bring jobs to male agricultural laborers desperate for work. After the breakwater project was terminated, however, the base offered virtually no employment. The service economy the admirals promised amounted to irregular waves of work for bartenders, prostitutes, shoeshiners, and washerwomen.

Male agricultural workers found their opportunities severely curtailed. The major source of formal employment in Vieques throughout the 1950s until the mid-1960s was a government-run sugar farm. Yet sugar production was dra-

_____ *Table 1* _____

Population Change in Vieques and Puerto Rico, by Sex, 1930-1960

	1930	1940	1950	1960
Vieques population				
Total	10,582	10,362	9,228	7,210
Male	5,612	5,367	4,724	3,660
Female	4,970	4,995	4,504	3,550
Male per 100 female	112.9	107.4	104.8	103.1
Puerto Rico population				
Total	1,543,913	1,869,255	2,210,703	2,349,544
Male	771,761	938,280	1,110,946	1,162,704
Female	772,152	930,975	1,099,757	1,186,836
Male per 100 female	99.9	100.8	101.1	97.9

SOURCE: U.S. Census 1930, 1940, 1950, 1960.

matically reduced by the navy's control of the land and provided only a fraction of the work it had in the past. Sugar production, moreover, was seasonal work, and the navy's control over the land impeded the important peasantlike subsistence activities people had long relied on to supplement work in the cane.

When the military restricted these economic activities, Vieques's population declined dramatically as residents migrated to Puerto Rico, the United States, and St. Croix. Although Puerto Rico's population as a whole grew, even in spite of mass migration to the United States, in Vieques the population significantly declined. The ratio between males and females changed as well. Once predominantly male, probably because the sugar economy relied on migrant male laborers, the proportion of men to women steadily dropped (see table 1). Although men remained a slight majority in Vieques, this demographic shift informed a perception that men were disappearing. A cultural festival program from the 1960s poignantly noted: "Most of the men of working age, and many of the women, have left the island. It has become an island of women, children, and old folks."

Carlos Quintero, a forty-one-year-old schoolteacher and antinavy activist, described the effect of these changing demographics on his own family:

My father left Vieques out of necessity. When the navy arrived in Vieques he had no place to work, he was a carpenter. He went to the Virgin Islands. He spent some time in St. Croix, but then later settled down in St. Thomas. He worked for the government and supported the family. The only thing that happened to the family was that he didn't return. One summer he brought us over to St. Thomas, we passed the summer and returned to Vieques. There came the moment when he stayed over there and my mother stayed with us. My mother had to struggle to raise the family. [What did your mother do?] She was a housewife, the work that there was, was washing and ironing. Listen, the contradiction of my life is that my mother washed and ironed clothes of the sailors from the base! My mother washed and cleaned for civilians, but there was a time when we benefited largely from the work she had from the sailors. As was the case with many housewives at this time.

The military presence altered the island's gender balance. It did this not only in prompting an exodus of working-age men, but in sending in truckloads of servicemen to town on liberty pass. Many middle-aged and elderly women recalled the influx of sailors as an invasion. Rosa Moreno was a teenager in early fifties and recalled: "There were eight thousand people here. At night the sailors would get passes to come to town. There could be six thousand of them. They were fresh and would start fights. Women and girls were afraid to go outside. My mother would hide all of us inside, my sisters and brothers, and lock the door and close the windows. The sailors would be roaming the streets, banging on doors, asking for 'Margarita, Margarita.' My mother wanted to protect her daughters. She was also worried about my brothers and my father, because they could be assaulted if they tried to defend our honor."

The lives of many women like doña Rosa were greatly circumscribed by hordes of drunken men. Rumors abound about women who were raped by sailors. Yet women's narratives often reveal ambivalence. Dulce Silva, a fifty-eight-year-old nurse, considered sailors' lewd behavior a natural male impulse: "Many years back there were many problems. Because in the beginning, when they gave passes to everyone after being on boats for so long, they came running into town on their own to get drunk. It was a natural thing because when a sailor goes out, he goes out to enjoy himself. . . . They were looking for women and to get drunk. Because they need to enjoy themselves and that's the truth. The only problem is that they get drunk and start trouble, destroy things." Doña Dulce stressed that she never had problems with the military, but admitted that she locked herself in her house from the early evening on. She downplayed the restrictions on her life, while confessing she was terrified of the sailors.

Well, I didn't have problems. It was in the late hours of the night that there would be problems. I was in bed. After 6:00 at night I kept the house all closed up, well closed up. Because many passed by, fighting. They were looking for businesses that were opened and women to go with them. Well, I kept my house all closed up. All closed up. And they passed by and I didn't have any trouble. They were drunk and running by. Because Destino [the entrance to Camp García] is close by. We lived in constant terror.

[KM: Were they on pass often? For example, how many times a month would you have to close your house?] They passed by every day. We closed the house for protection and out of terror. When there were maneuvers they would be running out in the evening. They were hot to leave for the mountains [where illicit sex took place].

"On a small island where we don't have eight thousand people, you can't give liberty to ten thousand!" asserted sixty-four-year-old Elena Portalatin. "Imagine selling beer to ten thousand men! The little businesses did well. Washing and laundry were busy; there were no dry cleaners in those days. There was a lot of work for bars, prostitutes, and washers," she added wryly.

Prostitution emerged hand in hand with the military presence.[8] Doña Rosa confessed that she was shocked to learn years later that her own brothers had acted as "mules" when they were children, bringing sailors to prostitutes for a small fee. "We were poor, but I never knew they were that fresh!" she exclaimed. Vieques spawned its own red-light district, a block called "El Cañón" on the outskirts of Isabel Segunda. The waves of troops on maneuvers drew migrant sex workers from the main island. A *San Juan Review* article notes planeloads of prostitutes traveling to Vieques from Puerto Rico (Wagenheim 1964). Doña Elena remembered that public cars took ten marines at a time to prostitutes in the countryside and came back an hour later for ten more. There were ten public cars running this route, she recalled: "There were not enough women on the island to give services to so many men."[9]

Intoxicated sailors provoked fights and occasional riots. Several municipal resolutions were passed in the 1950s and 1960s condemning sailors' conduct and chastising the bar owners who profited from such behavior. Despite the sexual conflicts, street fights, and riots, however, resentment for the navy did not crystallize around the abuse of local women or sustain nationalist resentment. In a case frequently recalled by antinavy activists, Julián Felipe Francis, the elderly owner of a local bar, was brutally beaten to death by eight drunken sailors when he came to the assistance of a woman they were harassing. A newspaper article described Felipe's body as beaten to a pulp, his skull so shattered that "a finger could be easily sunk in his encephalic mass." Another elderly man was severely beaten in the fracas as well.[10]

Although the case stimulated great outrage in Vieques, anger was focused on the navy's resulting decision to declare the town off-limits to military personnel. This declaration, said a local minister, amounted to an economic boycott of the impoverished community, presenting particular hardship to the women who relied on washing and ironing sailors' uniforms to earn their daily bread. A marine and a sailor were court-martialed, but a military court acquitted them of all charges.[11] Rather than provoking nationalist sentiment and spiraling into the kind of broader antimilitary movement that formed in Okinawa, however, grievances in Vieques remained focused on issues of land. The local municipal assembly adopted a resolution condemning Felipe's killing and calling for the navy to return twenty-six thousand acres of land. One factor accounting for the tempered response to these outrages was the fact that Viequenses did not view the sailors as clearly "foreign."

Doña Elena was a young schoolteacher in 1957 when she met and married a marine in Vieques. She was one of dozens of Viequense women of her generation who married sailors and left the island. "The funniest thing is that I didn't like the marines!" she remembered. "When I finished my B.A. at the university [of Puerto Rico] I returned to Vieques to work. I thought all the women hanging around the marines were stupid. 'Why are you hanging around the marines,' I asked my friends. 'You think they are rich because they are Americans. They are a bunch of hillbillies. They are dumb, stupid, and poor—they live in shacks in the South.'"

"I was an *independentista* in those days," she explained. "I had a boyfriend on the main island whom I planned to marry. I was not wasting my time with any dumb marines. Then I met one!" Doña Elena made a distinction between the flood of sailors on maneuver and the units of marines who were stationed in Vieques for six months to a year at a time. "These were the ones who married," she noted; "they became part of the town."

> The ones who came on maneuvers were different. They came only for six weeks and they came by the thousands. They thought they were entering a jungle. We didn't mingle with them. We all married men who were stationed here. The others you saw one or two times, you didn't get to know them. They were mean. They came on pass by the truckload, oh my God, there were so many. Even the marines from the subunit stayed away from them. And they protected us from them.

Unlike the gangs of sailors on maneuvers that would pour drunk through the town, the marines stationed in Vieques established steadier relationships with the townspeople, participating in community events, attending dances and religious services, and marrying local women. When asked if she had encountered hostility from local men because she had married a North American serviceman, doña Elena replied, "Oh no! Viequenses are good people, they are not like that."

Yet sixty-year-old Mario Moreno remembered the fights that used to break out between sailors and local youths who were jealous when sailors attracted women at a local dance club near the fort, which is perched on a hilltop above Isabel Segunda. "The sailors would come and take all of the women," he recalled. "Fights would break out. The young men would go to the top of the hill, climb the trees, and throw rocks at the sailors." In retrospect, don Mario commented, he realized that they could have killed someone. To avoid the rocks, the sailors would go running down the hill, which was steep and dangerous. Yet in the next breath, don Mario told how his father used to call out to sailors on the street and invite them to join the family for dinner. Don Mario's brothers were serving in the army, and his father would tell the sailors that he hoped their parents in the States would extend similar hospitality to his sons. Don Mario went on to serve in the military himself.

Viequenses' participation in the armed forces and social relationships with navy personnel militated against the development of coherent anti-American sentiment. People's direct experience with the U.S. military, whether through service, marriage, or family relations, bifurcated their sense of loyalty and belonging. Fernando Torres, a seventy-two-year-old U.S. Army veteran and antinavy activist, expressed these divided loyalties. He recalled the harassment of Viequense women by troops, a common spark to nationalist-inspired protest. "They would come to town on pass," don Fernando remembered, "and say, 'Hey señorita, look! I'll give you five dollars right now!' They would offer women five or ten dollars to sleep with them. They would harass women. Do bad things. Because of this we didn't want them to come to town."

Don Fernando expressed dissatisfaction with the local court system and the island's only judge, who he believed favored the navy. "Some of them were brought to court," he recalled. "The judge was easy on them. People talked about how he sided with the navy. He would say, 'Oh well, they're only here for a short time.' He would tell the sailors to improve their behavior, but he wouldn't punish them."

But rather than rallying against the navy, don Fernando defended the sailors, suggesting that their overall mission was good and that they were allowed to misbehave by a lax military code of conduct. He remarked: "Some Viequenses said, 'Well, let's see what happens if we kill one of them.' But I, Fernando, said, 'No, we don't have to kill them. They are here for only one reason: democracy and justice. The navy, the air force, and the army, they are here for just one reason: defense.' When they discharge them, they can't do what they're doing in Vieques. The law in civilian life is very different from military life."

Don Fernando's ambivalence was an expression of a broader political and economic context that was not conducive to the formation of nationalist senti-ment. At the same time, the continued tension of living with the military height-ened people's sense of attachment to the island.

The Emergence of a Cultural Identity

By the 1960s conflict in Vieques intensified. The fifties ended with a large-scale riot on the island, drawing political attention to the increasingly vola-tile situation.[12] Local political leaders, businesspeople, and farmers were in-creasingly resentful that the island remained essentially under wartime restrictions during a time of peace, and that the navy remained uncooperative about addressing the island's social and economic crisis.[13] In fact, as the de-cade progressed, the navy revealed itself as not only uncooperative but overtly antagonistic to the development of the local economy. The navy obstructed the island's major development scheme, the Woolnor resort, and revealed its in-tent to expropriate the entire island and evict residents. Vieques's future looked bleak.

In the late 1960s the navy appeared to budge and suggest it would relin-quish control over the resettlement tracts, where residents continued to live without title. Mayor Rivera, who had pushed for years for the navy to surren-der land, had renewed hope. At the same time a group calling itself the Cru-sade for the Rescue of Land in Montesanto and Santa María formed in an effort to claim the land in the resettlement tracts, further pushing Rivera's agenda. This group was composed mainly of independence advocates and different sec-tors of the political left.

Land talks, however, were derailed by growing tensions on the island. In the summer of 1967 Vieques was gripped by rioting. For two nights approxi-mately two hundred marines engaged in a rock- and bottle-throwing melee with three hundred townspeople.[14] In this context Mayor Rivera, who had long de-cried the island's ailing economy and lack of land, dissociated himself from the newly formed Crusade. He denounced the group, which was dominated by *independentistas*, as a bunch of communist agitators. The mayor's outspo-ken opposition to the Crusade for the Rescue of Land in Montesanto and Santa María hindered efforts to build broader support for the effort and illuminated the community's reluctance to associate with "radical" causes (Torres 1981).

The political climate in Vieques and Puerto Rico as a whole constrained the expression of grievances. The cold war shaped a climate in the United States in which individuals' patriotism and loyalty to the nation were constantly scru-tinized (Caute 1978; Fried 1990; Schrecker 1994). These tensions were all the more profound in Puerto Rico, where residents' citizenship remained ambigu-ous and position within the national polity unclear. In Vieques, residents re-

_____ *Table 2* _____
Vieques and Puerto Rico Population Change by Decade

	1920	1930	1940	1950	1960
Vieques population					
Total	11,651	10,582	10,362	9,228	7,210
Percentage change					
from prior decade	17.4	–9.2	–2.1	–10.9	–21.9
Puerto Rico population					
Total	1,299,800	1,543,913	1,869,255	2,210,703	2,349,544
Percentage change					
from prior decade	16.3	18.8	21.1	18.3	6.3

SOURCE: U.S. Census 1920, 1930, 1940, 1950, 1960.

sponded to the onslaught against them not by burning American flags but by digging in. One expression of this response was a growing concern for the island's decline in population.

Vieques's population dropped markedly between 1950 and 1960 because of the navy's usurpation of island land and diminishing economic opportunity. The U.S. Census documents that several other Puerto Rican rural municipalities also suffered declines in population during this time period, probably as a result of shrinking agricultural production. Vieques's rate of decline was more dramatic due to the particular hardships on that island.[15]

Despite the navy's role in stimulating out-migration, however, the decade of the 1950s did not mark the beginning of Vieques's population decline. The island's population reached its apex in 1920, registering 11,651 people, when the sugar industry was at its height. In the subsequent two decades, in the context of the Great Depression and local economic stagnation, the population shrank while the Puerto Rican population as a whole grew. Interestingly, however, much popular discussion of Vieques's population marked 1940 as the reference point for the beginning of the decline (see table 2).

Discussion of the population drop, therefore, must be understood in relation to pressure exerted by the navy on the civilian population. Concern for declining numbers paralleled a growing sense of urgency about the future of the island. Residents were not concerned about the population decline from 1920 on: they were concerned about the population drop from the 1940s on, because they felt threatened by the navy's intentions and worried about the viability of their community, now encompassed by the military. The military's efforts to expropriate land and squeeze the population off the island in the mid-sixties intensified this concern. *Patronales* festival programs started chronicling Vieques population statistics. In the midst of navy proposals to expropriate land,

Vieques's mayor Antonio Rivera visited Puerto Rican governor Luis Muñoz Marín to insist that the Commonwealth government intervene and adopt measures to "repopulate" the island.[16] Rivera adopted an increasingly urgent rhetoric, arguing that the navy had a master plan to strangle Vieques economically and "throw its children into the sea."[17] Such charged rhetoric echoed Abdel Nasser's threat to annihilate the new state of Israel. Rivera thus metaphorically linked Vieques's struggles not only with the struggle of the new Jewish state but also implicitly to its people's attempt to overcome attempted genocide.

While the intense focus on Vieques's declining population highlighted a sense of loss and anxiety over the future, it also demonstrated a growing sense of attachment to the island and a strong sense of peoplehood. Residents worried about demographics because they felt connected to and defensive of a particular place. Thus discussion surrounding the population drop ironically revealed an emerging sense of community.

The Fishermen

Another central expression of cultural identity on the island is found in its fishing economy. Fishing was an important subsistence strategy with roots in *agrego* relations to the ecology. The navy's control over three-quarters of the island only heightened its importance. In Puerto Rico as a whole, the rural past became romanticized after World War II in the context of profound social and economic change. In Vieques, one element of Puerto Rican rural identity, fishing, emerged as a vital expression of the community's resilience in the face of the growing hardship of life under the navy.

Fishing in Historical Perspective

The words of Pedro Vales, a Vieques fisherman, underline the nature of the contemporary island fishing economy, which has its roots in a way of like shaped by sugar cane production: "During the dead time there was work, but not much in the cane. It wasn't sufficient to live on—it paid only fifty cents per day. Because there wasn't anything else, we ate crabs and fished. That sustained us. There were a lot of fish."

In the early twentieth century, Puerto Rico was the most intensive large-scale sugar-producing territory in the Caribbean. The sugar industry employed nearly one-quarter of the total Puerto Rican labor force (Giusti Cordero 1996: 58). In Vieques, sugar dominated the local economy. As don Pedro makes clear, however, work in the cane was seasonal, providing employment for only a few months during the year. During the harvest (*zafra*), which lasted from March to June, men toiled long hours in the cane fields, cutting cane and loading it onto bullcarts or railway cars to carry it to the *central* to be ground, or onto barges to ship to Puerto Rico. When the harvest season passed, some laborers found work digging and cleaning drainage ditches, planting, weeding, and fertilizing cane (Giusti Cordero 1996: 64). By September there was virtually no work left, and working people struggled to put food on the table. During this "dead time," they relied extensively on the local ecology to survive. One of the ways people in Vieques survived was to fish.

Manuel Rosario, seventy-eight years old, worked as a cane cutter during the sugar cane harvest. During the dead time, he remembered, he used to tend cattle for a wealthy farmer, make and sell charcoal, and fish: "You could go to the beach and find conch and snails off the shore. You could catch them in ankle-deep water. You could fish by yourself, with a little trap and a little boat. There wasn't anyone to sell to as everyone caught fish. There weren't that many people who dedicated themselves solely to fishing, only three or four people. We all fished for ourselves."

Fishing was part of a host of peasantlike productive activities residents adopted to survive during dead time. In his classic ethnography of life in a Puerto Rican sugar town, Sidney Mintz (1956) describes fishing as one of the major "subsidiary economic activities" working people in a southern Puerto Rican sugar town used to piece together a living. Residents raised livestock such as goats, pigs, and chickens and cultivated subsistence crops on the plots of land allotted by the *central*. They fished, collected snails, trapped land crabs, and made charcoal. They gathered coconuts and fruit. They played the lottery and made bootleg liquor. Mintz writes, "Supplementary activities, for the most part, are of minor importance in terms of cash income but are valuable in terms of the meals they provide, the ceremonial obligations for which they may afford means of fulfillment, and the meaning and motivation they lend to the cultural life of a people. Work in the cane has lost much of its cultural meaning, while supplementary activity continues to be rich in it" (Mintz 1956: 360).

Fishing must thus be understood as a central element of working-class culture in Vieques. Juan Giusti Cordero (1996) takes issue with Mintz, arguing that these peasantlike subsistence activities were not "subsidiary" but central to both workers' subsistence and the social autonomy of laborers. Giusti argues for the fluidity between the proletarian and the peasant dimensions of rural life. This continuity is apparent in the recollections of Eduardo Negrón, a seventy-eight-year-old retired fisherman.

> Those who lived around the *central* were *agregados*. Something like a slave. These people had to work on the *central*, they were obligated to do different tasks, whether it was weeding, planting cane, cutting cane, loading it to be ground at Punta Arenas and sent to the U.S. Here the main source of income

was sugar cane. To survive during the dead time, many people had a piece of land to plant yams, bananas, *yautía* [a tropical tuber], corn, and pigeon peas. All of this until the harvest time arrived again. There wasn't any type of benefits for workers. And also they fished. Not like us. They would fish in the lagoons of Punta Arenas with open nets. They sold that fish or consumed it at home, or dried it, or salted it, smoked it, packed it in boxes or barrels, whatever they had. That's how we lived in Vieques.

Enter the U.S. Navy

The military expropriation of three-quarters of Vieques Island not only liquidated its economic base but severed people's relationship to the local ecology. When the navy restricted civilian access to most of the land and the coastal areas of the island, it effectively blocked residents from engaging in important productive activities—planting and raising animals, gathering fruit and coconuts, wood cutting and charcoal making, crabbing, collecting snails, and coastal and lagoon fishing—that were fundamental to island cultural and economic life. When asked how he would compare the quality of life before and after the navy arrived, Santiago Meléndez responded: "The food was lost. Those were the days in which food was abundant. There was more than enough food. There was an abundance of fish. There were a lot of crabs, a lot of fish. The coastal area below was agricultural. There were bananas, *yautía*, everything. There was a lot of food. Now came the moment when the navy arrived. When they arrived they put up the gate. We, the members of the household, had to get a pass with our names on it in order to enter and leave. If it was lost it was problematic."

Residents' access to the land was of not only material but cultural importance. People's relationship to the ecology was fundamentally connected to their understanding of the world, their sense of freedom and autonomy, their identity. The navy's restrictions on land created both economic hardship for and resentment from Viequenses who increasingly described themselves as caged in, imprisoned, and sandwiched by the boundaries of the base. In a context where the navy sought to evict people from the land, the importance of this connection was heightened. When the navy curtailed everything else—subsistence plots, animal raising, coconut gathering, crabbing—all that was left was fishing.

Fishing as a Form of Cultural Resistance

Fishing thus achieved heightened importance in Vieques for two major reasons. First, it was increasingly important in terms of subsistence, because residents' other activities were obstructed.[18] Second, it represented a link to a past way of life that was nearly extinguished by the navy. Fishing emerged not only as an important survival strategy but also as a profound cultural assertion.

Although fishermen represented only a small portion of the total population, they embodied the resilience of the community. Santiago Mélendez, the son of *agregados* and a displaced cane worker and manual laborer, is testament to this spirit of fierce attachment to Vieques Island. Don Santiago is a self-identified fisherman. "I started fishing for a living in the 1950s," he remembered. "I began fishing when I was a boy. I fished at Punta Arenas, near the tanks where molasses was loaded by Playa Grande. There were boats that came to pick up the molasses in this area. I fished since I was a little boy. Then from here [Esperanza] since the 1950s. When I got married in 1951, I was working in the cane at harvest time. During the dead time, when there was no work, I had to reach for the seas."

In a context where Vieques was losing its population to St. Croix, fishing was a way to remain on the island. In a context where men were seen to be disappearing because of a lack of economic opportunity, fishing provided work in a male arena. When asked if he had ever worked in St. Croix, a virtual rite of passage for men of his generation, don Santiago responded quickly: "Never! I never earned a cent outside of Vieques. Thank God. [Pause] Years ago I picked cane, I carried cane, I stripped cane. I was a driver in the cane fields. I've been a fisherman all my life. I worked in the cemetery making tombs. I broke rock. I've made charcoal. I've done everything."

Don Santiago's comments are noteworthy not only for the vehemence with which he stresses his work history on Vieques Island, but for the way in which he identifies himself as a fisherman, despite the fact that he was simultaneously engaged in other formal and informal economic activities. This was common among many fishermen. For example, don Eduardo, who described himself as a retired fisherman, also worked as a carpenter's assistant, repairing and building houses in town: "I did many odd jobs. One couldn't say, 'I was doing this.' You did what was available. Even the government provided jobs. There were no permanent jobs. It was necessary to grab them. I know how to do so many things. I also loaded sugar. I did carpentry, using a saw. Sometimes. We earned more or less. That's the way it was. No one could say they had a job for the whole year. If they said they had a job, it's a lie. We worked for two or three months. The buildings here were so small. When we finished building a house, we stayed jobless for a week."

To say that one is a fisherman is then less an objective description of one's livelihood than an expression of cultural identity. Interestingly, while the number of full-time fishermen on the whole is small, the number of men who identify themselves as fishers in the U.S. Census increases over time, from only eighteen in 1935 to fifty by 1990. This increase occurs within the context of a declining population, making the number of fishers proportionally larger than in the past. These numbers suggest in a very concrete way the growing significance of fishing on the island.

Those who declared themselves fishermen often emphasized both freedom and autonomy when describing their experience fishing. Like don Santiago, don Eduardo started fishing when he was a child. "It was like a sport when I was a boy," he remembered. "I started fishing at twelve. By myself. In different places. I had a little wooden boat. It was a present from a friend of mine." Later as an adult in the 1940s, don Eduardo fished during his free time. "I worked on the base for three years. When we were not working on the base, we went to the docks to fish. I used to fish a lot off the pier. There were good mutton snapper (*sama*), grey snapper (*pargo*), kingfish (*carite*), shark (*tiburóne*)."

Don Eduardo was emphatic that he never worked in the cane. "No! I preferred fishing," he declared. "I worked full time. I went to Salinas [Vieques's eastern tip]. I took a couple of rowboats, some food and water. I would tell my wife, 'I'm going.' I didn't know when I was coming back." Don Eduardo would go out for a week at a time, fishing and "storing" fish, as he described it, setting up traps (*viveros*) on the reefs to catch and cultivate live fish.

"There were fish in abundance," he remembered. "During the weekends, I had my coffee and at 3:00 A.M. I started harvesting and storing my catch. If I had snails, conch, lobster, I would bring it back. We fished for all of these fish."

Growing Tensions

While restrictions on land forced residents to turn to the seas for material and cultural sustenance, there was no escaping the navy's influence. Military exercises were devastating to the coastal ecology. Coconut groves were an early casualty of naval maneuvers. A marine's memoirs of his participation in maneuvers in Vieques in February 1950 offer an example of the type of havoc the navy wreaked on Vieques's environment: "We had also noted on these reconnaissances that the growth of coconut trees extended almost from the water's edge to a line about a hundred yards inland. We decided to use them in our defense of the beaches. We would cut them down, leaving about a seven-foot stump, and not completely sever the trunk so the entire thicket could be interlaced with barbed wire and demolitions. We hoped to make this the initial obstacle which would stop the landing forces at least long enough for us to place heavy concentrations of artillery and mortar fire on them" (Harris 1980: 20).

The coconut groves had ringed the beaches along the coasts of the island and were a significant source of cash and subsistence prior to the arrival of the navy. A number of older residents remember that coconut was a staple of the local diet, appearing in dishes such as coconut rice, coconut *arepas*, and coconut candies and custard. In addition, coconut husks were used for fuel and as brushes for cleaning clothes. Giusti (1996) describes coconuts as a "poor man's crop" and writes that in Piñones, Puerto Rico, wages earned husking and selling coconuts rivaled wages earned in the cane. A 1935 report notes that coconuts were the second-largest export crop on Vieques Island after sugar cane (R. Picó 1950: 211). Though in the 1930s an insect infestation devastated the island's coconut palms, a Puerto Rico Reconstruction Administration team was charged with rehabilitating the crop, a tacit acknowledgment of the importance of coconuts to the island. One elderly resident described the coconut palms as "the life of Vieques." Many older people independently mentioned the beautiful coconut palms of Vieques and lamented the loss of these trees, which were largely eliminated by the navy.

The fishermen tended to interpret changes in the natural environment in terms of the most visible elements of naval activities: bombs and bulldozers, tanks and maneuvers. Santiago Meléndez spoke with passion about the environmental destruction:

> It begins on land and ends in the sea. Because here in the '40s, when the Americans came to do maneuvers—before going to Korea, the infantry came here—they destroyed the coconut groves. On land, on sea, in the air, everything is contamination. This is tremendous with the navy here. This is the worst plague. The Bible speaks of seven plagues [*sic*] and this is the worst plague that has fallen on Vieques. [The snails, the conch, the crab] they don't exist anymore. The navy destroyed everything because they destroyed the mangroves and the lagoons. They brought bulldozers and tanks into the lagoons. The fauna—they destroyed everything.

Neftalí García Martínez (1979) has suggested that other, more subtle elements of military activity also shaped the ecology over time. Navy construction of roads along the coast and interior of the island closed channels between lagoons and the sea. The changing equilibrium of the water flow altered salination levels, leading to the slow destruction of the lagoons. The construction of the pier off the north coast of Vieques may also have affected tidal flows and salinity in the lagoons. Mangroves suffered from elevated water levels, hypersalinity, and sedimentation as a result of a complex interaction of factors, including the extraction of subterranean water by the navy, erosion, and the closing of channels to the lagoons.

The fishermen were the first to perceive the destruction of the ecology. "Before, there was an abundance of fish," noted don Eduardo; "now you don't find anything."

You can see the difference. Now there are no fish. They used to fish in these waters near the shore. Before people didn't have to go offshore. I used to set a trap over here [points to a nearby beach] in water a foot and a half deep. And the trap would be full of fish. All living things near the coast have disappeared. The first were the sea urchin. The food. They fed off this. Then the pig fish (*peje puerco*), parrot fish (*cotorro*), doctorfish (*médico*), yellow tail snapper (*colirrubia*), grey snapper (*pargo*), this was their food. But if there is no food, if it's killed, then they go. The big fish left when their food source was destroyed. When they killed the smaller fish, the big ones left—that's the situation.

According to don Eduardo, the size of fish diminished as well. Whereas he used to catch thirty-pound mutton snapper (*sama*), grey snapper, yellowtail snapper, and doctorfish off the northern coast of Vieques, he was now lucky if he found these same fish weighing more than half a pound. Crabs and snails, important sources of sustenance and income, were also affected: "We lived off this, catching snails. They would stick to the rocks. It's good food. We also caught crabs. And when the crab season arrived, we caught them and sold them at very good prices—better than fish—to hotels. All of this is gone because of the bombs. The crabs lived in the lagoons. The lagoons were dried out by the bombs. The crabs went running away, looking for fresh water to drink. The lagoons have dried up. The crabs have almost disappeared. The ones that remain now are small—not as they used to be."

The fishermen and the navy were on a collision course in a war that would play out in the seventies. Fishing, which had become an increasingly important form of subsistence and cultural refuge from the navy, was threatened by military maneuvers. Fishing became an expression of the community's resistance to the navy. To be a Viequense, to live on an island encompassed, invaded, and bombed by the military, became an act of defiance. Fishermen, by asserting links to a traditional way of life and the local ecology, signaled residents' commitment to stay despite the navy's efforts to remove them. All of the intensity of the struggle to survive on the island was played out in the fishermen's confrontation with the navy.

Three

The Fishermen's War

Vieques's long-simmering conflict with the navy exploded in 1978. The navy intensified maneuvers on Vieques after a militant anticolonial movement on neighboring Culebra forced the military off of that island. Heightened bombing and stepped-up maneuvers pushed conflict over the edge. A grassroots mobilization coalesced in Vieques in the late 1970s that aimed to evict the navy and reclaim island land. Political, economic, and cultural factors converged to transform local fishermen into the movement's primary protagonists. At the same time, tensions emerged between locally based economic grievances and broader issues of Puerto Rican sovereignty.

Vieques's struggle came at the peak of a period of social unrest and popular mobilization against the U.S. military presence in Puerto Rico. The Puerto Rican independence movement was expanding its influence, primarily through a series of charged confrontations with the U.S. military. In Vieques, however, residents were reluctant to link their local efforts against the navy to the broader cause of Puerto Rican independence.

The particular history of Vieques's conflict with the military was separate from the struggles waged by independence activists in the late 1960s. Conflict between residents and the navy stretched back to the forties and was based on a discrete set of economic and social grievances. As living conditions in Vieques deteriorated as a result of the intensification of maneuvers, however, popular discontent grew.

Protest erupted at a time of increasing international polarization. In the late 1970s, cold war tensions intensified between the United States and the Soviet

Union after the Soviet invasion of Afghanistan. A wave of revolutionary movements swept Central America and the Caribbean basin, heightening Washington's anxiety about the spread of communism and the growing influence of Cuba throughout the region. With U.S. public consciousness shaped by grim images of the hostages in Iran, the political establishment turned markedly to the right. The United States dramatically expanded its economic and military presence in the Caribbean, intervening in regional conflicts and arming and training security forces in the basin (Colón 1984; Young and Phillips 1986; Rodríguez Beruff 1986, 1988; García Muñiz 1987). Earlier confrontations between Puerto Rican activists and the U.S. military had occurred amid the turmoil of Vietnam and Watergate; now conflict in Vieques erupted in a changed political context, defined by the military's increased entrenchment. This polarized political climate shaped both the movement's expression and, ultimately, its outcome.

The central problem Viequenses now faced was how to articulate their particular grievances against the military without having their cause spiral into an overwhelming battle against U.S. colonialism. Fishermen became crucial in emphasizing the cultural and economic dimensions of a struggle within a highly charged political setting.

Crisis of the 1960s: Vietnam and the Student Movement

In the late 1960s the Puerto Rican left grew increasingly militant, and its struggle against the U.S. military played a defining role as the independence movement gathered momentum. A wave of resentment against Puerto Rican conscription into the Vietnam War solidified the strength of the independence movement, which emerged as a strong force in 1970 despite significant federal and Commonwealth efforts to destabilize it.[1]

In the late 1960s the political hegemony that the *populares* had enjoyed for nearly three decades had crumbled. Internal divisions within the PPD provided a space for the conservative prostatehood PNP to gain control of the governor's seat in 1968. The election of the millionaire industrialist Luis Ferré polarized a political climate defined by an increasingly militant left and strong student movement, on the one hand, and a socially conservative colonial administration, on the other.

In this period sectors of the Puerto Rican left converged in a struggle to block strip mining in the island's interior. This environmental struggle was overtly nationalist in character, defining itself as a fight to preserve the national patrimony from exploitation by foreign interests.[2] The clashes over strip mining extended to a mobilization to block privatization of Puerto Rico's beaches (Nieves Falcón, García Rodríquez, and Ojeda Reyes 1971).

At the same time student protest against the draft and the war in Vietnam gripped the island. While nationalists in the 1950s had refused to register for the draft, making a largely symbolic gesture against the U.S. military, the 1960s marked the first popular mobilization against the U.S. military presence in Puerto Rico. Never before had so many Puerto Ricans refused to serve in the U.S. armed forces, despite the threat of long jail sentences (Nieves Falcón, García Rodríguez, and Ojeda Reyes 1971). There were mass demonstrations against the "slavery of the draft" on the streets of San Juan.

The Reserve Officer Training Corps (ROTC) presence on the campus of the University of Puerto Rico (UPR) became a lightning rod for anticolonial sentiment. *Independentista* students organized marches and rallies to remove the ROTC from campus. For *independentista* youth, the ROTC represented the essence of U.S. colonialism. When a federal judge sentenced a student draft resister to jail in September 1969, the conviction triggered a student uprising at the university. Students ransacked the offices of the ROTC building, set it on fire, and burned American flags (Nieves Falcón, García Rodríquez, and Ojeda Reyes 1971).

Tensions on the UPR campus were explosive for the next two years. In March of 1970, clashes between *independentista* students and ROTC cadets spiraled into bloody riots. Students set fire to two campus ROTC buildings, and the university administration called in shock troops to quell the unrest. Fifty people were injured by gunfire, rocks, and bottles. The rioting spilled into the streets of Río Piedras, and one student bystander, nineteen-year-old Antonia Martínez, was shot dead as she stood on a nearby balcony of a guesthouse.[3]

One year later, in March 1971, confrontations between ROTC cadets and *independentista* students again turned violent. A fistfight snowballed into a full-scale riot. Hundreds of students were involved in a rock-throwing melee; Molotov cocktails set fire to two ROTC buildings. When the university called in the riot squad to contain the escalating violence, the riot squad commander was shot dead. Another policeman and a ROTC cadet were also shot and killed. By the end of the day, more than sixty people had been injured by rocks and gunfire.[4]

In response to the university unrest, a right-wing clandestine group calling itself the Anti-Communist Brotherhood of Puerto Rico launched a campaign against prominent independence supporters. Right-wing forces burned two *independentista*-owned businesses, a pharmacy, and a bookstore in Río Piedras to the ground. They also firebombed the homes and cars of outspoken independence advocates (Nieves Falcón, García Rodríquez and Ojeda Reyes 1971).[5]

The conflict between residents of the Puerto Rican island of Culebra and the U.S. Navy erupted against the background of this highly charged political context. Consequently, the naval presence in Culebra came to signify to the Puerto Rican left the very essence of Puerto Rico's colonial subjugation to the United States.

The Battle of Culebra

Culebra, a ten-square-mile island municipality of Puerto Rico to the north of Vieques, also existed under the grip of the U.S. Navy. Culebra and Vieques formed a strategic triangle with the Roosevelt Roads Naval Station on the main island. The navy launched amphibious assaults on Vieques and concentrated naval and aerial bombardments on Culebra. The struggle against the navy in Culebra became a cause célèbre of the Puerto Rican independence movement.

The navy had been interested in Culebra since the early days of the U.S. occupation of Puerto Rico. The navy eliminated the island's principal town, San Ildefonso, and removed its inhabitants in order to establish a marine base and gunnery range in the first decade of the twentieth century (Delgado Cintrón 1989). In 1941 President Roosevelt claimed exclusive military use of the airspace over Culebra and a three-mile radius of the surrounding water. In 1948 the navy expropriated 1,700 acres of island land in order to create a bombing range. The island's population, which once subsisted on sugar cane cultivation, shrank from 4,000 in 1900 to 580 in 1950. As a further emblem of military control, Culebra was governed by a series of appointed retired navy personnel until the 1960s, when island residents were first allowed to elect their own mayor.

Culebrenses existed under a surreal set of circumstances. The U.S. Navy owned one-third of island land and all of its coastline. A bombing range and bomb-laden harbor circled the civilian sector. Only a government-run ferry and a small air taxi traveled regularly from Puerto Rico to Culebra, and any nonresident who traveled to the island for any reason other than official business violated the law. The U.S. military's shift to missile technology in the late 1950s intensified the bombardment of the island. Low-flying helicopters and planes and extensive firing practice besieged residents. In a single year, 1969, Culebra was under fire by naval gunnery for 123 days and pounded by directed missiles for 228 days. Planes made between 35,000 and 40,000 target runs on the island that year.[6] There were a series of misfires and wild shots, bombs landing yards from private homes and mortar rounds sweeping waters where children frolicked in the surf (Schemmer and Cossaboom 1970; Schemmer, et al. 1970).

Starting in the mid-1950s, the navy drafted a series of plans to evict island residents. The Puerto Rican government resisted military efforts to completely usurp the island, citing a Commonwealth law that required a popular vote to abolish a municipality.[7] In 1970 the navy again tried to evict islanders in order to expand the bombing range. The irreconcilable differences between the navy and the resident population sparked a protest movement.

Emerging in the context of a wave of confrontations elsewhere between supporters of Puerto Rican independence and the U.S. military, the battle of this small island against the power of the U.S. Navy enjoyed widespread popular support throughout Puerto Rico. Like residents of Vieques, Culebrenses suffered material harm from the military presence, but their confrontation became defined in terms of the struggle for Puerto Rican independence.

While PNP and PPD leaders attempted to negotiate a settlement that would get the navy out of Culebra, independence forces pressed ahead with a direct action campaign. "The Americans are not paying any attention to the PPD and government pleas. The navy will only leave Culebra when it can no longer use the island as a firing range, not in response to government pleas," declared Puerto Rican Independence Party (PIP) president Rubén Berríos Martínez.[8] The PIP and the Puerto Rican Socialist Party (PSP) were instrumental in leading a direct action campaign against the naval presence. The PIP defined the battle as one of "pacific militancy" and organized demonstrations on beaches used for target practice, blocking ship-to-shore missile fire with human chains of protestors.

Construction of a chapel on the bombing range became the centerpiece of the movement. In February 1970, PIP president Berríos led demonstrators to the entrance of the base in order to construct a chapel on Flamenco Beach in the heart of the bombing range. Members of the U.S.-based Quaker Action Group joined the effort, which they perceived as a pacifist struggle. Police blocked their entry. Beyond the police, the navy had erected a wall of barbed wire, which in turn was guarded by a wall of armed marines. Demonstrators therefore took to the seas, wading through the surf to bypass the barbed wire and guns. They carried wooden beams and tools onto the beach and erected the chapel. Ecumenical services during scheduled target practice forced a halt to maneuvers. The navy tore the chapel down. Berríos and thirteen others were sentenced to three months in federal prison for defying a U.S. district court order against entering the firing range.[9] The conviction sparked student uprisings at the University of Puerto Rico.[10]

There was discomfort among Culebra residents about the involvement of the Puerto Rican left in the struggle. A group calling itself the Sons of Culebra denounced "communist" involvement in the movement, but most residents favored the exit of the navy. This support extended throughout Puerto Rico, and all political parties supported the navy's exit. The Culebra movement succeeded in uniting a society with deep political divisions. Resident Commissioner Jaime

Benítez commented, "If there is one single issue on which the whole Puerto Rican community feels profoundly and intensely, it is the Culebran question" (U.S. House 1973: 2).

Still, Culebra exposed the fundamental weakness of the Commonwealth government in the face of naval power. In January 1971 the U.S. secretary of the navy and the Commonwealth of Puerto Rico signed the Culebra Agreement, an accord that Puerto Rico understood as a commitment by the navy to find an alternative to the island by 1972 and to cease bombing permanently by 1975. In 1972, however, the secretary of defense announced that the navy intended to remain in Culebra indefinitely and at least through 1985. Puerto Rican officials expressed outrage at the navy's "cavalier attitude" and "duplicity" (U.S. House 1973: 4). In the face of continued tensions, in 1974 President Richard Nixon ordered the navy to leave Culebra by the following year.

The victory was fleeting, however. Although the navy was instructed to find an alternative training site to Culebra and Congress authorized funds for the transfer, the navy simply shifted its bombardments to Vieques (U.S. House 1994). Culebra thus was not only important as a parallel to Vieques's struggle against the navy. In a very direct way, Culebra's resolution created Vieques's problems. Vieques's antinavy movement emerged in response to the resulting intensification of bombing on the island.

Vieques: Prelude to Protest

By the mid-seventies it became apparent that Vieques had received the brunt of the Culebra "solution" in the form of increased bombing, maneuvers, and restrictions. The quality of life on Vieques, already affected by three decades of military occupation, deteriorated rapidly. Residents began to complain about the impact of maneuvers: roaring planes interrupted classes and bombing cracked the foundations of homes.

Although Vieques's grievances against the navy were deep-seated, forming a coherent antibase movement proved difficult. The Culebra movement had defined opposition to the navy as fundamentally anticolonial in character. While this framework may have been successful in uniting the Puerto Rican left, it proved more difficult in mobilizing a grassroots community movement in Vieques, where the majority of the population was supportive of continued political and economic association with the United States. Residents were fiercely opposed to naval incursions into their everyday lives, yet were reluctant to express grievances that might be construed as anti-American or "communist" in nature. Mayor Rivera had walked a delicate line in his 1964 confrontation with the navy, relying on his political position for legitimacy in confronting the military. Yet even in 1964 the Puerto Rican press viewed his message as potentially subversive. Ironically, when *independentistas* in Vieques later followed Rivera's lead and demanded title to the resettlement tracts, Rivera himself denounced them as anti-Americans and communists. Thus it became apparent that the packaging or framework of protest was crucial in this highly charged conflict.

In response to heightened maneuvers in Vieques, some of the same individuals from the political left who had been denounced by Mayor Rivera as communist agitators looked for new ways to confront the military.[11] Significantly, activists chose to channel protest into the cultural sphere. Activists took aim at the navy's participation in the annual *patronales* (patron saint festival), an important ten-day community event. In 1973, two hundred defiant demonstrators marched side by side with uniformed navy personnel in the festival parade, demanding their withdrawal from the *patronales*. Carlos Quintero, a forty-one-year-old schoolteacher and antinavy activist, explained: "The people began to organize. Make groups. Organize. Really what happened in this situation, in this type of struggle, was that the consciousness-raising came from the Left. . . . We considered the participation of the navy in the carnivals, the patron saint festival, to be a social and cultural aggression. It added to the constant assault of the maneuvers, the disorder, the lack of respect for the ladies in the street, to the marriages, to the children. It was all a type of aggression. Well, how were we going to let them participate in our patron saint festival?"

The navy withdrew from the *patronales* the following year, when violence broke out and a sailor wounded a demonstrator. These demonstrations signaled a changing political climate on the island. However tense relations had been in the past, there had always been cultural interchange between the military and residents. Now activists raised questions about military participation in various aspects of civilian life. Quintero continued:

> We made a committee to confront all these problems relating to the navy: their participation in the carnivals, their participation in these things, in school, and all of this. For example, as children, the school system allowed us to be brought to the military base in military trucks to see how they made military exercises. [There is outrage in his voice. KM: This happened?] Yes, not only this. They took us in helicopters to teach us, to give us the impression of how good the Americans are. This teaches us how to fight in wars, supposedly to defend democracy. We learned this as children. . . . This participation at the base and all . . . there was never a movement against this because. . . . It was a process of consciousness raising in many people. There was a small group that had consciousness that this shouldn't happen. Nonetheless, little by little we became aware of the way in which they were buying

us, buying the consciousness of the children. It was a birth of an understanding in general of the problems of the navy.

In 1977 new political developments in Vieques inspired outrage against the navy and encouraged the formation of new political alliances. In the aftermath of the Culebra compromise, Vieques politicians discovered that San Juan was negotiating changes for Vieques's future. The U.S. General Services Administration (GSA) had offered to sell Vieques resettlement tracts to the Commonwealth government in exchange for an aviation easement over the south coast of Vieques, the area regarded as having the greatest tourism potential on the island. Vieques politicians were outraged. Securing title to the resettlement land that residents had occupied since the forties had long been a political goal, but not at the high price the GSA sought, and not attached to an aviation easement. An easement would intensify military traffic over the south coast of Vieques and impose restrictions on construction and development. Coming on the heels of the attempted expropriation of this same area in 1964 and the recent increase in maneuvers, the negotiations were declared by the mayor of Vieques, Radamés Tirado, to be part of a subversive campaign of the navy: "The navy has attempted to take measures, that if successful, would have the ultimate effect of evicting the entire population of Vieques at little or no cost to the navy. Through the systematic elimination of opportunities for the development of the island and the destruction of its economy, the navy hopes to force the entire population of Vieques to migrate involuntarily to other islands. The navy could then gradually acquire all the land that remains at very little cost" (U.S. House 1981: 204).

The response to this crisis has generally been viewed in Vieques as a turning point in local politics. Opposition to the military, traditionally regarded as the cause of the left, of independence advocates, was expressed by the presidents of the four electoral parties in Vieques in reaction to the proposed aviation easement. A rally was held in front of the gates to Camp García in Vieques. The presidents of each of the parties denounced the proposed easement and gathered widespread public support. They traveled together to San Juan to lobby against the signing of the agreement.

This party unity in opposition to the military's proposal was hailed by Viequenses as a major achievement. Despite the significance attributed to it, however, the unified political opposition to the easement was not able to unite and mobilize the populace. This contrasts with a comparable political moment in Culebra—the extension of the bombing range—which unified residents on that island.

Vieques activists formed an organization, Viequenses United (Viequenses

Unidos), that sought to build on this political momentum and bring together Viequenses of all different persuasions in opposition to military activity on the island. But the unity that Viequenses United sought to build upon was short-lived at best. At the base of the group's collapse was its desire to challenge the military without changing the status quo. This type of ambivalence foreshadowed some of the problems that were to face the subsequent Crusade to Rescue Vieques. During a formative assembly, Viequenses United expressed a distrust of the political left and sought to prevent Mario Martínez, a prominent local leftist activist, from speaking. At this same meeting, called to address problems with the navy, however, organizers had invited a navy official to attend. Conflict erupted. Martínez remembered:

> In '77 Zenón [head of the fishermen's association] and the fishermen were having problems with the navy's ships and the maneuvers. I had the opportunity to talk with Zenón and strategize how we could coordinate their claims together with our claims. Viequenses United didn't think much of their struggle. Well, Viequenses United collapsed at an assembly to which they invited a navy official. They wouldn't let me speak at the meeting. They attacked me. Therefore, Carlos Zenón demanded to know how it could be that at a meeting in which we were to discuss the navy's treaty, how could we speak in front of a functionary of the navy while we were organizing to fight against them? It was as if the navy invited us to their house to discuss the treaty against us. This would never happen. Therefore the meeting collapsed. The people didn't like it and it disappeared.

Although antinavy activists often point to Viequenses United as an important political precedent, this organization is perhaps better seen as the counterpoint to the successfully organized Crusade to Rescue Vieques. While Viequenses United was organized at a key moment in Vieques's conflict with the navy, it lacked an effective framework for translating islanders' grievances into a movement for change. Basing struggle on the unified front of the different electoral leaders, Viequenses United dissolved into partisan politics. It was only the activism of the fishermen that was able to pull together a movement that could successfully confront the military. The fishermen succeeded in uniting Viequenses in large part because they avoided the partisan politics that had proved so divisive and instead anchored community struggle in the realm of the cultural and the economic.

The Rise of the Fishermen

By the late 1970s the navy's intensified maneuvers in Vieques created particular hardship for the island's fishermen. Not only did bombing cause great damage to coral reefs and fish in an already fragile marine environment, but as ship traffic increased, navy boats frequently severed buoy lines from the traps they marked, effectively destroying fishing gear and the financial investment the traps represented. Fishermen were prevented from entering waters they claimed were the best fishing grounds around the island. A newly organized fishing cooperative became a crucible of the antinavy movement.

The fishermen's co-op was not a political group, but rather an economic association. The co-op was one of a number of associations founded in Puerto Rico in the mid-seventies as part of a federally funded program administered by the Commonwealth government. The purpose of Vieques's co-op was to bring organization and resources to an extremely undeveloped yet important local industry. Many fishermen were operating out of wooden boats and had no centralized marketing, docking, storage, or meeting facilities. A fishing co-op promised better prices for both buyer and seller. It provided a place to store gear, a freezer, and better equipment, such as fiberglass, diesel boats.

The founding of the fishing co-op occurred at a critical time in Vieques's relationship with the navy. Just as fishermen were developing an economic co-op with shared interests and a coherent political structure, they were faced with increased damage and intransigence by the navy. Fishermen argued that they were drawn inevitably into conflict. For example, Rafael Cruz, the president of the fishing association, recalled:

> The struggle began in 1978 because for years Vieques had been mistreated by the navy. Women were raped. Men were killed in the streets fighting sailors in years back. I lost a friend on the base when a bomb exploded. But they continued with the abuse and the abuse eventually reached the sector of the fishermen. They bombed the most productive fishing areas. Dropped live bombs. Destroyed many fishing traps. . . . The situation in Vieques is that the fishers have families to support. The only factory that has its door opened to whoever wants to work is the sea. If you have a boat you can go fishing. And no one asks you if you are pronavy, antinavy, what political party you are. No one will ask you that. It's the only source of steady employment in Vieques. And here comes the navy saying for thirty days, you can't fish. This is terrible. Because fishers have bills to pay, they have families to support.

In February 1978 a ragtag contingent of eighteen-foot fishing boats halted NATO warships off the coast of Vieques. The U.S. Navy had organized an international training program, bringing together the navies of several countries to engage in amphibious exercises, electronic warfare, missile firing, and mock invasions. The planned training program would prevent local fishermen from fishing for thirty days of scheduled war games. The fishermen instead blocked the navy.

Positioning themselves in the direct line of missile fire, local fishermen successfully interrupted international military maneuvers. It was a triumphant moment in Vieques. With media headlines broadcasting David's battle with Goliath, international attention was riveted on the case of the humble fishermen of Vieques locked in combat with the U.S. Navy. Photographs showed bare-chested fishermen waving their fists from wooden boats and throwing stones as military helicopters attempted to buzz them out of the water. Fishermen declared their campaign to be a "fish-in," echoing the rhetoric of the civil rights protestors' sit-ins at segregated lunch counters in the U.S. South in the 1960s. They lambasted the navy for interfering with their ability to make a living.

Santiago Meléndez was arrested that day on federal trespassing charges. To don Santiago his arrest was a badge of honor, proof of his passion and commitment to the cause of Vieques and evidence of the abuse fishermen had suffered at the hands of the navy: "We went out to fish. I was arrested. Why? For looking for bread for my children. And it was with pride that I stood before a federal judge with my hands bound and my head held high. Because I had not committed any crime. To the contrary, there was prejudice against me because I was not permitted to look for bread for my children in my own land, in my own nation."

Don Santiago spoke with pride of his struggle to feed his family. He pointed to the injustice of being arrested for trying to make a living. The irony of the situation, in his opinion, was that he was denied this freedom and liberty, "in my own land, in my own nation." As became apparent in later conversation, he was not referring to Vieques or to Puerto Rico. Don Santiago's nation is the United States of America, and he was indignant that the U.S. Navy was interfering with his rights as an American citizen.

Over the course of roughly five years, 1978–1983, Viequenses backed the local "Fishermen's War" to evict the navy and reclaim land expropriated in the 1940s. Fishermen claimed that the navy's heightened maneuvers, destruction of fishing gear, and restriction of the seas prevented them from making a living. They argued that they had no choice but to rise up in defense of their community and their way of life. Yet how was it that an antimilitary movement came to be led by fishermen asserting their loyalty to the American flag? Why did a conflict that was rooted in the land become expressed in a battle of the seas?

Cultural Framing of Protest

Although the fishermen's claims were specifically material, their grievances cannot be understood in strictly economic terms. As researchers have shown, symbols and ritual can provide an important basis for resistance and revolt when the oppressed seek to challenge an overwhelmingly superior power (Kaplan 1992; Kertzer 1988; Nash 1979). David Kertzer, for example, illustrates the way Gandhi organized Indian resistance to British colonial rule around a relatively minor issue: the colonial monopoly on salt. "His choice of symbols was shrewd," Kertzer writes. "By ritually attacking the salt tax, he challenged Britain's right to rule; yet any colonial attempts to suppress the salt tax protest would appear disproportionate and inflammatory" (1988: 169). In Vieques, fishermen in wooden boats confronted warships in the open seas. The fishermen rallied not against U.S. imperialism but against restrictions on fishing waters and destruction of gear. They spoke not of Puerto Rican independence but of the right to make a living. The fishermen stood as cultural icons in Vieques and framed the conflict in terms of a set of discrete, local, material grievances. They did this by asserting a local identity, links to the land, and a "traditional" way of life.

The intensification of maneuvers clearly posed a threat to the marine environment that men had relied on to make a living. The fishing waters in Vieques were already in a state of crisis. In 1978 the director of Puerto Rico's Department of Natural Resources Fisheries Project testified in federal court that Vieques's fishing waters were threatened with depletion. Comparing yield figures between Cabo Rojo in southwestern Puerto Rico and Vieques over a ten-year period, this official noted that Cabo Rojo's catch had remained constant, while Vieques's catch had dropped 50 percent.[12] Now fishermen claimed they were losing access to the best fishing waters for extended periods of time, and that naval maneuvers were destroying traps, threatening their very livelihood.

Fishermen's claims did not focus on the most catastrophic element of naval maneuvers—the bombing. Rather, they stressed the restriction of the seas and the destruction of their fishing gear. Although there were legitimate economic repercussions, symbolic messages lay beneath the surface. The navy, which had usurped so much of Vieques's land, was now extending its reach to the seas. The gates and boundaries that cut across the island landscape were now being established in its waters. Don Santiago described the organization of an antimilitary movement in Vieques as the islanders' last stand against the navy's increasing encroachments: "The Crusade was organized because the navy had so many restrictions that we decided to organize ourselves into a united front. To demonstrate to the world that there was a people oppressed by the United States Navy. . . . They restricted [the waters] from the north-eastern part of the island to the southern part. On February 6, 1978, we stopped the maneuvers to show the navy that we didn't agree with the pressure they were putting on us." The military's restrictions of access to water, don Santiago asserted, were the ultimate blow that left Viequenses no choice but to organize in opposition.

The military restrictions of the seas echoed earlier seizures of land. They challenged the frontier the fishermen had established of relative freedom and autonomy, of male working-class identity, and of cultural continuity. In the context of profound social and economic change that was both challenging established gender relations and leading to a growing dependence on public assistance, the fisherman stood as a cultural archetype that was now under threat. Rafael Cruz remembered with great indignation a navy official's suggestion that fishermen turn to public assistance to make ends meet. The idea that an able-bodied working man take government hand-outs deeply offended him:

> We had a meeting with Robert Flannigan, who was at Roosevelt Roads in 1978. The mayor of Vieques, Radamés Tirado, who helped us, who was there for the struggle, went to Roosevelt Roads on a medical helicopter. And he said to the military, and 90 percent of them are arrogant, "Mr. Flannigan, Vieques has a level of unemployment of about 50 percent. About 75 percent of the people are living on food stamps. If you close the beaches of Vieques, restrict the area, especially where the fishermen fish, for thirty days, what will the fishermen do to support their families?" And do you know what he said? He said to Radamés, "Do you have food stamp service in Vieques?" He said, "Yes, we do." "Well, you people can go to the food stamp line because we are bombing here for the war games." I said, "Look, never before in the modern history of Vieques have we had problems." Can you imagine the power of the navy, the abuse? We have an immense problem. I came to Vieques and met with the fishermen and established that it was important that we fight this maneuver. On February 6, 1978, at 6:00 in the morning we were on the beach. And we went out to the maneuvers. There were about 95 of us. This attitude on the part of the navy, that they wouldn't let the fishermen go out to the sea for thirty days while they were doing their maneuvers. It's not possible. We had to fish.

Much of the fishermen's rhetoric and environmental claims centered on lost traps. Fishermen claimed that not only were they prevented from entering the most fertile fishing grounds by maneuvers, but navy boats were deliberately cutting the buoys that anchored and identified the traps. To the fishermen, this signified more than a callous disregard for their way of livelihood. The result, they claimed, was environmentally devastating: "When a boat cuts a trap, this trap falls to the depth of the sea. Fish die in the trap and continue to die. They go in and continue to die, continue to die. And neither I, nor my children, nor the children of my children, nor the grandchildren of my children are going to participate [in fishing in the future]. What kind of effect will this have? This is total destruction. The complete destruction of marine life." Charles Menzies asserts, however, that such claims should not go unexamined. A cheap, straightforward procedure can modify traps so that they do not become death traps for countless fish. If fishermen were truly concerned about the environmental consequences of lost traps, writes Menzies, they could easily make these modifications.[13]

Although it is possible that the fishermen were not aware of such modifications, it is also possible that the controversy surrounding the traps was more emblematic than economic. The charges leveled against the navy for deliberately destroying the traps and annihilating marine life connect to broader charges leveled against the navy for deliberately conspiring to annihilate the community of Vieques. Fishermen, signifying the island's authentic past, also embodied fears surrounding the island's future: the future of its youth in a context of economic stagnation; the sustainability of the environment in light of continued bombing; the future of the entire community in the face of efforts to remove them. The fishermen were such effective spokespeople in part because their claims and their campaign had multiple layers of significance.

Although antimilitary protest is commonly understood through the framework of nationalism, Vieques demonstrates both the material basis of conflict and the way in which a confrontation with a vastly more powerful opponent diverts the expression of protest away from the overtly political realm and into the realm of culture. Vieques may not be unique in this regard. At least two other highly charged confrontations between civilian groups and the military have had similar characteristics. In Hawaii, nationalists rallied popular opposition to naval bombing exercises on the island of Kaho'olawe by focusing on the island's sacred and religious qualities. The struggle to evict the navy became expressed as a struggle to revitalize traditional Hawaiian cultural practices (Linnekin 1983; Merrill 1994). Similarly, in a movement against the extension of a military camp in Lazarac, France, Alexander and Sonia Alland (1994) argue that protestors attempted to establish their legitimacy by rallying around a mythic peasant status.

The argument here is not that fishermen "invented" their identity to mask political purposes. Rather, fishing was an organic expression of a community's effort to survive on the island and resist removal. Fishing developed in opposition to the navy, much in the way Mintz describes peasant culture in the Caribbean erupting "like blades of grass pushing up between bricks" (Mintz 1985: 131).

Sidney Tarrow (1994) has emphasized the significance a movement's rhetorical framework plays in capturing and communicating a set of messages to a wider audience. Indeed, many writers have noted the centrality of symbols in affirming the legitimacy and expressing the principles and ideals of a movement (Geertz 1977; Hunt 1984; Kaplan 1992). The image of the fishermen at war with the navy on the high seas conveyed a heroic tale, and the media readily told the story of Vieques's David and Goliath battle to an international audience. The island's struggle was translated into a variety of different contexts and created a wider support network. But the framework also played an important role in organizing grievances in local terms that emphasized subsistence and avoided the larger realm of politics and issues of colonialism.

By the late 1970s this framework was key. Politics in the United States and Puerto Rico had taken a sharp turn to the right. The Puerto Rican independence movement, which in the early seventies was unified and strong, had splintered by mid-decade. There was an increased climate of violence and state repression. Radical factions of the independence movement set off hundreds of bombs across Puerto Rico and the United States (Trías Monge 1997). The incident most evocative of the period was the police shooting of two young *independentistas* and subsequent government cover-up of the incident. This case, which came to be known as Cerro Maravilla, after the mountain range where the youths were killed, shook the foundations of the Puerto Rican political system.[14] Within this volatile political context, the fishermen were crucial in defining Vieques's struggle in terms of local material claims.

Building a Movement: The Crusade to Rescue Vieques

"The abuse, the abuse of the bombing and maneuvers, really affected the fishermen the most economically. The areas where there were maneuvers were where there were the best fish. . . . We organized the people in general with the idea that the fishermen were suffering the most, because in reality they were the most affected. [The navy] damaged the ladies, they damaged the education, the children with the bombing. They damaged the marine life, the fauna, the reefs. But the economic point of view, they were affecting the families of the fishermen. They had to go out all day fishing and find areas closed off, boats on the beach, this affected the fishers and they organized themselves. The people in general got involved," recalled a teacher-activist, Carlos Quintero. Fishermen created unity where there were divisions. As the collapse of Viequenses United had demonstrated, there was considerable reluctance in Vieques to confront the military in a setting where protest was commonly construed as anti-American in orientation. At the same time, Viequenses United had demonstrated that there were significant local grievances that had the potential to mobilize the populace. The fishermen's struggle embodied those grievances, pushing protest outside the realm of politics and into a form that was simultaneously cultural, economic, and locally rooted. The fishermen's struggle became the basis of a grassroots movement. Shortly after the first confrontations between the fishermen and the navy at sea, a new community organization was founded that called itself the Crusade to Rescue Vieques (La Cruzada pro Rescate de Vieques). The Crusade drew together many of the same individuals who had participated in Viequenses United and who sought both to back the fishermen's campaign and to mobilize people on the island against the military presence. What was different from past efforts, and what established the success of the Crusade, was that it functioned as a coalition movement, bringing together a variety of people—teachers, merchants, workers—and anchoring struggle in the cause of the fishermen. Significantly, the Crusade expanded the fishermen's claims over rights to the waters to a call for the eviction of the navy from the island.

Ideologically, the Crusade distanced itself from the cause of Puerto Rican independence. This was different from Culebra, which had strident, anticolonial rhetoric and was led by the Puerto Rican Independence Party. Particular dimensions of the struggle in Vieques encouraged this expression. On the local level, strong opposition to military activity on the island came from sectors of the PNP, which was traditionally regarded as the most "pro-American" and "promilitary" of the various Puerto Rican political parties. Vieques mayor Radamés Tirado was outspoken against the navy, and a number of the leaders of the fishing association, like Santiago Meléndez, had strong links to the PNP and embraced the cause of Puerto Rican statehood:

> I am a statehooder. I believe in the democracy of the United States. I think that with the laws of the United States itself we can protect our rights as American citizens. But not through confrontation. Because we cannot fight against the American nation. No, but with the rights that would be ours if we were a state with a representative in Congress. Yes, those people would struggle for us. But not with the colonial system we have now, nor with independence either, because in Cuba, they have the navy and are communist and can't kick them out. I think that if we were a state—look, there are Congress people over there in the United States struggling and criticizing the navy's abuse against their citizens.

Antinavy activists in Vieques understood that Puerto Rican independence was an extremely controversial and divisive subject, and that they needed to develop a consensus to build a movement. Carlos Quintero explained:

> We invited the presidents of PNP, PPD, PSP, PIP—all so that there would be an authentic representation of all the parties and leaders that there were. This was not only *independentista*. We always had the vision that what the people want is not really a political movement, nor simply a movement to get the navy out of Vieques because, well, we are *independentista*, we don't want Americans. This was never the idea. There existed problems; there existed authentic problems about the military presence in Vieques. . . . Therefore we always tried to bring in the people, the population. The people came little by little. We always had this perspective that the more people we brought from the town, the better.

Furthermore, Vieques activists shied away from addressing issues of Puerto Rican sovereignty and colonialism because they were worried about sacrificing a focus on local grievances on the altar of Puerto Rican status debates. Leaders emphasized that the local movement was not about politics but, rather, about the "authentic" problems of the Viequense people—the concrete, material needs of the people that seemed to be ignored by the maneuverings of politicians and activists with broader agendas. Keeping the struggle focused on local needs meant, in part, keeping Viequense leadership at the helm of the movement and preventing it from spinning out of control and becoming merely a platform for the cause of Puerto Rican independence or subjugated to the interests of politicians. Fishermen were so important to the success of the movement because they characterized it as based on issues of quality of life and economic opportunity as opposed to broader anticolonial efforts.

The Crusade was crucial to supporting and broadening the fishermen's blockades. Over the course of the movement, the fishermen conducted dozens of "fish-ins" in which they disrupted military maneuvers at sea. The Crusade coordinated actions with the fishermen, organizing pickets, demonstrations, and activities on land. Like the struggle in Culebra, Vieques's mobilization relied heavily on civil disobedience and pacifism. The fishermen's blockades of maneuvers, like Culebra's human blockades of missile fire, used weakness as a strength. Since the fishermen clearly could not combat the navy on its own terms, their blockades dramatized the inequalities at the root of the conflict: the navy's seemingly wanton acts of destruction and disregard for human life, military control over land, and the fishermen's inability to enter their own waters. They also directly challenged military jurisdiction over the water—with dozens of cameras and newsreels spinning, leaving the navy stymied as to how to respond.

On land, the Crusade complemented the fishermen's campaign. On one occasion over one hundred demonstrators camped out on a beach on the southern coast of Vieques, symbolically planting coconut palms to mark an area where coconut groves had been razed to make way for maneuvers. A lawyer, Pedro Saade, who represented the Fishermen's Association, emphasized the expansion of the struggle: "This time the people of Vieques are not only fighting for their water, but also to recuperate their land."[15]

In addition to countless pickets and rallies, the Crusade organized a number of "fishermen's festivals," celebrating the valiant fishermen with food, song, and dance. Protest often took on a gadfly quality. Fishermen used slingshots to aim projectiles into the motors of navy boats. They learned that the license numbers displayed on the naval ships were important to the military, so they delighted in splashing paint on the sides of naval vessels. The fishermen were spirited and disruptive. Carlos Zenón recalled:

> One morning a new ship came towards Vieques. It started bombing the area waters at 7:00 in the morning. By 10:00 I said to my family and the other fishermen, "The bombing is going to stop!" I never heard anything like it before.
>
> So I jumped in my boat, got into the waters and met up with the U.S.S. *Dewey*. The bombing was so loud that I had to cut two pieces of cloth off my T-shirt to cover my ears. I thought my head would explode.
>
> I maneuvered right in front of the cannon, and the firing stopped. The navy says it lost $25,000 that day because someone halted its testing, though I can't understand how they lost much money if they were saving ammunition. (Zenón 1979)

The Crusade echoed the fishermen's tactics on land. One morning, one hundred demonstrators hiked two miles under cover of the early morning darkness to surprise a detachment of marines camped out on a beach. Bleary-eyed marines in their underpants were awakened by demonstrators singing "La Borinqueña," a nationalist anthem, and were dumbfounded to discover that demonstrators had pitched tents alongside their campsite. "We caught them with their pants down," Mario Martínez remembered gleefully: "One of the navy's justifications for its presence here is that they need Vieques to defend us. That they are here to protect us from whatever menace there is outside. . . . The purpose of our activity was to demonstrate to them that if we decided to conduct an enemy invasion, we could kill everyone. In this way we exposed their lie. They were not prepared to defend us. It was so easy for us to sneak up on them!"

Creating Linkages, Creating Divisions

In order for Vieques's grassroots movement to be successful, it was crucial that it build linkages beyond the shores of the island. Yet these same linkages created problems for the movement and contributed to its unraveling. The Vieques effort, like Culebra's before it, broadened the base of the movement by building a solidarity network that extended beyond the island. Links to the activist legal community would prove to be a key part of a support network. One of the first ways fishermen extended their struggle was to file suit. Almost immediately after the first blockade, Fishermen's Association president Carlos Zenón traveled to Puerto Rico to meet with lawyers from the Puerto Rico Project of the National Lawyers' Guild and the Legal Services Corporation to file suit against the navy. The fishermen were frustrated to discover that Puerto Rican governor Carlos Romero Barceló had beaten them to court, filing a suit against the navy that focused on environmental claims. A federal judge merged the fishermen's case with Romero's. The fishermen's lawyers worked to defend their clients' interests, especially when they diverged from those of the Puerto Rican government. Lawyers were also important because protestors were repeatedly arrested and charged with trespassing on federal property.

A number of other support groups sprouted up as well. In May of 1978, the National Committee in Defense of Vieques (Comité Nacional pro Defensa de Vieques) was organized to back the Vieques struggle and, over time, worked to coordinate several dozen different support groups that sprang up in different municipalities throughout Puerto Rico. In the United States, the Vieques Solidarity Network formed, linking together a number of different support groups in different cities to struggle to evict the navy from Vieques (McCaffrey 1998).

These support groups were instrumental in propelling Vieques onto a wider stage. "Remember, we didn't have any money. We didn't have access to newspapers," Mario Martínez recalled. The National Committee held press conferences, put out press releases, and organized conferences in universities. Members organized pickets, other activities, and demonstrations on the main island of Puerto Rico. They earned the support of various legislators in different cities in the United States and Puerto Rico and brought the case before Congress. They helped put Vieques on the international agenda, cultivating links between Vieques and supporters in Hawaii, Panama, Japan, France, and Spain and putting the case of Vieques before the United Nations Decolonization Committee.

In addition, the National Committee assisted the Vieques movement on the most concrete level, showing members of the Crusade how to produce propaganda, use sound equipment, and interact with the media. Committee members sent personnel to demonstrations in Vieques and lent organization to a community movement that wasn't well organized on the local level. This support was crucial, Martínez recalled: "The rhythm with which the movement developed didn't permit us to build an organization with structure. Remember, except for me [and another activist] nobody had any experience organizing. Many people didn't know how to interact with the media, respond on the radio, write a bulletin. They didn't have experience with anything. And this rapid development didn't permit us to develop a bit. We developed in the street."

At the same time that links to outside groups were essential to advancing Vieques's cause, they were also problematic on an ideological level. "It is easier to cultivate a broad base on a grassroots level than on that of solidarity," reflected Manuel Ramírez, who participated in the National Committee. While people in Vieques were motivated to struggle as a result of their living conditions and personal experience of the military, supporters from other sectors of Puerto Rico came to Vieques from a different perspective. A member of the National Committee interpreted the conflict this way:

> The large majority of the sectors that compose the support group [understand] the Vieques problem not as a regional one, but as a national one. The presence of the navy in Vieques, with its record of crimes and abuses against the Vieques population, is a concrete and vivid manifestation of the usurpation of our national sovereignty and lack of independence. To struggle successfully against the navy in Vieques is to advance the cause of Puerto Rican independence. And because they want to throw the navy out of Vieques and the rest of Puerto Rico, they sacrifice their free time, they defy the navy, they go to jail and they die. It is not a coincidence that the vast majority of militants against the navy in the big island are *independentistas*. (Feliciano 1980)

Despite near unanimous support for independence, the different sectors of the left who joined together to come to Vieques were divided on issues of strategy and tactics. Culebra had erupted at a moment when the PIP was extremely unified and militant; Vieques, however, erupted at a time when the Puerto Rican left was characterized by division and factionalism. "All of the conflict they had with one another, they handed over to us here," noted Martínez.

One of the most controversial and divisive moments between the National Committee and the Crusade occurred at a demonstration that the National Committee organized in front of the gates of Roosevelt Roads in Ceiba, on the main island. Martínez explained: "The people from the National Committee didn't have this vision of a broad struggle. They wanted to convert Vieques into a struggle for independence. For example, we understood that in Vieques you couldn't say 'Yankee go home.' The National Committee thought they could."

Demonstrators burned an American flag, an event that was broadcast on national media. The burning of the flag was a provocation that clashed with the more moderate sentiments of people in Vieques and of Puerto Ricans in general. The event threatened the fragile unity organizers had cultivated between Vieques and Puerto Rico, and the support of the various sectors that composed the movement's base. Cruz recalled: "On the national level, in the big island there were some who didn't approach the struggle as a socioeconomic one of the island of Vieques. They approached it as a political problem. We had a different vision. The large majority of us in the struggle, especially the leaders, considered and believed that Puerto Rico should be free, but that this struggle was our struggle. It is not a political issue. It is a matter of recovering Vieques. Because we want Vieques for our children. And many of them didn't understand this."

The leaders of the National Committee professed the burning of the flag to be an unplanned, spontaneous action, but activists in Vieques took it as evidence that the National Committee wanted to direct the struggle and transform it into a movement for Puerto Rican independence. Vieques activists increasingly felt that National Committee members were ultraleft, whereas Crusade leaders wanted to broaden the struggle.[16] Charges were leveled that the National Committee restricted membership in the support groups to advocates of Puerto Rican independence, stimulating a broad debate over the character of the support network. Increasingly activists in Vieques expressed ambivalence about the participation of the National Committee and asserted their sole right to direct the movement. When the National Committee planned an activity in support of Vieques the night before the annual Grito de Lares commemoration of the 1868 revolt in Lares, Puerto Rico, Vieques activists decried the National Committee for linking Vieques to a rallying cry for Puerto Rican independence.[17] National Committee members bristled at what they claimed were authoritarian and antidemocratic tendencies of the local movement. The Puerto Rican press made public the internal divisions that had begun to split the movement. News coverage highlighted the political affiliation of protestors, and assessed whether protestors were from Vieques or the big island. The media even covered an internal meeting of the Crusade and the National Committee where a "war" erupted between the Crusade and the support group.[18] The navy response came in the context of these increasing divisions

The Military Position

In the 1960s and 1970s, controversy in Cuba and Panama heightened U.S. military concerns over installations at Guantánamo Bay and the Canal Zone. With the Panama base slated for closure in 2000 and Guantánamo's status uncertain, Puerto Rican installations became all the more important to U.S. strategic concerns in the region (Langley 1985a).[19] Vice Admiral G.E.R. Kinnear II testified that Vieques was crucial to maintaining the U.S. edge in the balance of power with the Soviet Union: "The essential element that provides the U.S. Navy its advantage over the Soviets is our ability to deploy high performance aircraft; that is carrier aviation. They have us outnumbered in submarines and surface ships. Only in the area of high performance aircraft at sea do we have the edge. The Roosevelt Roads total training complex, of which Vieques is an integral part, is absolutely essential in enabling us to maintain that margin" (quoted in Langley 1985a: 274). These cold war tensions framed the intensity of the conflict that unfolded in Vieques.

Arrest of the Vieques 21

On May 19, 1979, dozens of fishing boats ferried approximately 150 demonstrators from the docks in Esperanza into restricted waters and onto a beach under military jurisdiction. Demonstrators were Viequenses and supporters from Puerto Rico, fishermen and lawyers, old people and young. Bishop Antulio Parrilla, an openly *independentista* Catholic clergyman, was celebrating mass on the beach when navy boats arrived. Matilde Rivera remembered the conflict that unfolded:

> Immediately, the fishermen and others got into their boats and started to maneuver them in the sea so as not to permit the boat from arriving on shore and disembarking. It was a brave and risky feat. The fishermen maneuvered their boats with magnificent dexterity; it appeared that they were going to crash into the boats and had succeeded in their purpose, but the navy began to spray them with a powerful hose. I could see that the water came out with tremendous force. On shore, the rest of us prayed to God that nothing terrible would happen. The force of the water forced the fishermen to retreat and all of us rushed to the shore where the boat was coming. (PRISA 1984: 15–16)

The navy boat disembarked with armed federal marshals and moved forward to arrest demonstrators, among them the bishop, wearing a stole with a Bible in his hands. A protestor recalled: "They had so many arms! Guns and bayonets and tear gas and bands of ammunition! They stood and they waited for the service to finish—people were telling them, 'Shh! Shh! This is a worship service!' Then, after we had finished, they started to surround the people they wanted. There was a lot of pushing and shoving and some people picked up handfuls of sand and threw it, but what could we do?" (quoted in Robson 1980).

A wild melee broke out. Demonstrators, facing armed marshals, refused to surrender placidly and dug their heels into the sand. Protestors screamed in outrage as groups of marshals forcibly dragged their compatriots across the beach and up the ramp onto the navy boat. News cameras captured photos highlighting the inflammatory nature of the operation. In one shot, a heavy female marshal, wearing a helmet and black glasses, a gun in her holster, kneels on the back of an old woman and handcuffs her, pressing the woman's face into the sand.

Of the dozens of demonstrators on the beach, only twenty-one were arrested. Of those, only two were from Vieques: Ismael Guadalupe, the leader of the Crusade and PSP president, and fisherman Ivan Davis, against whom charges were later dropped. The navy's public relations officer, Alex de la Zerda, was present and signaled to the marshals which protestors to arrest. The arrests effectively framed the movement as communist, run by outside agitators.

The arrests and the court cases that followed the fracas showed the navy's "community action plan" in motion. In an internal memo, the navy identified its design to divide and break the Vieques movement in a multitiered program it called its "community action plan" (U.S. Navy 1978). The strategy included assigning a Spanish-speaking public relations official to the island, making efforts to establish links with perceived or potential allies, and in the event of failure, taking harsher, punitive measures.[20] As part of this strategy, the navy responded to protest by arresting demonstrators who entered military land on trespassing charges and pushing Viequenses' conflict into the federal court system.

As Vieques's conflict with the navy played out in the federal court in Puerto Rico, it increasingly became a kind of cold war drama, in which protest was treated as a threat to national security. Although procedure governing the administration of the federal courts dictates that cases be randomly assigned, it was arranged that district court judge Juan Torruella, a conservative statehooder, would preside over nearly every one of Vieques's cases. His decisions betrayed a strong ideological cast. Torruella presided over the Romero suit, which he combined with the fishermen's claims, and issued a gag order prohibiting the lawyers and fishermen from talking publicly about the case. When the fishermen's lawyer challenged Torruella on the constitutionality of the gag ruling, Torruella reversed the order, but then threatened the attorney with an investigation into his possible disbarment. Torruella denied a series of motions by the fishermen for injunctions against the navy, but issued an injunction allowing the navy to prohibit fishermen from entering land under military jurisdiction in Vieques. Fishermen denounced the judge as prejudiced and attempted to withdraw from their lawsuit, but Torruella refused to let them do so. He ruled in favor of the navy in Romero's environmental suit, finding the navy in violation of several minor federal environmental laws but asserting the primacy of national defense in the case. Finally, he presided over the cases of the Vieques 21, convicting many of the demonstrators of federal trespassing charges and meting out maximum sentences of six months in federal prison in the United States in addition to a $500 fine.[21] Even the bishop was sentenced to one year of probation, ordered to stay off of Vieques, and issued a $500 fine.[22] These judgments sapped considerable energy from the movement and diverted attention and resources toward court cases and appeals.

Viequenses were riveted by the case of Ismael Guadalupe, one of the key leaders of the Crusade, who spoke passionately in court of the abuses perpetrated by the navy in Vieques before being sent to federal prison in Pennsylvania. Yet another conviction of one of the Vieques 21 proved to be more consequential to the movement: that of Angel Rodríguez Cristóbal, an *independentista* from Ciales, Puerto Rico. Rodríguez came to Vieques through the National Committee and was a member of the Puerto Rican Socialist League. Like Guadalupe, he was issued a $500 fine and sent to federal prison in the United States for six months. On November 11, 1979, two months into a six-month term, Rodríguez was found dead in his prison cell. Prison officials declared the death a suicide, but an independent autopsy the family had performed concluded that he was beaten to death. Photos of the cadaver showed that the face was heavily bruised, inconsistent with charges of suicide by strangulation.

With Rodríguez's death, a veil of terror and violence descended upon Vieques's struggle. The following month, clandestine factions of the Puerto Rican independence movement issued a response. On December 4, 1979, gunmen ambushed a busload of navy personnel in Sabana Seca, Puerto Rico, killing two sailors and wounding ten others. Several radical groups declared responsibility for the attacks, claiming retaliation for the death of Rodríguez and the two young *independentistas* murdered in Cerro Maravilla. The case sent shock waves across Puerto Rico and the United States and caused horror in Vieques.[23]

"We are not going to roll over to a small group of radicals," declared navy rear admiral Arthur Knoizen. "We are not going to change anything in the way we operate, what we are doing, or where we are going because of a few terrorists."[24] Increasingly the navy sought to undermine the Crusade by depicting it as a communist insurgency run by outside agitators. Already there was considerable ambivalence within the movement about the role of the support groups, and the murders in Sabana Seca further divided Viequenses.

The navy worked to shore up support for its cause on Vieques by creating a civilian constituency. It hired one hundred residents to work on the base as civilian security guards. There had previously been virtually no local employees on the base, so the hiring of one hundred civilians was significant. The loyalty of these people toward the military was questionable, but their employment effectively silenced them and their families. In addition, the navy organized another one hundred residents into two pronavy groups, the Navy League and the Pro-Navy Vanguard (Vanguardia pro-Marina), which drew heavily on the resident North American population for support. It was through these civilian advocates that the navy was able to successfully draw on its symbolic power, calling into question the loyalty and patriotism of antibase demonstrators. Alex de la Zerda, the navy's public relations official, proved key in advancing this agenda.

De la Zerda coordinated the Pro-Navy Vanguard, a militant group with Viequense and North American members that organized pronavy counterdemonstrations. The head of the Vanguard was allegedly an anti-Castro Cuban who owned a gunshop and firing range in Vieques. Viequenses membership for the Vanguard was drawn from individuals with links to the navy, often through marriage or employment, and from factions of the PNP who were alienated by Mayor Tirado's populist, antinavy administration. North Americans joined because they were politically conservative and financially secure and were upset by a vigorous antinavy movement. The Vanguard was linked to several violent episodes.

The Navy League was different from the Vanguard, functioning more as a social organization than a political group. The large majority of its members were North American, full- and part-time residents, and its major project was the founding and funding of the Sea Cadet program, which provided military training for island youth. The Sea Cadet program promised opportunity and adventure to young people on an island where the youth did not have much of a future. The intent was to win over parents through conscription of their children, and the program played an important role in dividing a population already characterized by considerable ambivalence.

Because these organizations tapped into Viequenses' ambivalence about the colonial state, about radical causes, and about outside interests and influence, they were effective in dividing the movement. The pronavy groups' most basic function was to reintroduce politics into a movement that assiduously sought to avoid all things political. The fishermen had oriented the movement toward economic grievances, and now the pronavy organizations refocused debate on issues of patriotism and political affiliation. Significantly, their political attacks were not aimed at the fishermen or at the economic grievances they raised, but at the support groups which they said were composed of outsiders who sought to control the movement.

If the ideology of unity, of the representation of all sectors, was a crucial tactic in building the movement, its undoing contributed to the downfall of the Crusade. The navy sought to undermine the Crusade by depicting it as a communist insurgency run by outside agitators. The Vanguard's pickets promoted this ideology. Members carried placards declaring themselves to be "100% *americano*." Other signs read "Navy Yes, Communists No," and "Socialists Go Home, Vieques for Viequenses." North American members of the Navy League and the Vanguard testified before a congressional subcommittee that the Crusade was run by outsiders who were socialist extremists. These tactics put members of the Crusade on the defensive. Activists continually denied that they were anti-American or communist.

The Vanguard and the Navy League acted as a kind of Greek chorus, underscoring a climate of growing repression. Movement activists charged that they were tracked and harassed by the FBI.[25] Time would show that a special unit of the Puerto Rican police maintained dossiers on dozens of Crusade activists, and that the secretary of the Crusade at one point was an undercover agent. General Electric, the largest private employer on Vieques, was widely believed to have blacklisted workers who got involved with the movement. Mario Martínez explained:

> The repression is transmitted between parent and child. "Don't get involved in this struggle, something will happen to you. Don't get involved in this struggle with the navy or you won't find work. Don't get involved in the struggle because they will blacklist you, investigate you, they will get you." Therefore this is repression. It was manifested also in the workplace. And here there was an undertaking at GE where their functionaries blacklisted people. This was a form of repression, a form of repression that occurred at many workplaces in Vieques. If the boss was pronavy, they would look for ways of repressing the employees. They'd follow them. This was all a form of repression.

The Vieques movement reached a turning point in 1980. On January 7, a right-wing underground group calling itself the Anti-Communist Alliance bombed the Puerto Rican Bar Association, claiming retaliation for the Sabana Seca incident. Two weeks later FBI agents arrested the navy's Vieques community liaison de la Zerda; Roberto Lopez Gonzalez, head of the Pro-Navy Vanguard; and a third man from Río Piedras, charging them with the Bar Association bombing and a conspiracy to bomb a Vieques Air Link plane operating between San Juan and Vieques. Federal judge Juan Torruella again presided over another Vieques case. Although the prosecution presented, among other evidence, taped conversations between de la Zerda and a navy ordnance man discussing the acquisition of explosives, and comments that indicated that de la Zerda plotted to bomb the Vieques Air Link flight in an effort to eliminate attorneys representing the Vieques fishermen, a jury ultimately acquitted all three men.[26]

The de la Zerda case confirmed not only the growing violence and repression that formed a backdrop to the movement but also the increasing polarization of the debate. More and more the terms of the debate shifted away from local claims about military control and the destruction of land and resources and toward a focus on patriotism and national defense. The heightened divisiveness spilled into the local elections that fall. Liche Castaño, the PPD mayoral candidate, who in 1977 argued that he was pro-American and antinavy, in 1980 ran on a platform that attacked the Crusade as anti-American and communist. The Crusade charged that he had been bought out by the navy. When Castaño won and PNP antinavy mayor Radamés Tirado lost, the results were widely interpreted as a referendum on the navy. And the pronavy side won. Santiago Meléndez elaborated:

> We were given the choice between god and the devil. There was a *popular* candidate for mayor here. And he took advantage of the opportunity. He was an opportunist who divided us into groups. He pulled together a group in favor of the navy. We were a group of statehooders who were behind Radamés and we were antinavy. He went and received support and help from the navy and bought votes and so on. He won the election as the pronavy mayor. I would say the election was a referendum. Navy yes or Navy no. That's when the Crusade began to die down.

Don Santiago also suggests the way in which partisan affiliation began to erode the unity the Crusade had built in opposition to the navy: "The people were divided. People who belonged to the Crusade with us voted for the pronavy candidate. If it was my decision, I wouldn't have done it. We have to vote for those who are in favor of the movement. [KM: I don't understand why people from the Crusade voted for a pronavy candidate.] They voted for the navy because they didn't look at the question of the movement. They looked at the political emblem."

Castaño's tenure in office heightened the divisions in town. In a highly controversial move, the mayor invited navy officials to the Vieques town square for the swearing in of a new admiral in a ceremony that would involve the participation of the Sea Cadets. Members of the Crusade regarded this event as extremely inflammatory. The change-of-command ceremony was hastily planned, but the Crusade was able to organize in response. The fishermen formed a blockade and prevented the admiral's boat from docking. Local activists and support forces from Puerto Rico rallied. The Sea Cadets were at the dock in uniform to join in the ceremony. The Vanguard organized a counterdemonstration in support of the military ceremony. The admiral was not allowed to dock and a melee broke out, with rocks and bottles exchanged between the factions. The next day, the conflict spilled over into the town's secondary school. Seventy-five Sea Cadets provoked a near riot in the school, forcing officials to close the school for a day.

The focus shifted from local claims to a scrutiny of patriotism. The Vieques movement, with local fishermen at the helm professing support for U.S. statehood, was perceived as a communist-led, anti-American insurgency, spurred on by outside agitators. A growing divisiveness took its toll. Lucia Meléndez spoke with bitterness of her husband's and sons' treatment by the navy and of perceived betrayal by other Viequenses:

> They were treated as if they were criminals. But who should we call criminals but the U.S. Navy? When they were arrested, what did they have in the boat? Only fish and lobster. And what were they doing? Surrendering a great feast when they hardly ever caught fish. Later they were arrested again. On this occasion they took my son and nephew. They were treated like animals. They abused them although they were trustworthy and honorable people who were only looking for their daily bread. Those who adored the navy and who are capable of killing their own brothers to defend the interest of the navy had a tremendous party, celebrating the arrest and wishing that they'd kill everyone. (PRISA 1984: 23)

Conflicts erupted within the Fishermen's Association, between the leadership of the association and the Crusade, and between the Crusade and the support group in Puerto Rico. When Puerto Rican governor Romero Barceló interceded, signing a memorandum of understanding known as the Fortín Accord with the navy in 1983, many people saw this as the solution to the island's dilemmas.

State Intervention

Although Viequense activists long struggled to assert local control over the movement and avoid the tangle of colonial politics, the ramifications of Vieques's case extended beyond the shores of that small island. From the outset Puerto Rican governor Carlos Romero Barceló established himself as a player in the drama, filing a federal court case against the navy within weeks of the fishermen's first blockade. Ultimately it was Romero who brought an end to the movement, signing an accord with the navy that effectively defused the local movement.

Romero had long acted as an ambivalent champion of Vieques's cause. On the one hand, the Vieques struggle served the ideological purposes of the PNP, which in the 1970s promoted the statehood movement as part of its demand for equality by second-class citizens of a U.S. colony (Meléndez 1993). The local involvement of the PNP and the retreat of the national PIP from Vieques made it possible for Romero to frame Vieques's struggle as a dramatic claim for full membership in the American nation. In the early part of the Fishermen's War, Romero was a forceful advocate of Vieques's struggle against stepped-up maneuvers and was happy to undermine the PIP "victory" in Culebra by suggesting that the navy's retreat was the result not of anticolonial mobilization, but of political manipulations by PPD governor Rafael Hernández Colón, who endorsed a shift of military maneuvers from Culebra to Vieques.[27]

On the other hand, it was clear that the Vieques case had the potential to derail the statehood cause. The navy pressured Romero, linking the acquisition of Puerto Rican statehood to the maintenance of military installations on the island.[28] The involvement of broad sectors of the Puerto Rican left in Vieques support groups undoubtedly alienated an administration that had dramatically demonstrated its hostility to the independence movement with the notorious Cerro Maravilla case. When the Vieques case grew more polarized in the aftermath of Sebana Seca, Romero started to retreat from his position of advocacy for Vieques, saying that the crisis in Afghanistan merited a reexamination of the national security issues at play in Vieques.[29]

When Romero announced his unilateral decision to drop litigation with the navy in exchange for a commitment from the military to bring industry to Vieques, local activists were furious. Romero came to Vieques with much fanfare on October 11, 1983, to meet with navy officials and sign a memorandum of understanding at the nineteenth-century fort outside Isabel Segunda. Angry protestors shouted from the sidelines that he was surrendering Vieques's cause. Romero responded that they were surrendering nothing—it was the navy that had agreed to concessions. Yet because the governor had dropped a multimillion-dollar lawsuit for what amounted to an unenforceable good neighbor agreement, critics speculated that he must have received money under the table, possibly in the form of military contracts for Puerto Rico. Zenón was furious and swore that Vieques had been handed over to the navy on a silver platter (Nazario 1986).

Still after years of bitter struggle and divisiveness, many Viequenses embraced the accord signed at Vieques's *fortín* (fort) as the answer to a long, difficult struggle. By bringing the navy to the bargaining table, the Fortín Accord seemed to acknowledge the legitimacy of local claims and offer at least a symbolic victory. The navy, which had long dismissed all local claims as unfounded and had characterized the movement as a communist insurgency, now admitted that it had been wrong. Promising to help the local economy and make efforts to mitigate its damage to the environment, it recognized its obligations to be a good neighbor and strive to improve the welfare of island residents. Years later, don Rafael Cruz would reflect that the accord was the single event that more than any other cause contributed to end of the local movement and the decline of political activism in Vieques:

> This accord between Romero and the navy, I think it was the most important victory for the navy. Because it was the governor, the biggest leader to come to this town. The people believed that with the agreement, all of our problems had ended. But what happened? Even now there are few people who will get involved in the struggle. "Let's wait because . . . the navy signed this agreement with Romero. An agreement is an agreement." With the accord began the decline of the movement. The people of Vieques have the tendency of believing in people from the outside rather than from here. We, the leaders of the Crusade and the fishers, said it's not true what they are saying. The people didn't believe us before. If you interview anyone from town, they will tell you that we won. I'll tell you that not even 5 percent of what they offered has been completed. They did nothing.

Conclusion

Vieques was changed by the Crusade. Although Romero represented his accord with the navy as the most significant outcome of five years of struggle, there were other, less noticed changes that occurred as a result of the protest. First, in 1980, in the middle of the protest movement, the navy turned over the resettlement tracts, where the majority of Vieques residents lived without title, to the Commonwealth government. Few people in Vieques mentioned the transfer of land as a movement victory, probably because the shift in ownership did not result in the transfer of title to residents.[30] But the turnover of land suggested that the military conceded the permanence of the population that it had long maintained on military-controlled land under the threat of eviction.

Second, and perhaps even more significantly, the navy shut down Camp García's marine installation. Interestingly, not a single person in Vieques mentioned the shutdown of the base as a consequence of the antinavy mobilization, while the navy conceded that pressure from protestors forced it to close the camp (Zeimet 1985: 353). The marine base represented the institutionalized presence of the navy in town: the marines attended local dances at the Ocean View Hotel, participated in holiday parties, brought schoolchildren in trucks to see helicopter landings, dated and married local women. Yet perhaps because the pullout of three hundred sailors left unresolved broader issues of stepped-up maneuvers and bombing, the event seemed to pass unnoticed in Vieques. The fact that the shutdown of the base provoked so little reaction also suggests that protest had a basis not in anti-Americanism but, rather, in material grievances. The symbolic presence of the marines seemed of little importance to residents. Rather, the control of land, the island's economy, its natural resources, and its future were what mattered to Viequenses. Those remained under the power of the navy.

More generally, however, Vieques signaled a changing relationship between Puerto Rico and the U.S. Navy. Fifteen years of struggle against military encroachment on civilian life—as represented by the antidraft, ROTC, Culebra, and Vieques mobilizations—suggested that military hegemony on the island would not continue uncontested. These subtle shifts are at times hard to read. Yet when the Commonwealth government and community activists converged to resist the extension of an army base in Salinas, Puerto Rico, because this would signal the "Viequesization" of this community, evidence of change bubbles to the surface (Berman Santana 1996: 40). After the Fortín Accord, however, it would take nearly twenty years before changed consciousness would again transform itself into organized protest in Vieques.

Four

There are places in the world, on American soil, where one
cannot do certain things because there are animals, flora,
and fauna. Nonetheless we are people and no one takes
us into account. We are a species in danger of extinction.
We, the people of Vieques, are in danger of extinction. And
no one heard us.
—Radamés Tirado, former mayor of Vieques

We Are a Species in Danger of Extinction

The Aftermath of the Fishermen's Crusade

The Fishermen's War of the late 1970s and early 1980s made clear
the underlying tensions that stemmed from the navy's virtual stranglehold on
Vieques Island. Although the navy continued to represent the protests as ideologically inspired, the Fortín Accord it signed with Romero conceded that the
military had caused the community material harm and proposed a remedy. The
navy's promises of work quelled organized protest, but the accord ultimately
failed to resolve conflict.

In the absence of an organized movement, residents reverted to vigilante
acts of protest to address their grievances with the military. A series of "land
rescues" in the late 1980s, however, failed to change the status quo and exposed the fault lines within Vieques over the control of land. Residents were
left deeply divided and reluctant to engage in further acts of confrontation.

Various tensions and social divisions emerged in the aftermath of the
antinavy mobilization and failed accord. Despite the reluctance of most
Viequenses to involve themselves further in conflict and controversy, the navy's
failure to live up to its promises and its ill-advised public relations campaign
heightened tensions between the military and island residents. In an increasingly polarized climate, residents often expressed feelings of victimization and
loss. This discourse about loss and victimization, about annihilation and extinction, ironically reveals the fundamental resilience of the community. The
pressure of living with the navy continued to heighten the importance of local

identity, a cultural context that ultimately became a key component of the re-surgence of protest.

The Collapse of the Fortín Accord

The Fortín Accord purported to offer a solution to what had become a protracted and contentious struggle. The navy's failure to meet its promises triggered widespread disillusionment.

In the accord the navy recognized that its "activities on the Island of Vieques may have a potential detrimental impact on the social and economic develop-ment of the island." In order to alleviate this effect, the military pledged to work with the Commonwealth government to bring full employment to the island.

The navy's stated commitment to improving Vieques's economy, however, was belied by the fundamental contradiction with the navy's own goals. The navy had long viewed the development of Vieques's economy as contrary to its strategic interests. This was the story of the demise of the Woolnor resort, which the navy torpedoed in 1961. This was the underlying rationale behind efforts to expropriate land in 1964. The navy was concerned that the develop-ment of the local economy would lead to an increase in population, traffic, and the development of a constituency opposed to the use of the island as a bomb-ing range.

In the Fortín Accord, the navy attempted to resolve this apparent contra-diction by developing an economy with strong links to the military, encourag-ing top defense contractors to subcontract work in Vieques. The navy's goal was to provide the island with five hundred manufacturing jobs. Although the navy's plan was specific to Vieques in its attempt to resolve a sensitive strate-gic situation by relying on its strongest allies in industry, the idea of attracting industry to the island followed the Operation Bootstrap industrialization-by-invitation economic model that has generally been viewed as successful in Puerto Rico as a whole (Grusky 1992).[1]

As Sara Grusky (1992) demonstrates, this model was not sustainable on a local level. Vieques had a unique set of "disincentives" that stemmed from the military presence: a lack of available land, a lack of access to natural resources (aquifers, coastline), poor infrastructure, and transportation problems that dis-couraged contractors from committing to the island. The local economy was fragile, and the navy's singular focus on bringing in several large contractors did not anticipate the potential harm that would be caused by any internal dis-ruption in one of these enterprises. Two unconnected problems—mismanage-ment of funds by the parent company of a food dehydration plant, and bribery charges leveled against Dandie, a military shirt manufacturer—shut down those operations and proved devastating to Vieques's economy. On the Puerto

Rican level, bureaucractic snafus and intense party rivalries compounded the difficulty of advancing economic projects in Vieques. In short, the navy failed to live up to its promise to bring full employment to Vieques. By the early nineties, unemployment rates were higher than when the navy signed the Fortín Accord. The shells of abandoned factories littered Vieques's landscape. Residents were embittered.

The environmental elements of the 1983 agreement also proved disappointing. The navy's environmental commitments seemed more rhetorical than real, aimed mainly at improving the military's public image. The accord left unresolved the catastrophic effects of toxic dumping and weapons testing. As a public relations strategy, the Fortín Accord was more than a failure. The environmental elements of the accord inflamed antagonism because they celebrated the navy's role as an environmental protector, arguing that the navy had protected Vieques's habitat from development. While bombing and military maneuvers continued, the navy spent $70,000 on a program collecting sea turtle eggs from beaches used for military maneuvers and relocating them to a cage on the other side of the island. The military spent another $35,000 building ten wooden beach shelters on the shores of three beaches on navy land. The navy spent half a million dollars planting 150 acres of mahogany trees, an "expensive waste of effort," admitted a navy lieutenant commander, for a bunch of "pathetic-looking trees."

The navy erected signs declaring certain zones under military jurisdiction to be "environmentally sensitive conservation zones." One small islet immediately off the coast from the military target range was declared an environmental reserve for nesting brown pelicans. The navy erected more signs prohibiting the trapping of crabs on military land and suggesting that poachers were responsible for the decimation of these species. These signs intensified local antagonism; they highlighted residents' lack of access to the land and were seen as blaming them for the destruction of the environment.

Most fundamentally, the Fortín Accord failed to redress underlying grievances about the control of the land. While it brought an end to organized protest, the accord did not dispel the core resentment that had motivated that movement. The navy maintained control over the majority of island land and resources and, with it, the future of Vieques. Although the navy had transferred control over the resettlement tracts to the Commonwealth government in 1980, Puerto Rico failed to devise a strategy to resolve the tangled mess of land ownership. Residents continued to languish without title to the land they occupied while responsibility for the chaos passed from one Puerto Rican agency to the next. Although the immediate fear of eviction seemed to have lifted, residents' status remained ambiguous. Without title to the land, individuals were unable to qualify for a mortgage or buy homeowner's insurance. The municipality received no property tax revenue.

For the navy, the collapsed accord represented a lost opportunity. The accord had the potential to resolve conflict by providing a minimal number of jobs, in essence a small commitment to shore up support at a naval facility the military had deemed so vital. The community's acceptance of the accord revealed how fundamentally moderate residents' aspirations were. Most perceived the struggle not as one of national liberation, but rather as a struggle for a right to make a living and obtain a certain quality of life, uninterrupted by relentless bombing raids.

In the absence of real resolution, conflict again exploded in 1989. The manifestation was different, and to many Viequenses, particularly old-time activists, the politics were troubling.

Monte Carmelo

In the spring of 1987 the navy began eviction proceedings in the U.S. District Court for the District of Puerto Rico against Carmelo Félix Matta and his family, charging them with illegally residing on navy territory. The Félixes were one of a number of Vieques families who had established residence in the so-called military buffer zone, an unmarked swath of navy-controlled land that bordered the resettlement tracts. It was typical for most people in Vieques to live on navy-controlled land for decades without title to the plots on which they built their homes, but some residents staked a claim to parcels of navy land in an organized movement in the mid-seventies.[2] Many more people like Carmelo Félix simply fanned out from the cramped resettlement tracts to the quiet, empty fields on the fringes of navy territory. The navy turned a blind eye as residents took out personal loans to build homes or constructed houses piece by piece as the cash came in. Migrants poured foundations for one-day dream houses to return to after years spent working in New York City or St. Croix. These homesteaders carved erratic roads snaking to homes that sprouted like mushrooms on the hills. They pressed the municipality to deliver electricity, water, telephone service, and mail to homes that had no addresses. The Félixes were just one family who had staked a claim in this no-man's land. Their home was modest, built of concrete with no plumbing or electricity. It was unclear why the navy sought to evict the Félix family at this particular moment; a number of families had been living unchallenged in the same area for years.

In a move that showed the strong political undercurrents of this confrontation, Carmelo Félix sought and received legal help from the office of a leading PIP politician. The lawyer argued that Félix was willing to pay the navy rent, and had not willfully trespassed, as there were no fences, signs, or warnings that would have alerted him that he was building on navy land. The U.S. district court denied the motion and entered judgment against Félix. Félix's case quickly drew attention and roused public sympathy in Vieques.

By the time U.S. deputy marshals and unarmed navy reinforcements arrived at the Félix homestead to evict the family, local forces had mobilized and rallied to stop the eviction. At least one hundred neighbors and protestors blocked the road to stop navy vehicles carrying the Félixes' possessions. Tensions flared and a navy truck was doused with gasoline and set afire. As the situation escalated, the marshals called for reinforcements. A U.S. Coast Guard helicopter was dispatched, bringing in a group of heavily armed marshals wearing bulletproof vests and brandishing submachine guns and automatic rifles. By the end of the day, the marshals declared the Félix family evicted and order restored. The truck burned on until the next afternoon.

But the eviction of the Félix family only sparked resentment. The case received extensive media coverage in the Puerto Rican and U.S. press. Within days of the eviction, Carmelo Félix returned to his home with the support of fifteen to twenty Vieques families and local and main island groups. He basked in the limelight and vowed never to leave and to personally battle the U.S. Navy, if necessary, to defend his family and home. Félix's hilltop homestead, a humble little house flanked by a Puerto Rican flag, became celebrated as Monte Carmelo, Mount Carmelo. Vieques's David and Goliath battle against the navy was revived.

The Félix case exploded tensions over the land and latent resentment toward the military. Although Félix had never before been active in the antinavy movement, and indeed during the seventies had accused antinavy activists of being communists, he now became a central figure in the antinavy movement. With a new rallying point and revived antinavy sentiment, local activists decided to use the Félix eviction as a stepping stone for reclaiming land. A handful of veteran activists and newly inspired individuals mobilized. In May 1989, five hundred well-organized people seized eight hundred acres of vacant military land. Called a "land rescue" by proponents and a "land invasion" by opponents, the squat was so well planned that it included registration forms and a $10 membership fee administered by an executive committee. Leaders called the takeover an act of self-defense and survival of the Viequense people. The land rescue was the most recent and dramatic effort by Viequenses to claim unoccupied land on the perimeter of the base. Like those in neighborhoods formed in the sixties and seventies (Bravos de Boston and Villa Borinquén), residents took advantage of the navy's lax security and seeming indifference to squatters on the borders of its territory. Now the navy was left struggling for a resolution that would not bring about another embarrassing confrontation.

Many activists hoped the land rescue would revitalize the valiant struggle of the Crusade, but the new movement turned out to be of entirely different circumstances and character. Though there were participants who were motivated by concerns of social justice, there were also many individuals who were merely interested in seizing tracts of land to sell them off as vacation lots to wealthy Puerto Ricans. The movement dissolved into infighting and speculation. Félix's involvement and values were viewed with skepticism. Born out of bitter disenchantment rather than idealism, the land rescue became a form of vigilante justice, a self-interested free-for-all. The cause of the recovery of the island was abandoned to cynical individualism as people looked for ways to make up for past wrongs and strike it rich while they were at it. Many veteran activists retreated from the movement in disgust.

The land rescue came to a precipitous conclusion in August 1989 when Hurricane Hugo struck Vieques and wiped out the settlements. Seizing on the opportunity provided by the resulting chaos, the navy quickly moved in to erect fences and reclaim its jurisdiction. The land rescue officially came to an end.

The land rescue of 1989 can be read as a response to the aftermath of the antinavy mobilization. In the absence of a resolution of conflict, with resentment toward the navy and the Puerto Rican government for the failure of the Fortín Accord, cynicism and vigilantism infused popular sentiment and activity.

The Legacy of Monte Carmelo

The kind of chaos and speculation unleashed by Monte Carmelo sent shock waves across Vieques Island. For decades popular discontent had focused on the negative impact of the navy; now the land rescue, for the first time, suggested the possibility that the navy's exit might be worse than the status quo. Such uncertainty created deep divisions among residents, who, while upset by the collapse of the accord, were also disturbed about the island's future. North American residents were particularly rattled by the land speculation, and the event further polarized this insular community from the rest of the civilian resident population.

The North Americans

One morning in the spring of 1994, I drank lemonade on the patio of Betty and Jack Wilson's Caribbean vacation home. The Wilsons are retirees from New Canaan, Connecticut, who are part of a community of self-described snowbirds who flock to Vieques for the winter.

The Wilsons first vacationed in Vieques in the late 1960s, at the urging of friends. "It was described as less expensive than other Caribbean islands," Mr. Wilson remembered. "And less developed because of the navy," Mrs. Wilson added. "And that is what attracted us to it. The lack of big high-rise or fancy hotels."

The Wilsons were part of a wave of North Americans who bought up land in Vieques in the late 1960s as the island's *colono* class sold off cane and pasture land that was no longer viable after the collapse of the sugar industry. Many *colono* families left Vieques for Puerto Rico and were replaced by seasonal North American residents who were attracted to the island's tranquility and "bargain" prices. The Wilsons bought a forty-five-acre family farm with four other "rich friends" from Connecticut and built their winter vacation home. In those days they felt the political climate was less divisive. "I would guess that the navy was significantly better accepted," Mr. Wilson said. "Not that more people loved them, but the reverse. Less people hated them. Hardly anyone would admit to being fond of the navy, except for people like us."

The Wilsons' home is perched in the western hills of Vieques and has unobstructed, breathtaking views of the Caribbean. The week before, helicopters on maneuvers buzzed in their line of vision, but on that morning, a solitary hawk circled silently, carried over acres of abandoned farmland by the trade winds. "You can see why we don't want [the navy] to give up the land," Mrs. Wilson said, as we settled down to chat.

The Wilsons are members of the Navy League, as are most of their snowbird friends, yet they had no personal connection to the military and expressed no deep affection for the navy. "I think most North Americans who have homes here enjoy having the navy here and the limits [on development] the navy establishes," explained Mr. Wilson. "By the same reason, most, 99 percent, of the Puerto Ricans feel the reverse."

Mr. Wilson went on, "The natives complain about not having an opportunity. And if I were a native I think I would complain about the lack of opportunity. I think the navy has an uneconomic result—not planned, or looked for, or hoped for—but that's the way it works out. But I'm not surprised that there's all this, 'You've got to give back what we sold to you.'"

"It wasn't expropriated," Mrs. Wilson interjected. "You know [an activist] uses that word. They did buy the land."

"But they bought the land at a price that the government decided was a fair price," Mr. Wilson added. "Not a haggled price, if you know what I mean."

The Wilsons, like most of the older seasonal residents of Vieques Island, spoke no Spanish and had little interest in local politics. But the land speculation and free-for-all unleashed by the Monte Carmelo incident disturbed them. They were concerned about what they believed to be the navy's laissez-faire attitude toward residents who had encroached upon the boundaries of navy land.

> JW: Incidentally, the navy had a policy of allowing people to squat on navy land. Stand up and look at the houses down there. They are squatting on navy land. If you keep your nose clean, be a good citizen, eventually they are likely to give you a title to the house. Then you sell it and it has some value. Prior to that it had zero value. For reasons known only to God and the navy, some three or four years ago . . .

> BW: [Interrupts] Oh, well, you must know about this, the Monte Carmelo incident . . .

> JW: [Interrupts] They turned the trucks over and burned cars downtown. And there were fellows selling lots for fifty bucks. And another fellow to guarantee them for another fifty. It was unpleasant. It was extremely unpleasant. And we wrote the navy and said that our inconvenience was not the navy's problem, but in our opinion, the navy had left this island lawless—without law. And the navy ought to protect its own rights and get up and do something! And lo and behold, they got up to do something and the goddamn hurricane came along and did it for them. Every piece of wood that was on this land down here ended up in the Atlantic Ocean! [Laughs.]

The land rescues of the late eighties had a profound effect on local politics. For North Americans like the Wilsons, the rampant speculation and lack of law enforcement confirmed suspicions that the Puerto Rican government was inept and incapable of governing its own land. At the time I spoke to the Wilsons, Carlos Romero Barceló, the governor who had become Puerto Rican resident commissioner in Washington, D.C., had submitted legislation calling for the navy to return the western part of its landholdings to the municipality. When I asked the Wilsons what they thought about Romero's proposal, Mrs. Wilson responded with mock indignation: "This is *our private property!*" Mr. Wilson was more shrewd in his assessment: "The charm of this house would disappear. The *value* of the house would increase significantly! We think. So it's kind of a fail-safe. You wouldn't want to live in the house. But a lot of people would." The Wilsons thought the idea of returning land to the municipality was futile.

> BW: I don't see that it's going to help very much. I mean, I think the minute they give—if they give this end of the island it's all going to be in the hands of a few people who will make a lot of money, and maybe the natives will get jobs as . . . menial jobs. I don't . . .

JW: [Interjects] Dishwashers!

The Wilsons' pessimism seemed firmly rooted in their desire to preserve the status quo and reflects an important political reality in Vieques. North Americans form a political and economic bloc on the island. Their organization, comparative wealth, and coherence give them power to influence the island's future.

Politically, the North Americans profess nearly universal support for the navy and formally back it through their membership in the Navy League. In addition, the North Americans advance their interests through the Vieques Conservation and Historic Trust (VCHT), a conservationist group founded by wealthy North American seasonal residents that is particularly concerned with the preservation of Vieques's spectacular bioluminescent bay.[3] The membership of the VCHT almost entirely overlaps with the Navy League, and the environmental message the group espouses ideologically parallels that of the navy. The VCHT celebrates the role the navy plays in keeping the island undeveloped and worries about "native" sources of environmental contamination: trash on the beaches, gasoline-powered boats in the bioluminescent bay. For years the VCHT refused to take a stand against the bombing of Vieques Island and the destruction of the coastal ecology by military maneuvers, professing that such a position was political in orientation.[4]

Economically, the North Americans own a significant portion of the island's titled land and have carved inroads into prime beachfront property on squatters' land. They have also come to dominate Vieques's modest hospitality trade. The original wave of snowbirds was followed by a wave of entrepreneurs who came to Vieques to escape the fast-paced life and crowded urban centers of the North and the demands of corporate work. North Americans now own the majority of the small hotels on Vieques. They also control what passes for the entertainment industry, leading trips to the bioluminescent bay and snorkeling, scuba, and diving tours.

North American real estate agents and brokers lease and sell vacation properties owned by North Americans. They own the majority of the island's restaurants, serving chicken wings, Texas barbecue, and crab enchiladas, a sort of southwestern, laid-back "Latino fare," if not authentic Puerto Rican food. They own small gift shops selling sarongs and toucan earrings, "tropical" items totally disconnected from any native production, custom, or dress.

Significantly, many North Americans refer to Vieques Island's capital not by its proper name, Isabel Segunda, but by a derivative form, "Isabela." More than a careless error, this misnomer reflects a shift in consciousness, a lack of concern for local history, customs, and language, a separateness that defines the North American community.

In short, the older seasonal residents are invested in the idleness of the landscape, while those in the North American entrepreneurial class fear an expanded economy and corporate power that might squeeze them off the island. At the same time, these North Americans complain bitterly about wilted lettuce that comes too late on Vieques's unreliable ferry and about garbage strewn on the beach, marring the view from their small hotels. They blame the island's malaise on the Puerto Rican government, on the ineptitude of local officials, or on the laziness and irresponsibility of locals. The navy, they believe, acts as the primary force that has "saved" Vieques from the Puerto Ricans.

What becomes of Vieques land influences the future of North American residents and their investment on the island. As the Wilsons recognize, a turnover of land might raise the value of their property, but it could also destroy their underdeveloped enclave. Thus a number of North Americans are adamantly opposed to any turnover of land and are threatened by antinavy sentiment. Frank Jones, the president of the Navy League, interpreted much of the antinavy sentiment on the island as generated by communist-influenced outside agitators. Jones linked what he believed to be unfounded claims against the navy to unfounded claims to the land:

> They complain about the navy—say they're destroying the island—say Vieques has more craters than the moon. I've been to the bombing range— it's a very small section of the base—it doesn't look like the moon. They claim that the noise is unbearable—that children are shell shocked, that they can't hold classes because of the noise from the planes. I'll tell you—it's a hell of a lot more noisy by the airport in San Juan than it is here. They hear more noise in St. Thomas—that's where they complain. There's a hill behind the place where they bomb so you hardly hear anything here. . . . They claim that the navy stole the land—they bought it. Bought it from the sugar plantation owners who were more than happy to get rid of it. There were people squatting on the land and the navy built them houses.

Jones depicts Viequenses as little more than squatters, for whom the navy built houses. This view not only denies the legitimacy of local claims to land but illuminates a major anxiety of North American residents—the specter of squatting that was raised during the land recovery of 1989. In Jones's opinion all Viequenses are squatters with no rights to the land the navy occupies. Turning over land, it is feared, would only open up military borders to rampant, uncontrolled squatting, one of the most intense, pervasive fears expressed by North American residents.

Hillary Clark, who owns a local tourist shop, articulated these fears one Saturday afternoon following hearings in Vieques on Romero's proposed legislation in Congress. Though the hearings, which were the most significant political event in Vieques in years, were held two blocks away from her home, Clark did not attend. Still, she expressed deep concern that the proposal would only unleash squatting. "I don't want to see that happen to Vieques," she remarked, "but on the other hand, if the island is going to go to squatters I want to be the first one there."

For all their stated disdain for squatting, North Americans have been at the forefront of land speculation in Vieques. They have bought up plots of beachfront property on the island's north coast to build walled mini-castles with minarets and, indifferent to the ravages of tropical storms, they have built vacation homes with three-storied walls of glass.

Discussion of any changes in the island's status deeply concerned North American residents. Frequently, their opposition to change was framed in environmental terms, a striking ideological development in the years after the Fortín Accord. The navy's campaign to depict itself as the environmental steward of Vieques was well received by the North American population. For example, Fred and Susan Meyers, who have operated a bed-and-breakfast on the island for several seasons, were somewhat ambivalent about the impact of the military presence on their business. Fred felt that the controversy created by the navy's bombing of the island probably deterred tourists, although once they arrived they could see that the navy was not really a problem. "The navy has kept the land pristine," he noted. "If it weren't for the navy, Vieques would be just like St. Thomas. On the other hand, if you talk to Carlos [his neighbor] he'll point to the areas that used to be fishing villages and where people used to live and all of that was taken from them. It's hard for us to relate, but if that had happened to us, we'd feel the same way."

Susan Meyers felt more strongly in favor of the navy. She was upset by talk that some of the base land would be returned. "I hope if the navy does leave that the land is turned into a national park," she commented. The Meyers were less invested in debates over whether or not the navy bought the land that it occupied; in fact Fred seemed to concede that there was injustice in the way the land was acquired. But the Meyerses seemed convinced that a larger good had occurred: namely, that the navy had protected the island against uncontrolled development. And they favored the continued estrangement of Viequenses from the land, either by the military or by the National Park Service, as a guarantee of the island's "preservation."

Figure 1. In the 1970s, the navy's imposition of new restrictions on the waters surrounding Vieques provoked clashes between local fishermen and the military. Fishermen organized a flotilla intended to block naval maneuvers that they claimed prevented them from earning a living. *Courtesy* El Nuevo Día (*Ramón Korff*).

Figure 2. As the 1970s' conflict intensified, the navy blasted high-power water hoses to disperse fishing boats. *Courtesy* El Nuevo Día (*Ramón Korff*).

Figure 3. Fishermen used their superior knowledge of the coastline to evade navy ships in a series of cat-and-mouse chases. *Courtesy* El Nuevo Día (*Ramón Korff*).

Figure 4. Support from the Puerto Rican left sustained and expanded the fishermen's mobilization. Hundreds of activists traveled to Vieques from elsewhere in Puerto Rico and the United States to attend rallies, pickets, and marches. Here dozens of protestors defied naval authority to march on a Vieques beach under military jurisdiction. *Courtesy* El Nuevo Día (*Ramón Korff*).

Figure 5. In 1979 navy police broke up an ecumenical service and arrested twenty-one demonstrators on federal trespassing charges. Demonstrators threw sand when Angel Rodríguez Cristóbal was dragged onto a navy boat. Rodríguez, a member of the Puerto Rican Socialist League from Ciales, later died under suspicious circumstances in federal prison. Authorities declared his death a suicide, but activists believe he was assassinated as a message to the Puerto Rican left to stay out of Vieques. *Courtesy Roso Juan Sabalones.*

Figure 6. Fishermen charge that bombing exercises are devastating the marine ecology. A fisherman is shown netting one of the countless unexploded bombs that litter Vieques's coastal waters. *Courtesy* El Nuevo Día (*Xavier Araujo*).

Figure 7. Following the example of Culebra activists thirty years earlier, in 1999 pro-independence activists from El Congreso Nacional Hostosiano built a schoolhouse on the bombing range. The schoolhouse was one of over a dozen resistance sites erected there. *Author's collection.*

Figure 8. By putting themselves directly in the line of fire, activists blocked live-bombing exercises on the target range for over a year. They lived in a *casita* on a bomb-scarred hilltop covered with unexploded ordnance. The Monte David protest camp became the heart of the Vieques mobilization in 1999. *Author's collection.*

Figure 9. The worn flag of Vieques is raised high on a battered tank on the top of Monte David. Once used as a target for firing exercises, the tank became a symbol of the resistance effort when activists from many Puerto Rican municipalities staked flags to mark their pilgrimages. *Author's collection.*

Figure 10. A wall of crosses memorializes those in Vieques who have died of cancer. The hilltop of Monte David overlooks a panorama of destruction, a lagoon obliterated by bombs and littered with rusted tanks. *Author's collection.*

Figure 11. The arrest of leading Catholic and Protestant clergy for civil disobedience signaled a dramatic change in the movement. The new religious leadership helped to maintain the commitment to nonviolent passive resistance. *Courtesy* El Nuevo Día (*Xavier Araujo*).

Figure 12. Demonstrators continued entering restricted military areas to disrupt maneuvers after the navy dismantled their protest camps. This demonstrator surrendered peacefully to military authorities and was led off the base in plastic handcuffs. *Courtesy* El Nuevo Día (*Xavier Araujo*).

Figure 13. The commitment to passive resistance transformed the protest effort from the militant campaign of the seventies. This activist passively collapsed into the arms of navy personnel, who cuffed and dragged him off the range. *Courtesy* El Nuevo Día (*Xavier Araujo*).

Figure 14. The revived Vieques movement, transcending partisan politics, mobilized broad sectors of Puerto Rican civil society. Hundreds of federal employees formed their own chapter of "Peace for Vieques" and traveled by ferry to the island to march in solidarity. *Author's collection.*

Figure 15. The threat of cancer has mobilized many women to join the struggle to end military bombing exercises on Vieques. These members of the Vieques Women's Alliance traveled to New York City to protest, carrying white crosses to memorialize island children who have died of cancer. *Courtesy* El Diario-La Prensa (*Humberto Arellano*).

Figure 16. Riot police blocked supporters from the gates of Camp García, as navy police arrested "invaders" who scaled navy fences to enter the base. Cheering picketers were pepper-sprayed in a tense standoff. *Author's collection.*

Figure 17. Governor Pedro Rosselló stirred controversy and resentment in the winter of 2000 when he signed an agreement to allow limited bombing and the use of Puerto Rican police to guard U.S. military property. The new policy was a dramatic reversal of his pledge that "not one more bomb" should fall on Vieques. *Author's collection.*

Vieques at Large: The Fear of the Worse

It is not surprising that the land speculation would elicit a strong reaction from North Americans, who are the group most invested in the status quo on the island. Many Viequenses, however, particularly the elderly, were also shaken by the aftermath of Monte Carmelo. This was not because they regarded Vieques as a pristine Caribbean vacation land, but because of their fear of the "worse." Over a decade after the navy relinquished control over the resettlement tracts to the Puerto Rican government, most Viequenses continued to live on land to which they held no title. The idea that the fragile balance of life, the order people had established without law or support from the government, could quickly be thrown into disarray frightened many people. After the land rescue, the navy, for many people, stood as a force of order and stability, an emblem of the status quo.

Luis Ramírez is an elderly resident in his mid-seventies, a retired schoolteacher, who has long been antagonized by antinavy activism. Don Luis belonged to a faction of the local PNP that was deeply alienated by former mayor Radamés Tirado's antinavy position during the Crusade. Don Luis was loosely associated with the Pro-Navy Vanguard during these years. In don Luis's opinion, the Crusade was "anti-American antagonism more than a protest about Vieques. All that was American was bad. Except for the money, except for the money. There was no basis [to the protest]." Don Luis asserted that the majority of people in Vieques have always been in favor of the military presence. But when pressed to elaborate whether he believed Viequenses were really in favor of the navy or the status quo, he explained:

> LR: The status quo more than anything else. Because we are in favor, not out of lack of interest, but we believe that they bought it, as you buy your house, it is yours. If they bought the land and the government of Puerto Rico seeks little by little the return of all the land they are not using, I am in favor of this. Because they are not using it.

> KM: What do you think of Romero's proposal to return land?

> LR: Romero is saying that what they aren't using they should return. This is logical. I agree with this. And everyone agrees, because what they are not using here, should go to the people . . . not the people here, no, to the government of Puerto Rico. Because here, if you let them, they will grab and sell to get ahead. What have they done with Bravos de Boston [a "rescued" barrio]? What have they done? The others, from here, from Vieques have taken land to sell it to outsiders. What happened to the money they collected? If the government had that land, it would make housing plots, highways, who

knows what? But here many people took land for their own benefit, not for the benefit of the people.

Like don Luis, sixty-year-old Isolina Mendoza supported the navy as an emblem of the status quo, although her political and personal perspective is different. Doña Isolina is an avid *popular* and a relative of Liche Castaño, the PPD mayor who backed the navy during the Crusade. Doña Isolina has been married for over forty years to a marine she met at a dance in Vieques in the 1950s. She traveled all over the world with her husband while he was in the service, but returned to Vieques with him when he retired. She was the treasurer of the Pro-Navy Vanguard in the late seventies and was one of the few Viequense members of the Navy League. She lived in a modest, one-story concrete home and endured a grueling daily commute to Puerto Rico to work in a Commonwealth agency. She admitted that she believes Vieques does not benefit economically from the military presence, but attributed the island's malaise to the tenure of the current PNP mayor who took office after Liche Castaño. Her defense of the military combined patriotic sentiment with an economic rationale.

KM: Do you think the majority of people are in favor of the navy?

IM: Yes, I would like there to be a vote to prove this.

KM: Do you think that most people are in favor because they like the navy, or because they like Vieques as it is now?

IM: Because we like Vieques as it is now. Because this is the defense of our nation. If the navy leaves Vieques, they will have to pull the base out of Ceiba. If Vieques goes, Ceiba has to go. And there are thousands of people working over there in Ceiba. In Vieques there are fifty to seventy people who work [for the navy].

KM: How do people feel about the navy now?

IM: The people are in favor, more or less. There's a small group that pickets and does damage.

KM: Why?

IM: Because they want, according to them, to rescue the land for progress, to make hotels, to cultivate the land. And they don't do it, because look. Bravos de Boston belongs to the navy. The people invaded that land. And they sold it to the Americans. The majority of people living in Bravos de Boston are Americans.

Doña Isolina impugned the patriotic sentiment many activists profess, noting the prevalence of North Americans in a "rescued" section on the north coast of Vieques. She not only questioned the motivations of activists, but clearly saw the navy as a check to the kind of land speculation that has plagued Vieques.

One of the main subcurrents that runs beneath the surface of "promilitary" sentiment is the issue of access to land. Antinavy activists decry the military occupation of two-thirds of island land and the stifling of the local economy. But many of the Viequenses who defend the navy fear that they would have less access to the land and to the productive potential of the island if the navy pulled out. Political support for the navy often masks a class-based concern for control of the island's productive potential and resources. Vieques, many residents fear, would be snatched up by wealthy Puerto Ricans and North Americans and built up like San Juan, St. Thomas, and St. Croix. They fear that local residents would be excluded from the island's development, triggering the kind of alienation, racial antagonism, and violence many Viequenses have witnessed firsthand in the Virgin Islands.

Underlying the polarized debate of pro- and antinavy factions, then, is a broader debate about colonialism that mirrors wider status debates in Puerto Rico as a whole. The language of plebiscite is instructive here, for it reveals the way in which people's perspectives are framed by what they see as limited options. The vote for the status quo is less a hearty embrace of the military than an expression of the fear of the worse. Vieques follows the pattern of the rest of Puerto Rico, in which islanders' support for continued political and economic association with the United States often reflects a political pragmatism, shaped by the perception of limited options (Grosfogel 1997).

This pragmatism was reflected in the comments of Pedro Vales, the seventy-eight-year-old retired fisherman. In the 1970s, don Pedro spearheaded direct confrontations with battleships, but now he declared that he was no longer interested in protesting the navy. Don Pedro was involved in a bitter dispute over the leadership of the fishing co-op, and ultimately left fishing to turn his attention to evangelical ministry. He claimed to have "changed his mind" about the navy: "I said to the fishermen, we have to give up the pickets, because the navy is not going to leave Vieques. What we have to do is to picket the navy to bring us jobs and give up land. But the navy is not going to leave. Because one hundred or two hundred 'cats' are not strong enough to get the navy to leave. We can live with them." Don Pedro expressed both resignation and a willingness to work toward some reconciliation. He seemed resigned to living with the navy, but committed to the idea of pressuring the navy to provide jobs, which was the essence of the 1983 accord. His pragmatism characterized the outlook of many Viequenses: "I'm not a fanatic. If I am asking you something at gunpoint, you won't listen. But if I explain to you the reason, maybe you will understand and your heart will be touched. If I go to you with a threatening attitude, you're not going to listen. The navy is not leaving. This is an important base. The navy is part of Vieques."

If the navy had met the promises it outlined in the Fortín Accord, it would have satisfied moderates like don Pedro, who were willing to settle for a compromise. The collapse of the Fortín Accord, however, eroded support for the navy from even some of its strongest adherents on the island. Flora Lebredo, for example, is widely regarded as one of the most pronavy Viequenses on the island. Her links to the military are strong. As a child, she grew up in barracks on a U.S. military base where her father was in the military police. Later, she herself served in the marines. Yet the failure of the navy to live up to the promises it made in the Fortín Accord soured her view of the military. Doña Flora asserted that she was neutral on the subject of the military presence on Vieques Island: "I have tried to stay away from this. Distance myself. Not say anything. Neither yes, nor no, in favor or against." Doña Flora's husband was the head of VEDCO, a civilian board that worked with the military to implement navy-initiated development projects. As she refused to comment, however, she began to talk more and more: "The navy was supposed to bring in factories. Everything flopped. They came, they did damage, they left. I don't have anything to do with the navy now. I'm not a member of the Navy League. I don't go to Roosevelt Roads anymore. I do keep in touch with Admiral Knoizen. I send him a Christmas card every year."

Doña Flora dated her disenchantment with the navy to the collapse of VEDCO projects in 1986. "I've had a lot of pain and suffering because of the situation with the navy," she asserted, "including an employee who went to jail." Doña Flora is the head of a Commonwealth agency, and some of her employees were jailed during the Fishermen's War for trespassing on military property. "During the hard times things were really tough here," she reflected. "It wasn't worth it. It wasn't worth it." Doña Flora continued:

> There are a lot of people here who have tunnel vision. They put blinders on and don't want to see other perspectives. Carmelo Félix Matta. He's a fanatic. He rants and raves, says he's against the navy, and he's selling land left and right. Including one plot of land he sold three times to different people. People here say that they want the navy to go, give back the land so that there can be tourism and development. They say they're against the gringos, but then they turn around and sell all our land to the gringos. People here all have two houses. And cars. All these people see only one way. Not me. This is a small island. Everyone knows one another and has to get along. That's why

I don't get involved. . . . Things were so bad. At the height of the bad times I went out and bought a magnum. Yes. That's right. That's how bad things were. Fanatical. It wasn't worth it.

Doña Flora's comments reveal the reluctance of many Viequenses to involve themselves further in controversy over the navy. What was striking about popular sentiment in the early nineties was that even in light of the failed accord, Viequenses were still willing to compromise. Tensions remained high over the control of land, but people were willing to settle for jobs. Even Carmelo Félix, whom doña Flora dismissed as a fanatic, took to the local airwaves in an attempt to start a movement looking for jobs or some sort of compensation in exchange for the continued bombing of the island. The navy, however, squandered this opportunity to make peace. It failed to bring any work to the island, and it inflamed tensions with a poorly conceived public relations campaign and a general arrogance toward the civilian population.

The Navy

The navy's public relations campaign in Vieques was poorly managed. Despite the significance the military attached to Vieques, the navy did not devote attention or resources to building a climate of goodwill. This failure of commitment was an expression of a much longer legacy of antagonism, stemming from the navy's wish to see the island emptied of its inhabitants. Simply put, the navy was not much concerned with building goodwill because it did not see the civilian population as vital to its interests; rather, the navy viewed civilian residents primarily as an encumbrance that blocked its unfettered access to the range. This perspective shaped an attitude that was openly adversarial. Such a posture heightened tensions on the island.

A tour of the Roosevelt Roads Naval Station near Ceiba, Puerto Rico, with Chief Anne Bradford, the navy's public relations officer, made this adversarial climate apparent. Chief Bradford picked me up at the gates of Roosevelt Roads and drove me around the base. She started the tour by providing me with an overview of the geography of the base, mentioning that the complex has 150 miles of roads and occupies 9,000 acres. I asked her if those numbers included Vieques. "No. With Vieques the complex is 33,000 acres," she said, and quickly added, "The navy paid fair market value for the land at the time, which they bought from the local sugar barons. It's not like the navy came in and took it from the locals," she said, "which is what they like to say."

We reached a high point on the road where we could see a good part of the base and all of Vieques. Chief Bradford indicated where the ammunition was stored on Vieques and where the range lay. People complained about the range, she acknowledged, but noted, "There's a ten-mile radius between the civilian sector and the bombing area. Even if they're slightly off target, it's not like bombs are falling on their laps." Chief Bradford had little sympathy for local grievances, and argued that without the navy, Vieques wouldn't survive. "They think that if the navy pulled out that they would build a Conquistador or Palmas de Mar type of complex," she said, referring to two large Puerto Rican resorts:

There isn't any developer in his right mind who would develop that place. First of all, there is the problem of transportation. They'd need their own fleet of airplanes to get to the place. Furthermore, there isn't anyone with the knowledge or wherewithal there to do that. We help as best we can, but they're very poor, and the island is undeveloped. They don't have the where- withal to develop it. The navy helps as best we can. The problem is basically a few malcontents who believe they will have paradise if the navy leaves. They may for a while, but it's another thing to see that to fruition.

Although Chief Bradford seemed to suggest here that protest emanated from a handful of extremists, she went on to extend blame for tensions to the entire civilian population. Bradford argued that conflict between residents and the navy stemmed from residents' misplaced sense of entitlement. "The mili- tary can't support the locals in the manner to which they'd like to become accustomed to. We do a lot of good deeds," she noted, "but I became very dis- appointed when I got to understand the local mentality. Everyone wants some- thing for nothing. They're not used to doing things on a big scale. Everyone's out for themselves on a local and national [Puerto Rican] level." As a case in point, Chief Bradford noted that the mayor in Ceiba had recently approached several different navy offices on Roosevelt Roads, requesting that the navy sponsor a Christmas party for underprivileged children. "Rather than going to Walmart they come to the military," she stressed. When I asked her if it wasn't the case that in the past the navy had sponsored Christmas parties in the community, she admitted that it had. The government has public relations funds from which the navy purchases toys, she noted, but there was less money every year.

"Vieques is a sensitive issue," she told me bluntly, abandoning any attempt at diplomacy: "They want something for nothing. If the navy left, it would take anything of value. They're not going to just leave it behind. The locals have been doing things their own way for hundreds of years—ever since Colum- bus arrived, as a matter of fact. There has been very little progress. They don't understand what the navy is about. It's like a third world country. They can't understand—it's like expounding on Newton's theory to an eighteen-month-old baby." Bradford argued that the navy contributed an "awful lot" to Vieques, but was constrained by budgetary limitations from extensive involvement. "It's not like we are the bad guys," she explained: "We do as much as we can, given the facilities. We can't build schools, we don't have the material. It's not like there's a four-hundred-foot fence. They have the run of the place. They have access to all of the facilities. To make it a resort would take a lot of money, and then it would be the developer who got the island, not the locals."

Although Bradford repeatedly emphasized residents' false sense of entitlement, her remarks seemed to acknowledge the tension that emanated from local desires to see Vieques's land and economy developed. Such tensions should have been mitigated by the 1983 accord, which promised to bring jobs to Vieques. In the absence of any improvement in local economic conditions, however, the troubled relationship between the navy and Viequenses remained unchanged.

Chief Bradford's distrust of the local population informed the perspective of Lieutenant Commander Tom McDonald, a government liaison officer and self-described "leg-man" to the admiral who had been enlisted to help carry the sagging mantle of the 1983 accord. After the failure of the defense industry to bolster Vieques's ailing economy, the navy was again faced with the incompatibility of its strategic interests and the development of a strong local economy. In the early nineties, the military focused its efforts on encouraging a smattering of small-scale projects in Vieques. Whether these efforts were sincere is not clear. Lieutenant McDonald admitted that his job was not well defined and that his predecessors' work did little to orient him to his responsibilities. The first liaison officer had been a lawyer who spent a lot of time drafting the Fortín Accord. The subsequent officer, McDonald said, spent a lot of time at cocktail parties and reading the newspaper. McDonald decided to devote himself to Vieques's development and claimed to allocate 80–85 percent of his time to Vieques. There were obvious problems, however. This career navy officer was stationed in San Juan, with no background in economics or development, with no command of Spanish, with no familiarity with Vieques, and yet was held single-handedly responsible for the economic resurrection of the island.

McDonald discovered that he had little support from the mayor's office, which by the early nineties was tired of working with the navy. He built a web of acquaintances on Vieques among the North American resident population, who were more supportive of the navy and could speak to him in English. He was quickly frustrated by a tangled maze of political alliances, government regulations, and fundamental obstacles such as transportation. He was enthusiastic about a number of small-scale projects. He embraced a proposal to build a slaughterhouse in Vieques, because it would provide jobs hosing down cattle stalls. He was enthusiastic about a condiment company owned by two North American entrepreneurs and was determined to use his position to influence the commissary at Roosevelt Roads to stock its shelves with Vieques hot pepper sauce. But he was discouraged that local Viequenses did not share his enthusiasm for the condiment company. "Do you know that Ellen Smith from the condiment company has to buy peppers from Puerto Rico because no one was willing to raise them here?" he exclaimed with indignation. "She looked all over, was willing to supply the seeds, but couldn't get anyone who was willing to grow them!" There is very little privately owned land or capital to invest in Vieques. Furthermore, the North Americans are not well linked to the local Spanish-speaking population. McDonald was convinced, though, that Ellen Smith could not find anyone to grow peppers for her because Viequenses lack a work ethic. "When you get down to it, they're lazy," he concluded. "They don't want to work. If there were industrious people here we could do so much."

With his efforts to develop the local economy floundering, McDonald turned to the local newspaper in an effort to build public goodwill. McDonald began running a series of articles in the *Vieques Times* aimed at communicating the navy's latest plans for the economic development of Vieques, thus demonstrating the navy's continued commitment to the 1983 accord. McDonald had a strong belief that locals needed to be educated about the public good the navy contributed to Vieques. He highlighted the leading role the navy played in preserving the natural environment, and argued that Viequenses should put aside concern for the past and focus on the future. McDonald's articles, rather than building the goodwill he imagined, instead stirred significant controversy and a stream of angry letters and editorials in the newspaper. One resident wrote:

> The admiral [*sic*] claims that the navy has maintained Vieques' beauty. Well, how would he know? He just got here today! I am a retired senior citizen who remembers before World War II, digging for turtle eggs in the sand and eating turtle soup. The turtles were never endangered, there were plenty for us. Admiral, what tore down Vieques and endangered our wildlife were the naval bombardments, military land maneuvers, and the stationing on this tiny island of 10,000 to 15,000 men in Camp García during World War II and the Korean War. The Vieques whose beauty the admiral praises and claims credit for is nothing to what it was before the navy got here, and can be again if the navy leaves.[5]

McDonald failed to perceive that though North Americans celebrated the navy's self-declared role as environmental champion of Vieques, there was no more ideologically inflammatory notion he could present to Viequenses. In general, the navy's efforts toward environmentalism were the most provocative and ill conceived of its poorly executed public relations campaign in Vieques. The navy's fundamental understanding of environmentalism rested on the notion of excluding the population from the majority of island land and blaming Viequenses for destruction. This perspective was articulated by Fred López, a conservationist employed by the navy. López remarked that he had recently read an article in which local fishermen complained that the navy maneuvers were impeding their access to the island's best fishing grounds. "This is a contradiction," López argued. "The reason why the waters are abundant is that the navy's conservation programs have made them that way." Beyond monitoring and moving turtle eggs off of beaches used for amphibious landings, however, the navy played no active role in preserving the coastal ecology. López believed that the navy protected the island's fishing grounds by restricting access to these waters during military maneuvers. This was the kind of statement that polarized the navy from the community at large. Despite the population's overwhelming political moderation, the navy's insensitive public relations took its toll on its relationship with the community.

The tension created by the navy's failure to bring jobs to Vieques was only heightened by the military's environmental campaign that blamed locals for the destruction of the ecology. In response to assertions that the navy worked to protect endangered species, it was common to hear Viequenses assert that they themselves were the primary victims of the navy's presence on the island. Vieques's PNP mayor Manuela Santiago, who for years struggled to work with the navy and strike a neutral posture on the military presence, eventually abandoned her efforts at neutrality and spoke out against the navy. Like her predecessor Radamés Tirado, she became convinced that the navy threatened the existence of Viequenses themselves: "Forty-four years of bombarding including napalm in Vieques has been painful to the environment of the island. The navy nevertheless has been careful not to destroy the turtles and pelicans because they are protected species but now it is time to protect the people of Vieques which to us are at least as important as turtles and pelicans" (U.S. House 1994: 85).

Santiago's comments speak to a sense of victimhood that was widely asserted on the island. Beneath expressions of powerlessness and defeat, however, there was evidence of a fierce resilience and determination to exist as a people that was also the legacy of the continued conflict with the military.

The Military Presence and Local Identity

On a local level, Viequenses have not framed their conflict in terms of a national struggle, nor have residents been motivated primarily by ideological concerns. Grievances always have been fundamentally material. Nonetheless, the military presence has had a profound affect on people's identity and sense of connection to Vieques. Despite the difficulties of living on an island bombing range with few opportunities to work and no clear sense of the future, residents are surprisingly determined to stay. One of the continued effects of the military presence has been to create a heightened sense of peoplehood and a commitment to remain on Vieques despite the hardships of daily life.

A major preoccupation in Vieques continued to be the size of the island's population, even though it increased between 1980 and 1990 from 7,662 to 8,602. Antimilitary activists pointed to the island's perceived population drop and the loss of the island's youth as among their primary reasons for opposing the navy presence. As Chapter Two showed, major discussion about Vieques's population decline first emerged in the 1960s, fomented by military efforts to expropriate land on Vieques's south coast. By the nineties, however, residents expressed growing concern about the changing character of the island, in particular the process of gentrification whereby North Americans, Europeans, and Puerto Ricans from the main island have come to Vieques to build vacation homes (Rivera Torres and Torres 1996). Viequenses expressed fear not only at being evicted by the navy but at the loss of local culture and ways of life, extinguished by the growing presence of North Americans. One individual concluded, "Vieques has the threat of the base, and the threat of the American civilians."

Mario Moreno, the forty-eight-year-old schoolteacher activist, evoked images of genocide to describe the process of gentrification on the island: "The Americans who come here are very distinct. Economically, they're well off. The first thing they do when they buy a place in Vieques is construct a wall. They absorb the beaches; they don't want us to enter. In the Caribbean, there are not many people who can afford to buy. It bothers the natives. It's like when the Spanish came and killed the Indians. In the same manner, they are killing us, little by little."

Perceptions of the North Americans, like perceptions of the population drop, are shaped by relations with the military. The North Americans have acted as the major source of organized support for the navy and base of opposition to the antinavy movement. The North Americans' links to the military arouse suspicion and fuel conspiracy theories about the nature of the community's presence and intentions on the island.

Viequenses' feeling of being surrounded by hostile forces is coupled by a sense of betrayal by the Commonwealth government. One of the themes that frequently surfaces in dialogue about the navy in Vieques is the omnipotence of the military and the collusion between the navy and the Puerto Rican government. Many residents believed that the navy paid Puerto Rico for the bombs it dropped on Vieques. "They get the money and we get the bombs," one fisherman remarked in disgust. "The government's big chiefs have sold us out."

The sense of victimization, of betrayal and isolation, of being under siege, has spawned an explicitly and aggressively local sense of identity. Nancy Morris (1995) has described the strong feelings of regional identity expressed by Puerto Ricans throughout the Commonwealth. The particular sense of regional identity that people in Vieques express is all the more extreme and vehement in light of the onslaught the community has faced—by the navy that bombs and usurps the island and by the North Americans who seek to take whatever is left over. This conflict has heightened the significance of the land in people's sense of self-identification. These factors create a peculiar, essentialist form of identity that is perhaps best seen by considering the controversy over Vieques's hospital.

The Death of Birth

One afternoon I interviewed twenty-six-year-old José Moreno, a young antinavy activist. When I asked him to describe what he felt the most pressing issues were facing Vieques, I expected that he would talk about the military's control over the island. Instead, he remarked: "What worries me the most about Vieques is that—before anything else—there are no more Viequenses anymore. In Vieques you don't find Viequenses anymore. People aren't born in Vieques. The other is—those who were born here have had to leave. In Vieques there is no place to work. There is no place to study. You have to leave. This is one of the things that worries me the most, that really bothers me. That people have to leave from Vieques. They have to leave out of necessity, out of obligation. Not because they want to leave, you understand." When I asked José to clarify what he meant when he said that there were no more Viequenses on the island, he responded: "You are from the town where you are born. If you are born in Vieques, you are Viequense. If you are born in Fajardo and raised in Vieques, you are Fajardeño. People aren't born in Vieques anymore. This hurts, this is really sad. You have to leave your land out of obligation, because it is inevitable. This is the saddest of all."

José's comments piqued my interest. He was expressing a form of regional primordialism, in which birthplace alone conferred identity. José's conception of identity seemed oddly reductionist and exclusionary, an assertion that denied the history of migration and diversity that has long characterized the island's people. José's ideas, however, were commonly expressed in Vieques. The concern about the lack of babies born on the island was one of the pressing social concerns people consistently raised. This problem is linked to current controversies over the state of the local hospital, but people's understanding of the problem is uniquely colored by their relationship to the navy. The significance residents assign to birthplace is inseparable from struggles over the land and the struggle to stay on the island in the face of the navy's efforts to evict them.

In the mid-1980s the Vieques hospital was regionalized, part of a broader process of the privatization of Puerto Rico's health services. Such processes have been devastating to poor communities like Vieques, whose cash-strapped municipalities are now in charge of hospitals they lack the funds to run. In Vieques, privatization has turned the local hospital into little more than a glorified first-aid station. Residents must travel to Fajardo on the main island for lab work, X rays, and any kind of "specialty" care. Although the Vieques hospital has an emergency room, the most it can do is stabilize patients before transferring them to the main island for care. Among the services it no longer provides are prenatal care and childbirth facilities, forcing pregnant women to travel to the main island for check-ups and to deliver their babies. This poses particular risks and hardships for women and their babies, but few people express concern for any dangers involved in traveling. Instead, wide concern is expressed over the simple fact that babies are no longer born on the island. To understand the significance of this, consider the case of Margarita Sánchez.

Margarita Sánchez is a thirty-five-year-old elementary school teacher. She is originally from the Dominican Republic, but married a Viequense and settled on the island. She was one of the casualties of the hospital crisis. Margarita lost her first child in her seventh month of pregnancy. She had been traveling from Vieques to Fajardo via a twenty-two-mile ferry ride on rough seas to receive treatment for intermittent bleeding throughout her pregnancy. She was in Vieques one day in her seventh month when she started hemorrhaging. The hospital in Vieques was unable to manage her case, and by the time she was transferred to Fajardo the baby had died.

Margarita eventually did give birth to a full-term baby, María, who is now six years old. When she was pregnant with María, Margarita's doctor ordered her to bed in her fourth month. Still, she had to travel to Fajardo for check-ups, which, she noted, was extremely dangerous. She traveled this time by airplane, a considerable expense for her. But ultimately, unaware she was in labor, she took the ferry to the hospital. Thank goodness, she reflected, she didn't run into problems on the boat.

What was most surprising to me about Margarita's tale was the focus of her sadness and regret. She expressed little anger at the circumstances surrounding her first baby's death, or frustration at the risk or expense she assumed traveling to Fajardo for care during her second pregnancy. Instead her sadness was focused on another issue: the place of María's birth. "María was born in Fajardo," she told me wistfully. "She's from Fajardo, not Vieques. Little by little, soon there will be no one from Vieques." I took note of Margarita's experience and perceptions, finding them unusual. But her story took on new meaning for me when I spoke to Eduardo Negrón.

Don Eduardo is a seventy-eight-year-old retired fisherman who lives on his wife's social security check. Don Eduardo's wife, Elena, suffers from debilitating arthritis and has to travel to Fajardo for medical care. She is usually accompanied by a son, which leaves don Eduardo free to spend most of his days reading newspapers on his doorstep. He is very up to date on politics and current events. One day I was discussing with don Eduardo the mayor's proposal to turn Vieques into a free port. This economic strategy, don Eduardo felt, was better than nothing, and could be initiated regardless of whether the navy pulled out of Vieques. He paused and added: "One belief is that the navy could help us by giving us a decent hospital here in Vieques, so that we do not have to go to Fajardo. So that women should not have to travel there to give birth. Children are not from Vieques, they are from Fajardo. Clearly." I was interested in the fact that don Eduardo brought up the hospital and implied that the navy had a responsibility for the state of health care on the island. I thought it curious, furthermore, that the focus of his concern was women traveling to Puerto Rico to give birth, rather than the plight of his own wife, who had to endure exhausting travel while she suffered with a chronic illness. It was apparent that don Eduardo was concerned more with the fact that children were being born off island than with any personal risks the mothers might assume traveling in labor. This same perspective was echoed by Rosa Moreno, a sixty-year-old former school secretary, put out of work by crippling osteoporosis.

Doña Rosa is a widow who lives alone in a section of town one mile from the ferry (her three adult children live in the United States). The process of commuting to Fajardo is exhausting. To make a 10:00 A.M. doctor's appointment, doña Rosa rises at 5:00. On a good morning, she can reach the ferry on foot in an hour, walking slowly with a cane. (There is no system of municipal transportation in Vieques.) The ferry departs at 7:00 and arrives in Fajardo between 8:30 and 9:00. From there, doña Rosa takes a public taxi to the hospital to keep her appointment. Her illness requires her to make frequent visits to the hospital for check-ups, and often she stays with a sister in Fajardo overnight, to lessen the impact of the grueling trip.

Given these circumstances, I was not surprised that doña Rosa pointed to the hospital as Vieques's single most pressing social problem. She was quite passionate in arguing that the situation was a disgrace. Doña Rosa's concerns, though, centered not on her own struggles for adequate health care, but, as don Eduardo had, on the hospital's lack of a maternity ward. Like don Eduardo, her concern was not for the health of the mothers but for the fact that babies were being born off-island. Doña Rosa explained: "The fact is we had no problems until the navy came. We were fine. But when I see now that no babies are born here, when I see the high unemployment, I believe there is some subtle hand at work. It's like there is a plan—it's like some hidden hand is orchestrating this. . . . We want a hospital; we've been asking for one. We used to have a hospital with everything, a dentist, specialists. Now we have nothing and it's getting worse." Doña Rosa's conviction is that Vieques's lack of a maternity ward is part of a plot by the navy to eliminate Viequenses. What the navy had not accomplished by expropriating land, doña Rosa maintained, it would achieve by gradually squeezing the lifeblood out of Vieques. One expression of this was the navy's squelching of the economy. The other, more sinister effort was the shutdown of the maternity ward.

There is no evidence that the navy had any role in the closing of Vieques's maternity ward. Although the navy has occasionally offered medical clinics for residents, and from time to time provides its assistance in medical evacuations of the critically ill, the military has had little involvement in issues of health care on the island.

The concern for the lack of babies born on Vieques Island is an expression of the polarized relationship between the navy and the civilian population. The maternity ward becomes the locus of anxieties about loss and continuity, powerlessness and victimization. From residents' comments one might conclude, however, that the community of Vieques is disintegrating, that its people have scattered, and that there is little left but a skeleton crew of old timers tenuously clinging to survival. The controversy surrounding the maternity ward points instead to an important legacy of the military occupation of Vieques: the strengthening of links to the island, the creation of a resilient, stubborn identity.

Here in Vieques, we find an expression of local identity that is not defined by genes or blood composition. It is not defined by common kinship or a "soul." It is not defined by a set of cultural practices or participation in the political sphere. Instead, identity is narrowly defined by birthplace, by territory. In Puerto Rico as a whole the importance of birthplace is frequently asserted, framed by a larger debate on the role and importance of the diaspora of nearly three million U.S.-based Puerto Ricans.[6] But in Vieques, the significance of birthplace takes on particular meanings. The experience and continued threat of expropriation color most perceptions of the navy and understandings of social change on the island. In the face of massive migration, of efforts to usurp and buy up real estate, Viequenses define themselves in relation to the land.

The emphasis on a primordial connection to the island speaks to an obstinate resilience of the people in the face of efforts to remove them. It is a definition that anchors people to the island. In Vieques, one is hard pressed to find an adult who has lived his or her entire life on the island. Defining identity by birthplace is a way of expressing a right to return, a birthright to the island. In the same way that Viequense maintain plots of land during the years they work in New York City or St. Croix to preserve a right to return to the island, they have created an identity that is rooted in the land.

Territorially based definitions of identity are often read as exclusionary, as constructions of identity that fail to incorporate the broader diaspora. In Vieques, cultural identity, with its emphasis on a primordial link to the land, is less exclusionary than it is the product of exclusion. The heightened importance of land in popular notions of identity emerges from a visceral struggle over the right to exist on the island. Territorially based definitions of cultural identity serve to anchor a population that is perceived to be dispersing, vanishing. The defining emphasis placed on birthright suggests that Viequenses, wherever they go, wherever they live, are eternally Viequense. The perceived threat to this link, as expressed in the shutdown of Vieques's maternity ward, sparks an intense, emotional response.

This cultural context is crucial to understanding the persistence of protest on the island. As Crusade activists demonstrated, and the next chapter will consider, activists' ability to harness the intensity of local identity politics has been a critical element in propelling organized protest. Viequense cultural identity has acted as the lifeblood of the island's resistance to the navy. The Monte Carmelo incident, however, suggests that discontent, without a structure or clearly defined politics, dissolves into vigilantism and cynicism.

Five

Organizing for Change

In late October 1993 a navy jet, in a botched training exercise, dropped five five-hundred-pound bombs six miles off target, on the buffer zone between military and civilian territory. The explosions rocked homes in the neighborhood of Santa María, on the eastern limits of Vieques's civilian sector. Residents, well accustomed to the routine sound of bombing, besieged the mayor with panicked telephone calls, describing a "new kind of bomb" or perhaps a crashed bomber in their neighborhood. The navy did not answer phone calls from the mayor's office until the next day, when the military officials called to apologize for "excessive noise" emanating from navy property.[1] Members of a newly formed group seeking the closure of the base were outraged and organized a picket the following Sunday.

One week later, on a brilliant Sunday morning, thirty protestors picketed in front of the gates of Camp García to denounce the incident. They carried colorful homemade placards and chanted antimilitary slogans in front of a handful of civilian security guards. Although the group succeeded in publicizing the demonstration in the Puerto Rican press, the local reaction to the picket was lukewarm. Beyond several passing cars, it seemed few people in Vieques were aware of the protest. One veteran antinavy activist was upbeat after the demonstration, however, noting that it was the first picket in Vieques since a small group of demonstrators had protested the navy's use of napalm on the target range the previous year. But a more cynical observer dismissed the picket as nothing but the same old group of hacks, beating the same old drums, chanting, "*Que se vaya la marina.*" "What are they going to accomplish?" he asked.

Less than six years after this small picket passed seemingly unnoticed in Vieques, another training mishap triggered a groundswell of outrage, protest, and popular mobilization unprecedented in Puerto Rican history. The death of a civilian security guard in Vieques in 1999 reignited the decades-long movement against the military presence. What factors brought about such a dramatic change? Why did the first training mishap pass with so little public reaction, while the second triggered such outrage and popular mobilization?

Four elements were crucial to the resurgence of organized protest in Vieques in 1999. First, the end of the cold war had opened new space for Viequenses to articulate their grievances. The restructuring of the U.S. military, including the widespread closure of key military installations, fundamentally changed the political climate surrounding Vieques. At the same time, the U.S. military's new focus on the "war on drugs" presented particular challenges to activists in Vieques who sought to evict the navy.

Second, activists founded an organization, the Committee to Rescue and Develop Vieques, that was consciously broad based and inclusive. The Committee's ability to accommodate diversity and forge alliances was crucial in creating a foundation for the current mobilization. Third, the Committee was able to adopt a framework for political mobilization that tapped the intensity of local identity politics and moved discussion outside the realm of debates over Puerto Rican sovereignty.

Finally, the navy's own unwillingness to compromise in the face of rising social discontent was a key factor in the development of protest. The navy's determination to erect a radar installation in Vieques and Lajas, Puerto Rico, not only stimulated outrage but gave its opponents focus and coherence that coalesced in 1999.

The Founding of the Committee to Rescue and Develop Vieques: In Search of a Moderate Course

For five decades Vieques languished as a cold war hostage. The island suffered direct material harm as a consequence of U.S. military expansion and rivalry with the Soviets. To protest these conditions, however, was deemed subversive and anti-American. The collapse of the Soviet Union in 1991 shifted U.S. military priorities and commitments. The United States cut back operations at 275 overseas sites, including 14 major bases, and pulled thousands of troops out of Germany, the United Kingdom, South Korea, and Latin America (Goodno 1997). The closure of long-contested bases in the Philippines and Hawaii signaled a changing political climate and a new opening for Vieques residents to challenge the navy. In light of this wave of closures, activists formed a new group with the specific purpose of including Vieques in discussions of which bases to shut down. They decided to take their case directly to the federal government, petitioning the Federal Base Realignment and Closure Committee to add Vieques's name to the list of facilities to be closed.

In the spring of 1993 the Committee to Rescue and Develop Vieques (Comité pro Rescate y Desarrollo de Vieques) launched a door-to-door campaign in Vieques, collecting signatures on a letter to Secretary of Defense Les Aspin to close the military facilities on Vieques. The Committee represented the efforts of a handful of veteran antinavy activists to rebuild the organized struggle for the recovery of Vieques's land from the military and shape the planning process for the island's socioeconomic development.

The Committee's name alluded to the defunct Crusade to Rescue Vieques, and the new group sought both to link itself to this organization and to distinguish itself from past political formations. While a number of the same key activists from the seventies came together in this new effort, they aimed to broaden their membership. One of the most controversial and divisive charges leveled against the Crusade had been that it was a communist-led, anti-American agitation. Although the core of the new Committee was *independentista* and politically leftist, these activists worked hard to build bridges to more moderate, centrist constituencies. At their founding meeting, they drew in a young factory worker with no prior history of political involvement. They also attracted a policeman's son who aspired to the police academy himself, and a return migrant who had married a marine. Significantly, founding members of the Committee enlisted a retired doctor, Rafael Rivera Castaño, a prominent epidemiologist and public health official and the son of Vieques's former mayor Antonio Rivera Rodríguez. They also drew in a Catholic deacon from one of the island's remaining *colono* families. The Committee thus successfully joined disparate elements of Vieques's working-class and social establishment. From the outset, the group consciously sought to act as a broad-based coalition movement, and the *independentista* founders shared power and authority with more centrist members.

One of the major ways the Committee attempted to distinguish itself from the Crusade was by organizing and planning for the future. Given the aftermath of the land rescue, one of the Committee's main objectives was to develop a coherent vision of Vieques's future, one in which the majority of island people would enjoy the fruits of development, rather than wealthy, off-island developers or politically suspect local speculators. Mario Martínez, a founding member of the Committee, explained: "More than anything you have to work with concrete issues. We can't be very idealistic. And we have to establish alternatives. We [in the Crusade] didn't establish alternatives. We have to establish alternatives to what we want if the navy leaves. What are we going to do with this land? Why do we want the navy to go? We want them out just to get rid of them, or because we plan to develop the economy. This is important."

The group solicited the opinions of a variety of urban planners and development specialists from Puerto Rico and the United States who volunteered to chart a thoughtful and coherent plan for the island's social and economic development. The Committee also expended significant energy in lobbying. Although a militant *independentista*, Martínez felt that political circumstances demanded a new approach to the struggle to evict the military. He described the pragmatism that now shaped the Committee's tactics in its use of legislative channels, such as petitioning the local municipal assembly, and its willingness to compromise.

> This historic moment is different from 1978 . . . we are more pragmatic—we are slower. In part because of reality. The navy has control of the island of Vieques. The possibility that the navy might leave entirely is difficult. Therefore we founded another group, not necessarily committed to the total departure of the navy from Vieques. We might consider the possibility of recovering pieces of land. In 1978 we were committed to the rapid departure of the navy, and the departure had to be total. We understand that the recuperation of part of Vieques is a triumph. And that it won't impede us from struggling for more. In this sense we distance ourselves. Another element is the fact that there's a base closure commission. This gives us an opportunity. This doesn't mean that we reject the previous style of struggle. The pickets are present. The direct confrontation we can't use. At the moment we don't confront the maneuvers, the boats, etc. But it's the reality that has changed our vision.

Carlos Quintero, another longtime activist, expressed some ambivalence, however, about the movement's shift to the center:

> It is not a struggle as before. Conversation, dialogue, presenting evidence [before Congress] that they themselves have gathered! Congress did a lot of studies about Vieques, the environmental impact on Vieques. And they recommended to stop this, to cease the assault against the ecology, against the marine life, the flora and fauna. Nonetheless, they spent the money on these studies, they presented recommendations, nonetheless [the navy] stayed. We have to have faith to continue the struggle. This type of struggle that we are doing now of diplomacy, to bring the case of Vieques to the entire world. Because I don't think we are going back to the moments of aggression.

I don't think we are going back to the type of struggle that was made necessary by those times. Now we are in diplomacy. Whether we will succeed, I
don't know.

One of the major lessons the Committee absorbed from the Crusade was
the social cost of divisiveness in a prolonged conflict. In the aftermath of the
Crusade, the fishermen's co-op dissolved into bitter factions and contentious
lawsuits over co-op property. Activists discovered that friends and neighbors
had acted as police informants during the Crusade. Individuals who risked their
reputations and jobs to resist the military and, as they saw it, save their island
were charged by fellow Viequenses with being controlled and manipulated by
outside agitators with a communist, anti-American agenda.

The Committee's concern for unity, eschewing partisan affiliation, responded to this divisiveness. Its politics echoed older attempts by Viequenses
to organize to evict the navy. Recall the group Viequenses United, which in
the months prior to the Fishermen's War tried unsuccessfully to bring together
a unified, nonpartisan group to resist the military. Ultimately its efforts to avoid
partisan affiliation revealed how powerful such associations were, and the
group collapsed with charges that various members were *independentistas*. It
was only the highly charged, confrontational, and emotionally resonant campaign of the fishermen that propelled a movement, giving substance and di-
rection to the battle against the navy without dissolving into political infighting.

In its commitment to political moderation and the nonpartisan unity of all
sectors, the Committee to Recover and Develop Vieques seemed to be the resurrection of Viequenses United. There existed tension within the Committee
over strategy and ideology. Zoraída López was one of the new activists to join.
She was born in New York City, but had married and settled in Vieques twenty-
five years earlier to raise her family. She was not involved in the Crusade. Now
in her fifties, she was attracted to the Committee in part because of her own
growing political consciousness and in part because she viewed the group as
politically centrist. López noted that the Committee had been criticized recently
on the local television station as being headed nowhere. The critic felt that
rather than lobbying, the Committee should organize thousands of Viequenses
to come forward to block the next scheduled military maneuvers, scaling fences
if necessary. López was irritated by this advice:

Who the hell are you going to get to do that? The last three times there have
been demonstrations, there have been no more than thirty people. At least
the cards got people to put their names on something. People aren't willing
to climb fences. At least putting their name on something was a positive step.
Most citizens accept this way of going about the navy situation. The only thing

that is really a unifying force is a desire for people to see Vieques whole. Many people won't come out and say, "*Que se vaya la marina.*" They are afraid to be labeled communist, *independentista*.

Yet Julia Ramos, a veteran activist originally from Puerto Rico, who came to Vieques after working with Puerto Rico–based solidarity movements, expressed dissatisfaction over the Committee's politics and momentum. Despite efforts to incorporate people with different political backgrounds, *independentistas* like Ramos formed a majority of the group, and Ramos struggled to suppress her personal feelings and strive for consensus:

> [All we do is talk.] We don't have an ideology. [Laughs.] No. I think it's a committee without ideology. Because we are so different. Unfortunately, unfortunately, unfortunately for *me*! [Laughs.] Everyone has a different position. Some are conservative, others, less. Some more revolutionary. I don't know if we'll be successful. For me, the Committee is really conservative. I'm trying to maintain myself on the line of dialogue, without controversy and without confrontation. This is the ideology you will find. Trying not to appear to have a partisan political position. The *populares* try not to criticize Manuela [the PNP mayor]. The *independentistas* try not to criticize the other leaders. Everyone is trying to keep their own political opinions and political projects to themselves.
>
> It's difficult. Because my political experience from years before is that the committee in one form or another has a political opinion. That's not what we are trying to do here. Before this, I was involved in ten different groups. But all were *independentista*. All picketed, wanted to get rid of the navy, etc. . . . Now nobody will say they are *independentista*. You understand? We just talk.
>
> When we started to talk about a picket, people were getting uncomfortable. We can't talk about this, because it makes people uncomfortable. We don't accept violent expressions. Only expressions of fraternity. At times it's okay, at other times it's a little difficult. But it works, because we've been together for a year. It hasn't broken up.

Despite reservations, Ramos acknowledged a major strength of the Committee: the fact that it had held together despite marked internal differences. Furthermore, the group succeeded in mobilizing both the local municipal government and the Puerto Rican resident commissioner in Washington, D.C., to take a stand on Vieques. Although the Committee did not have a strong base or identification in the community, at the same time it had no real opponents or vocal critics. Most Viequenses seemed comfortable with lobbying and signature collecting, and the selection of Dr. Rivera as the group's spokesperson communicated that the Committee was respectable and moderate.

In Search of a Framework for Political Action

While antinavy activists founded an organization, their efforts did not immediately translate into a movement. Initially the Committee faced an uphill struggle. After its letter campaign, one of the group's first public actions was a picket to protest the navy's botched bombing exercise of October 1993. The reluctance of some group members to engage in what they saw as an act of open confrontation foreshadowed the response of the community at large. Several of the more radical Committee members drove through town in a car rigged with a loudspeaker, denouncing this "brutal assault" and announcing that the Committee would picket in response to the bombing. Few townspeople showed up to participate or even watch the spectacle. In contrast, a beach barbecue sponsored by the PNP later that day attracted hundreds.

The irony was that this picket might actually be described as a nonconfrontational confrontation. Demonstrating in front of Camp García was a tactic used during the seventies, and the picket was clearly intended to draw on this legacy. Marching in front of the gates to the camp, an emblem of the navy presence, the protestors symbolically took civilian grievances directly before the military. In reality, however, it was one or two Viequenses security guards who stood witness to the event, while the operational and command center of the small navy presence was located on the other side of the island. Meanwhile, the military officials responsible for the mishap in all likelihood were located not on Vieques but rather in Puerto Rico at Roosevelt Roads. The gates of Camp García lie away from town and beyond the major residential areas. Sunday afternoon is a sleepy time on the island, and few cars travel past the base.

The picket revealed the ambivalence of the Committee over engaging in acts of open defiance. Significantly, the group chose Dr. Rivera as its spokesperson, rather than one of the more charismatic veteran *independentista* activists. Dr. Rivera delivered a prepared statement denouncing the bombing mishap and calling for an end to the bombing and the withdrawal of the military. He noted that during that week the mayor had signed a card as part of the Committee's new postcard campaign to President Clinton calling for closure of the base, and the mayor had asked Resident Commissioner Romero to deliver the 3,750 signed postcards from Viequenses to the president. Essentially, the doctor was using the picket as an avenue to broadcast the Committee's more moderate measures: lobbying and collecting signatures. His calm, measured reading of the statement set the tone of the demonstration.

Although the picket did not appear to stir the passions of most Viequenses, it was not a failure. The protest was covered in the Puerto Rican press, drawing public attention to the continued conflict between residents of Vieques and the navy and to the navy's bungled training exercise. The picket also demonstrated the Committee's willingness to work through internal differences to forge a consensus.

Still, the picket raised questions about how the Committee could effectively mobilize Viequenses to remove the navy. Many people had been horrified, even angered, by the navy's bombing mishap. But to mobilize these individuals to take action was a challenge. "Viequenses don't know how to distinguish—or they don't want to distinguish—that one thing is not the other," noted Aurora Vélez, a sixty-three-year-old veteran activist. "That if you're against the navy you're not necessarily against the American government. You're against the navy because of what it is doing, not because you are against the American government." In this political context, where expressions of opposition were seen as subversive, it was crucial that the Committee find an effective framework to channel popular discontent.

Fishermen

The Committee initially looked to fishermen to revive Vieques's movement to regain its land. Iván Meléndez, the son of Santiago Meléndez, a fisherman leader, had recently founded the Vieques Fishermen's Rights Group (Grupo pro Derechos de los Pescadores Viequenses). The Committee sought to build an alliance with this organization.

As Chapter Three argued, the emergence of fishermen as protest leaders in the late seventies was the result of a confluence of specific events at a particular moment in time. While the fishermen remained folk heroes, changed circumstances precluded resurrecting them as protagonists in the nineties. Turning to the fishermen to lead the struggle would have placed faith in an association that had dissolved into fractious infighting and still palpable hostility. Furthermore, one of the earlier problems in placing fishermen at the leadership of Vieques's movement was the tension this created between locally based grievances and the broader, colonial dimensions of Vieques's case. Fishermen had earned grassroots support in Vieques because they focused protest on the specific acts of material harm the navy was committing. But the local emphasis created friction with solidarity groups who wanted both to support and to expand the significance of Vieques's struggle to address Puerto Rico's colonial status.

The current incarnation of the Fishermen's Association was even more circumscribed in its focus. Although Meléndez's new group claimed to struggle for fishermen's rights, in practice the group devoted most of its time to acquiring compensation for lost traps. This effort was not as evocative and inspiring as struggling for a right to fish in the island's waters, and it impeded any expansion of the group's influence. Though there were several clashes between navy boats and fishermen, the fishermen did not reemerge as protagonists.[2]

The Cultural Realm

The fishermen were successful in the seventies in part because they framed grievances in not only economic but cultural terms. In Puerto Rico, writers have noted the importance of the cultural arena for defining and reinforcing identity and political consciousness (Dávila 1997; Quintero Rivera 1991). Despite Puerto Ricans' support for political and economic association with the United States, they express strong feelings of cultural nationalism (Duany 2000; Morris 1995). The fishermen's mobilization suggests some of the ways in which cultural nationalist sentiment can be directed into political action.

Activists in Vieques were conscious of the potency of the cultural realm. A number of the same veteran activists who belonged to the Committee worked to gain leadership positions in the Vieques Cultural Center, a local organization run under the auspices of the Commonwealth's Institute for Puerto Rican Culture.[3] They were quite savvy about using the institutional structure and financing of the center to promote a nationalist agenda. Activists' ability to tap into Viequenses' fierce sense of local identity suggested a possible framework for organizing against the military presence.

A cultural event organized by the Vieques Cultural Center in 1994 illustrates the significance of the cultural realm. To commemorate the 150th anniversary of the founding of Vieques municipality, the Cultural Center planned an excursion to the ruins of the Playa Grande and Resolución sugar *centrales* on military base land. Although the excursion received the sponsorship of the municipality and required the consent and cooperation of the navy, initiative for the outing came from the Cultural Center and the several activists who dominated it. The community response to the excursion provides a counterpoint to the picket organized by the Committee several months earlier. The event suggested that Viequenses were potentially mobilized and radicalized, depending upon the packaging and perception of the event.

The Excursion to the Ruins of the Sugar Centrales

On a Saturday morning in January 1994, hundreds of Viequenses filled the town plaza to participate in a tour of the ruined sugar *centrales*, located behind navy fences on military-controlled land. The turnout overwhelmed the planners, who had secured only two school buses for participants. Approximately three hundred people had gathered that morning. Emotions ran high.

The crowd included older Viequenses who had worked in the mills and were evicted by the navy in the 1940s. Others had been born on sugar land and had never been allowed to return to the place of their birth. Families arrived carrying coolers. While many people wore Vieques T-shirts and a handful carried Puerto Rican flags, this was not a hard-core *independentista* crowd. Some sported camouflage and one person wore an Operation Desert Storm T-shirt. There were a few North Americans, but on the whole, Navy League members were conspicuously absent. The main organizer for the event, Samuel Rivera, a high-profile antinavy activist who was a member of both the Committee and the Cultural Center, rallied the crowd with fiery words about the struggle to reclaim Vieques. The crowd cheered and clapped. There was a scramble to board the two buses and a much slower process of forming a caravan of public taxis and private cars to carry the rest of the crowd to the base.

In order to arrive at the site of the old sugar *central*, the caravan had to pass through the base's main entrance. There was considerable delay. The navy, expecting only two school buses, was overwhelmed by the caravan. It was a busy day for the guards, who copied license plate numbers and collected signatures. The base commander was on hand in her dress whites to act as an escort, but ended up supervising chaos. In the meantime, people aboard the idling buses started singing nationalist and folk songs. Two elderly North Americans aboard one of the buses looked decidedly uncomfortable.

Finally the procession was under way. The trip was emotional for many. One woman sat clutching a tissue, looking out the window. Another shouted out as she recognized stopping points for the old locomotive that ran from the cane fields to the *central*. An elderly (and imaginative) antinavy activist lamented that land now overrun with vines and scrub brush once nurtured sugar cane that grew to "thirty-six-foot" heights.

When the group arrived at the site of Playa Grande, Rivera gave a brief speech. "This was the center of the social, political, and economic life of Vieques before the navy expropriated it in the 1940s. This is where people lived, worked, and died." Rivera gave a brief chronology of the owners, and then encouraged people to share their experiences, especially urging young children to listen to their elders.

The crowd started milling about. What little had been left of the Central Playa Grande has been largely destroyed by Hurricane Hugo in 1989. The site was mainly crumbling, vine-entangled brick walls, overrun by mesquite and thick vegetation. People reminisced and poked among the debris, collecting rusted nails and pieces of broken pipe. Parents took photos of their children in front of the ruined walls. The local television station conducted an interview among the ruins, talking to an older man who had worked and lived at Playa Grande. The man explained that the navy arrived and offered the people a choice between working at the base or the *central*. They all chose the base, he remembered. His family was paid $25 to leave. The base never ended up providing the work they had all expected, he noted. People were videotaping the interview, taking photos and notes.

I spoke to a young man on the tour. I recognized him as one of a group of unemployed young men who passed most of their days on the roadside, drinking rum and beer from bottles in brown paper bags. He sported a cap emblazoned with the Puerto Rican flag and seemed enthusiastic about the tour. I asked him what he thought of the ruins. "It's nice," he answered in English, then switching to Spanish as a sailor passed by, "but we need this land. They have two-thirds of the island; we have only one-third. With this land, Vieques could develop. What do they need all this land for? They're not even using it. The navy should go. I'm not anti-American, only antinavy."

At noon the buses left for the ruins of Resolución. The caravan passed through magazines cut into the hills before arriving at a site similar to that of Playa Grande. Again Rivera gave a brief historical introduction to the *central* and encouraged people to share their experiences. There were a few brief testimonies. One woman grabbed a mike and said that even though she was born here, this was the first time she had returned to this soil in fifty-two years. An elderly man and prominent artist in Vieques said a few words about his experience working at Resolución. Again the crowd milled about, collecting nails and taking pictures, exchanging stories and memories. People began to break out coolers and bags of food and drink—*arepas*, the little savory balls of dough that are a culinary legacy of Vieques; fried chicken; juice and water.

The caravan made a final stop at the beach in front of the base headquarters. By now the tour had transformed itself into a town picnic. The atmosphere was festive with food and drink everywhere. Rivera said a few final words. He thanked the base commander, who sat to the side of the crowd, for her cooperation in planning for the day's activities. There was polite applause. "But," he continued, "we come here today on behalf of no organization, because of no one's permission or approval. We come here today as our right as the people of Vieques, to our own land. This is not just a historic tour of our past, but a visit to our present and future!" The crowd erupted into loud applause and cheers. The festivities continued, and by the time the buses returned to the plaza they rocked with loud nationalist and folk songs. In the following week, poems of loss and longing were printed in the local newspaper, describing the bittersweet experience of visiting Vieques's supposedly glorious past, now in ruins.

Mobilizing Culture

The limited success of the picket pointed to Viequenses' antipathy toward acts of direct confrontation. Although many were deeply upset by the bombs dropped on the outskirts of town, they seemed equally troubled by the idea of picketing in front of the base. The tour to the sugar *centrales*, in contrast, allowed for freer expression of sentiment and commitment. While the picket evoked the specter of communism and anticolonialism, the tour was safely ensconced in the realm of culture; the excursion, after all, was a historical tour organized by the Cultural Center. Most North Americans stayed away from the event because they associated the trip with a particular antinavy activist, but Viequenses were more willing to accept the stamp of institutional legitimacy given to the tour by the Institute of Puerto Rican Culture (as backer of the Cultural Center); of the municipality, which cosponsored the event; and of the navy, which authorized the entry onto military lands. Strong nationalist feeling, with assertions of historical links to the land and claims to its future, came from a heterogeneous assemblage of townspeople. Like the fishermen who focused grievances in the realm of the cultural and the economic, the excursion to the base offered a rallying place for nationalist sentiment within a circumscribed and "safe" locale.

The officially sanctioned tour suggested the importance of the cultural realm for reinforcing identity and political consciousness. The poignancy and power of the brief journey derived from its connection to the expropriations narrative that dominates popular discourse. The local newspaper described participants as pilgrims to a "living history classroom" of what had once been a thriving agricultural area and residential community.[4] The tour to the ruins evoked feelings of loss, tapping into nostalgia for Puerto Rico's "authentic" agrarian past. The tour, however, not only heightened nostalgia but made apparent the current social inequality of the military landholdings and the abandonment of the terrain. The excursion created not only a sense of a historical link to the land but also a feeling of entitlement to land that was clearly not used. As such the tour politicized the populace, within a context that the navy itself unwittingly authorized.

The excursion pointed to the possibility of radicalizing the population in a domain outside pure politics. The tour was particularly effective in rallying residents because it connected to grievances against the navy. A visit to the remains of two sugar *centrales*, a tour the navy approved as a seemingly harmless "historical excursion," proved a volatile reminder of the squelching of the economy, the loss of land, and the destruction of terrain by the military.

The essential problem with the cultural realm, however, was how to connect feelings of a distinctive cultural identity to a progressive political program. The challenge activists faced lay in harnessing the intensity of emotion evident on the excursion into a movement to evict the navy.

It was the navy, ultimately, that solved the dilemma. In its efforts to maintain its presence on Vieques Island, in its failure to compromise in light of rising discontent, it unwittingly spawned a new movement that challenged its hegemony.

Military Retrenchment

Although a special U.S. Armed Services Committee panel concluded in 1981 that the navy should find an alternate training site to Vieques, the military remained firmly entrenched. While activists declared the cold war over, and with it the primary justification for the military's use of the island, the navy asserted that the Vieques installation remained vital. The end of the cold war, it seemed, had only created new reasons for the navy to stay in Vieques. In a world of "violent peace," the navy argued, Vieques served as a crucial training ground for U.S. forces deployed across the globe. Pilots patrolling the skies of Bosnia, troops on the streets of Haiti's Port-au-Prince, and U.S. forces in Kuwait, Libya, and Lebanon had all been trained in Vieques (U.S. House 1994: 19).

Puerto Rican resident commissioner Carlos Romero Barceló introduced legislation that appeared to suggest a compromise. Earlier, as governor of Puerto Rico, Romero had signed the 1983 Fortín Accord with the navy and was well aware of the failure of that agreement to bring a resolution to continued conflict. In light of rising discontent and agitation to close the base, he intervened with a compromise.

The Vieques Land Transfer Act of 1994 proposed turning over roughly eight thousand acres of land in western Vieques to the municipality of Vieques for public purposes. Although the navy used land in the east of Vieques for weapons testing and maneuvers, its land in the west was mostly vacant, checkered with 102 magazines, 40 of which were inactive. Sixty bunkers monopolized eight thousand acres, nearly one-third of Vieques Island. The navy itself estimated that Roosevelt Roads could accommodate the bunkers on 646 acres of land, albeit at a cost of $300 million (U.S. House 1994: 47). Romero's bill might act as a pressure valve, allowing the navy to keep its essential holdings while appeasing the civilians by returning significant acreage currently used for ammunition storage.

The Committee, though struggling to regain the entire island, decided to back the bill. Dr. Rivera explained that the Committee saw the legislation as an initial step for the recovery of all Vieques land (U.S. House 1994: 115). The group recognized that the western territory was particularly valuable, because it represented the shortest transportation route between Vieques and Puerto Rico.

The navy, however, firmly opposed the bill. Admiral Ernest E. Christensen, Jr., argued that the ammunition depot was an integral part of the Vieques complex, because the munitions stored there were used primarily in training exercises on the island. Furthermore, with overseas bases closing, particularly Panama bases, the navy might need even more munitions storage facilities (U.S. House 1994: 26). The admiral inflamed tensions at the congressional hearings with a poorly worded statement:

> I believe the issue which is before you today is not the absolute value of the land of Vieques to the United States Navy, nor to the Nation, nor is it the issue of the eastern side of Vieques where significant training occurs. I believe that the issue here today is rather the western side of the island, which comprises somewhere between 7,600 and 8,000 acres, and whether the ammunition which is stored on the western side is worth more than the municipality of Vieques to this Nation than to the Nation in its national defense. It is my firm conviction it is worth more to the United States Nation and to the national defense. (U.S. House 1994: 19)

Romero challenged the admiral, asking if he intended to imply that the ammunition depot was worth more to the nation than the municipality of Vieques. Though the admiral struggled to extricate himself, the public relations damage was done. At best, Christensen was asserting the navy's unyielding intent to hold on to eight thousand acres of land used to house sixty bunkers, despite the hardship this caused the community and despite the failure of the navy to live up to its good neighbor agreement. At worst, he was implying that the value of this depot, or perhaps the ammunition it stored, was more valuable than the people who lived on the island. In any case, the hearings sealed the fate of the legislation. The navy refused to budge and the bill languished. Without any real advocate, the bill went nowhere. The navy, however, sought to make clear its commitment to stay on Vieques.

Vieques in the War on Drugs

The apparent political space opened by the collapse of the Soviet Union proved fleeting. Although the end of the cold war suggested that Vieques's strategic significance would diminish, in the early nineties the U.S. military redefined its mission in the Caribbean. The menace of communism in Cuba and

Nicaragua passed, the defense of the canal was no longer crucial. Instead the U.S. military found new meaning in the war against international narcotics trafficking and arms smuggling. The Caribbean would be critical to drug interdiction efforts and the defense of the U.S.–Mexican border (Rodríguez Beruff 1999).

The U.S. military's redefinition dovetailed with a growing sense of crisis in Puerto Rico caused by the expansion of the drug trade. By the early nineties, drug-related homicide rates had skyrocketed, and Puerto Rico became the U.S. capital of carjackings. The media kept a sensationalist chronicle of the daily carnage of the drug wars, broadcasting gruesome accounts of cadavers on the evening news (Rodríguez Beruff 1999). The headlines of the tabloid *El Vocero* blared a daily tally of rising murder rates.

In 1992 pro-statehood governor Pedro Rosselló was elected on a campaign promise to get tough on crime and drugs. His administration aggressively expanded the presence of the police and armed forces into civil society. The National Guard was called in to restore order to the island's public housing projects, widely perceived to be infested with drugs. Dozens of housing projects became the primary battlefields for the government's war on drugs, raising serious questions about the erosion of civil liberties (Colón Morera 1997; Rodríguez Beruff 1999). Middle-class communities across the island, gripped with fear, blockaded public streets and hired security guards to control access to neighborhoods. This was the context that framed the navy's decision to erect an antidrug radar system in Vieques.

The Irradiation of Vieques

In the spring of 1994 the navy announced its intent to erect a $9 million "Relocatable-Over-The-Horizon-Radar Installation" (ROTHR) in Vieques with the cooperation of the Puerto Rican police, the Puerto Rican National Guard, and the Puerto Rican Economic Development Administration (Fomento Económico). ROTHR was developed by the Raytheon Company during the cold war to monitor Soviet fleets in the Pacific Northwest. The sophisticated radar system now had a new purpose: to scan the Caribbean and Latin America for aircraft carrying drugs to and from the United States.[5] Governor Rosselló hailed it as an important contribution in the war against drug trafficking.

The installation would consist of three parts: a transmitter located in Vieques, a receiver in Lajas, Puerto Rico, and an Operation Control Center in Norfolk, Virginia. The Vieques transmitter would include 34 vertical towers ranging in height from 71 to 125 feet, requiring approximately 100 acres of leveled land. The navy considered three potential sites for the installation: one on the western part of the island, near the Playa Grande Lagoon on the site of the old sugar cane *central*, and two others in the east near the Camp García airstrip.

The significance of the project's timing was not lost on members of the Committee. Although the project was described as part of the war on drugs, Committee members felt such a claim was a subterfuge for entrenching the military presence. After all, it was shortly after Romero visited Vieques to describe his efforts to reclaim the western part of the island, and in the midst of the Committee's work to close the Vieques base, that the navy suddenly found new use for lands that had lain idle for decades. Committee members were furious and found a new focus for their energies: alerting the public to the potential health dangers of electromagnetic radiation and resisting what they perceived as new efforts by the navy to maintain its presence.

Public hearings on the project were held in Lajas and Vieques in early June. In the weeks preceding the hearings the Vieques television station ran a number of programs describing the potential health risks of the radar installation. In Vieques, a growing concern for the health effects of the naval presence dated back at least five years, when an article had been published in a Puerto Rican engineering journal about high concentrations of explosives in the local drinking water (Cruz Pérez 1988). Residents were increasingly concerned about contamination from military explosives and reports of high levels of certain types of cancers in the community. The secretive nature of military activity and the community's lack of access to information intensified fear and suspicion. So while the announcement of the radar installation initially received little attention in Lajas, in Vieques it raised activists' fears that the military was plotting a new way to ensure its presence on the island and that electromagnetic radiation could expose the population to new risks of cancer. The early hearings in Lajas passed without notice. In Vieques, the public response to the hearings and the radar project was explosive.

On Saturday morning, June 11, the Committee organized a boycott of the public hearings and a picket on the plaza in front of city hall where the hearings were taking place. Approximately 150 people joined the demonstration, blocking traffic for hours and drawing considerable attention as they chanted and marched in the hot sun. The Committee had contacted the Puerto Rico–based leftist environmental group the Misión Industrial, and a member arrived to distribute leaflets describing the dangers of electromagnetic radiation. Inside city hall, a handful of concerned residents posed critical questions about the impact of the proposed radar installation. They inquired about the energy requirements of the station, the aesthetic appearance of the facility on land locals hoped to conserve for ecotourism, and the health effects of electromagnetic radiation. The hearing, the public concerns, and the protest all received extensive coverage in the local paper and attention in the Puerto Rican press. The local newspaper described the demonstration as composed of "sympathizers from all parties, various religious groups, municipal assemblypersons and even government employees, many not considered antinavy types."[6] It was clear that the Committee had successfully surmounted fears of communism and anti-Americanism to organize a high-profile picket joined by a diverse group of people from the community.

In the ensuing weeks, there was a growing schism in the Committee over how to continue the momentum established that Saturday morning. One member had been quoted in a San Juan paper expressing his belief that the radar project was nothing more than a military plot to ensure military control of the island. He represented a faction of the Committee that felt strongly about emphasizing the military conspiracy part of the equation, rallying popular sentiment against the radar station as a thinly veiled attempt to derail efforts to reclaim the land. Several other Committee members, however, wished to avoid statements of direct confrontation with the navy and instead focus attention on the health dangers of the radar station. The threat of cancer, they felt, would be more effective in building popular opposition to the navy and its project. They wished to deemphasize the military objectives of the navy, a focus that they felt alienated people, and concentrate more on the environmental repercussions of the project as a way of attracting as many people as possible. Ultimately the faction that wanted to emphasize the health risks and environmental consequences of the facility dominated, and the struggle over the radar proceeded based on those concerns.

Forging a New Consensus

From the earliest days of the radar controversy, it was clear that opposition to the ROTHR installation united people in Vieques as never before. One clear expression of this new unity was seen in the concern of North American residents over the radar installation.

In a startling development, in July 1994 the board of directors of the Vieques Conservation and Historic Trust announced its unanimous opposition to the navy's ROTHR station. The VCHT, as mentioned earlier, was the pet project of a number of wealthy, North American seasonal residents, and it claimed to focus on preserving Vieques's environment, particularly its unique bioluminescent bay, but over the years it had alienated itself from sympathetic Viequenses because of its refusal to oppose the naval bombing exercises. The VCHT maintained that speaking out against the bombing would be an exercise in politics and that it wished to engage in environmental preservation, not political controversy. In reality most VCHT members, who were often Navy League members as well, were strongly supportive of the military presence on Vieques and were not willing to compromise their loyalties, even in the face of this apparent conflict of interest. Thus activists were surprised when the VCHT issued a strongly worded statement declaring its unequivocal opposition to the radar station, which aside from representing a visual blight on "one of the loveliest unspoiled islands in the Caribbean" and a potential health threat to island residents, would almost certainly adversely affect the island's environment, in particular the bioluminescent bay.[7] For the first time, the interests of antinavy activists and those of a locally based North American organization had converged.

Concerns about the radar installation also rattled some of the navy's other most loyal supporters. This fact surprised me one afternoon when I arrived on the doorstep of María Rivera, a seventy-two-year-old woman whose daughter had married a marine. I knew little about doña María when we first met. A friend of a friend insisted I talk to doña María about what she thought about the navy, since her daughter had married a marine. The friend called doña María, told her that she didn't have to answer any questions she didn't want to, and that I was on my way over. I was then shuttled over to an interview I wasn't sure I wanted, at least under these circumstances.

When I arrived at the house, doña María was reticent, bordering on hostile. I tried to describe my project, telling her that I was interested in knowing what relations between the navy and residents were like over time, and how Vieques had changed. She told me that she didn't know much about these things, that they didn't interest her at all, and that she didn't want to get involved in them. What exactly did I want to know? I asked her if she knew if there were any dances or social events between the navy and the town in the past. "There was a dance hall in town," she answered curtly. Now there were no more dances. What about marriages between soldiers and Viequense women? Her daughter and cousin. That's all she knew. Both left the island. I asked her some questions about the 1950s. She said she wasn't here. She had left for New York, where she lived for twenty-five years.

I was prepared to leave when doña María started to warm up. She told me that most people in Vieques were in favor of the navy. There were only a few who were against them and they were communists. Well, it is said that they are communists, she clarified, but admitted she didn't know for sure. But it's a small group and they are opposed to everything, she went on. They like to start fights. For example, take the radar. They are against the radar. It's always the same people against everything.

"Are you in favor of the radar?" I asked. "Of course," she responded. "It's to fight drugs. Just the other day they dropped $60 million worth of drugs on Vieques." (In a widely publicized incident, authorities discovered that empty base land in Vieques was being used as a new cache for drug smugglers.)

Doña María started to talk a little more about the navy. She said they had some clubs on base that they allowed "Hispanics" to attend. They gave them passes. Of course they don't give passes to communists. They're not even allowed on base. There's only a few of them. One of them they say is a Jew, she noted, as if to highlight the activist's alien nature. He's against everything and he's not even from here. So it's none of his business anyway. He's married to a woman who is a teacher in the school, and she's not from here either. There are two or three of them from here that they won't let on the base either.

"So do you think that most people here are in favor of the navy?" I asked. "Oh yes, definitely," she assured me. "Most people feel that way. If it went to a vote we would win."

"Why are people in favor of the navy?" I asked. "They bought this land," she responded. "This island is poor. Before there was sugar cane and the navy gave people land. That's what they say," she qualified herself.

I was interested then when doña María turned the conversation back to discuss the proposed radar installation. "Why don't the communists want the radar?" she asked me. "Does it cause cancer? They wouldn't put something in that caused cancer, would they?" She was completely sincere and appeared truly worried.

I discovered later that doña María had been a member of the Pro-Navy Vanguard, the militant pronavy group that organized in opposition to the Crusade to Rescue Vieques in the late 1970s. Despite doña María's strong support for the navy and her hostility toward antinavy activists, the potential health threat of the radar installation troubled her, penetrating an ideological curtain of sorts. Doña María had absorbed some of the navy's major representations of the antinavy protestors—that they were a communist minority, dominated by outside agitators, and that local claims to the land were unfounded, because the navy bought its holdings and gave parcels of land to the poor. Yet her fear of cancer was genuine and raised questions for her, though so much else seemed to be black and white.

This encounter with doña María suggested the significance of the radar mobilization in forging a new consensus in Vieques about the military presence. The radar issue was so effective because it diverted attention away from politics, which, as doña María's comments indicated, were still extremely divisive, and focused attention instead on the environmental and health effects of the military presence.

No al Radar!

Within months of the navy's announcement of its intention to erect the ROTHR station, opposition to the radar began to grow not only in Vieques but in Lajas, Puerto Rico. In Lajas, a group calling itself the United Front to Defend the Valley of Lajas formed to oppose the project, bringing together a diverse group of local landowners, veteran independence advocates, and military veterans. The Lajas front succeeded in significantly expanding the radar struggle. The coalition the Committee to Rescue and Develop Vieques forged with Lajas activists is fundamental to understanding the broad-based antinavy movement that erupted in Vieques in 1999.

The struggle in Lajas took on a different character from the one in Vieques. While in Vieques the navy proposed erecting towers on military-owned land, in Lajas the navy planned to lease 950 acres of land from eight landowners. The Lajas Valley was once agricultural and had a complex irrigation system installed in the 1950s when owners intended to turn the land to grain production.[8] Over the next several decades, however, economic policies in Puerto Rico proved devastating to the island's agricultural sector (Dietz 1986; Pantojas-García 1990; Weisskoff 1985). The Lajas Valley was largely undeveloped and used for cattle grazing.

Interestingly, despite the lack of agricultural development in the Lajas Valley, opposition to the radar installation there focused mainly on the perceived military expansion and usurpation of agricultural land. Although the navy stated that 750 of the proposed 950 acres of land it wanted could still be used for agriculture, it did not quell opposition. The Lajas mobilization against the radar took shape as a struggle to conserve agriculture. The navy was depicted as usurping the Puerto Rican agricultural heartland, at the center of the national identity.

Lajas's movement quickly built momentum and was strengthened by the high-profile involvement of a group of Vietnam veterans, who built an encampment at the entrance of the valley consisting of tents and shacks, festooned with U.S., Puerto Rican, and veteran flags. The veterans handed out pamphlets describing Lajas's struggle against the ROTHR, the dangers of electromagnetic radiation, and problems facing veterans.[9]

The Vietnam veterans were crucial to the mobilization on two levels. First, with decorated war heroes on the front lines of the mobilization, the struggle could not be dismissed as a nationalist agitation. The veterans lent legitimacy and moral authority to this confrontation with the military. Second, the veterans focused attention on the issue of military contamination in a charged, emotional manner. One veteran at the encampment, on crutches because his bones were slowly dissolving after exposure to Agent Orange, crystallized the anger and anxiety over the toxic legacy of military practices. This decorated war hero, victimized by the U.S. military itself, undermined the navy's authority in asserting the safety of the ROTHR installation. The veterans became the lifeblood of the Lajas mobilization and provided a crucial symbolic link between Lajas, which emphasized land and agricultural usurpation, and Vieques, which highlighted health and victimization in opposition to the radar.

The radar mobilization grew on both fronts. In May 1995 the Committee organized a candlelight march in opposition to the radar that was attended by over a hundred Viequenses. In July 1995 thousands protested the radar installation at a fair in Lajas.

In light of the surge of protest, the navy struggled to assert its project and failed once again at the art of public relations. Navy spokesperson Lt. Commander Michael McCloskey declared that Puerto Rico "is a territory of the U.S. and the Pentagon decided it is the best location to raise the radar." The radar would be erected, with or without the consent of the Puerto Rican people. McCloskey's comments outraged even the statehood party that had supported the radar installation in the war on drugs.[10]

In October 1995 opponents of the ROTHR installation organized one of the largest mobilizations in Puerto Rico in years. Tens of thousands converged on the streets of San Juan to voice their opposition. Even demonstration organizers were surprised by the massive turnout. An effigy of Lt. Commander McCloskey was burned at the demonstration. Delegations from Lajas and Vieques had effectively mobilized both cultural nationalist sentiment about the land and fear of electromagnetic radiation. Confrontation over military expansion and encroachment had been channeled into discussion about the environment and health.

The struggle over ROTHR continued over the next two years. The Puerto Rican Environmental Quality Board halted the project briefly, demanding detailed information about the health and environmental implications of the installation. A victory seemed on the horizon when the navy announced that it would abandon plans to install the radar. Then in 1996, in a reversal, the navy announced its intentions to go forward with the ROTHR project. It would abandon Lajas as a potential site for the installation, and instead erect the radar antenna in nearby Juanas Dias on military-owned land at Fort Allen. The Vieques antenna would be erected on the western part of the island, despite continued opposition to the project there.

In January 1997 the Committee to Rescue and Develop Vieques organized what it declared to be the largest antimilitary demonstration in Vieques in twenty years. Over five hundred people gathered in front of the gates of the Western Ammunition Facility, the proposed site for the ROTHR. Leaders of the local political parties and churches delivered messages of opposition. The demonstration was coordinated with the movement in Lajas, which held its own protest simultaneously in front of the gates of Fort Allen.

In February 1997 the Committee organized yet another well-attended protest, this time a "Walk for the Health of Vieques." The purpose of the walk was to dramatize the community's concern over high cancer rates and other illnesses stemming from environmental contamination, and residents' fears that electromagnetic radiation from the proposed radar installation could exacerbate rates of illness. As in January, over five hundred people attended.

Conclusion

In focusing on the health and environmental consequences of the proposed radar installation, the Committee succeeded in rallying opposition to the navy on the island. Opposition, however, was carefully framed around the threat of cancer. The Committee deemphasized its belief that the radar project was a military subterfuge designed to derail land reclamation. It organized residents not to protest the navy, but to "walk for the health of Vieques." Fears of association with an anti-American cause dissolved in the face of what was understood to be a real threat of cancer.

The Committee's emphasis on moderation and respectability turned out to be an important asset in organizing around the radar issue. Dr. Rivera, the epidemiologist and prominent public health official whose presence the Committee had sought to highlight as a voice of reason, gave legitimacy to health concerns about the radar installation. When the doctor talked about cancer rates and the risks of electromagnetic radiation, people listened. Even the North Americans, who had never displayed any sympathy for antimilitary causes, were swayed by the concerns the Committee raised about the installation, even if those concerns (predominantly the bioluminescent bay) differed from those of Viequenses. The Committee thus succeeded in building tentative bridges between the Viequense and North American populations.

In the radar struggle, we again see the way in which the issues that mobilize Viequenses have symbolic resonance that connect to deep-seated grievances against the navy. The historical excursion, for example, actively revived romantic memories of the sugar era and the more painful story of the expropriations, reinforcing claims to the land. The struggle against the radar station and perceived cancer threat connected to pervasive fears of military conspiracy and "genocide." Although the Committee felt that the public would shy away from a focus on the calculated political motives behind the proposed ROTHR station, activists recognized that the public was generally sympathetic to the notion of military conspiracy. The idea that the military still secretly plotted to remove all island residents remained strong, as was the belief that navy maneuvers and bombing had created a toxic legacy. By focusing on the theme of cancer-causing radiation towers, the Committee was able to tap into these fears and rally the community against the military.

The navy project ultimately prevailed. A number of activists in Lajas were dejected. Although they managed to block the radar antenna from the valley, the navy simply shifted its project to a neighboring town. Numerous residents in Vieques were outraged at the erection of the antenna in the face of the health fears of the community. But the ROTHR struggle ultimately laid the foundation for the mobilization that erupted in 1999. Through the radar struggle the Committee had successfully organized and mobilized Viequenses' concerns about health and safety, called upon their intense emotions and attachment to the island, and built linkages to a wide web of supporters in Puerto Rico.

Six

The first time that I went to the target range, I brought a cross, representing my mom. I placed it on Monte David. I pretty much broke down in tears because. . . . It's such a shame, such a beautiful piece of land. It hit me. The fact that my mother died of cancer just like my aunt died of cancer, even friends. . . . It was like, what's going on? Why isn't anybody taking any action?
—Juan Silva

From Pescadores to Rescatores

The Resurgence and Transformation of Struggle

On April 19, 1999, David Sanes Rodríguez, a thirty-five-year-old civilian security guard, was patrolling the Vieques live-impact range when explosions rocked the navy firing-range observation post (OP). Two F-18 jets, traveling between 500 and 1,300 miles per hour, missed their mark by one and a half miles. The jets dropped two five-hundred-pound bombs not on the range, but on the barbed-wire ringed complex where the navy surveyed the shelling. The navy's range control officer and three security guards inside the OP were injured by fragments of shattered glass and concrete. Sanes, standing outside, was knocked unconscious by the explosion and bled to death from his injuries.

Several days later, hundreds attended Sanes's funeral mass in the Monte Santo Catholic Church in Vieques. Following the ceremony, the Committee to Rescue and Develop Vieques organized a group of fishermen, antinavy activists, and members of the Sanes family to enter military lands and erect a twelve-foot-high white cross in honor of David Sanes. It was supposed to be a religious ceremony. Sanes's family wanted no part of politicizing his death. The Committee's effort to involve fishermen in the activity reflected a prolonged and largely unsuccessful effort to recharge the leadership of the fishermen in mobilizing against the military.

When the group arrived at a hill in the center of the impact zone, events took an unexpected course. The contingent staked its cross, according to plan, and christened the spot Monte David, in memory of Sanes. But then a member of the group, Albert de Jesus (Tito Kayak), a self-proclaimed environmental "warrior" from Vega Baja, known throughout Puerto Rico for his high-profile acts of disobedience, stole the spotlight.

De Jesus gave an impassioned speech against the navy and vowed to remain, to personally block the resumption of military maneuvers. Members of the Sanes family who were ambivalent about confronting the navy were upset about politicizing the memorial. Committee members, who for years had painstakingly organized against the military presence, were indignant that de Jesus, an outsider, was imposing his individual agenda on the group. The contingent left de Jesus on the target range, where he remained alone overnight, while antinavy activists struggled over how to proceed. The next morning, Eleida Encarnación de Zenón, the wife of fisherman Carlos Zenón, called Julia Ramos, a member of the Committee, and argued that de Jesus could not be left alone and that he deserved support. The Zenón sons joined de Jesus on the target range, bringing food, water, and supplies and eventually founding an encampment. More followed.

For over a year activists positioned themselves as human shields on the bombing range, bringing military maneuvers to a halt. To get there, protestors scaled fences or shuttled into the range by fishing boat. Over a dozen encampments sprang up on the target zone. Thousands of supporters from Vieques, Puerto Rico, and the United States visited the campsites to express their solidarity. Viequenses traipsed over dusty fields littered with live ordnance to stake white crosses on the silent ridge of Monte David in memory of loved ones who had died of cancer, they believed, because of the navy's bombing.

David Sanes's death opened a new chapter in a decades-long story of conflict between the U.S. Navy and the residents of Vieques Island. The Committee to Rescue and Develop Vieques had laid the foundation for a movement to evict the navy over the course of six years of organizing and coalition building. During the six years that the Committee denounced the navy as a persistent threat to safety and health, it created a context for understanding the death of David Sanes. The Committee developed an organizational structure and links to a broader network of supporters that would prove vital to sustaining more spontaneous and creative forms of protest. The Committee's work made possible the much broader mobilization that grew from de Jesus's individual act of defiance

A key element of the Committee's success was its ability to create a resonant cultural framework that shifted the focus of Vieques's conflict outside the realm of colonial politics. The white crosses, signifying Christian martyrdom, emerged as particularly important symbols that fused local cultural meanings with more universal messages. The encampments on the bombing range, a series of tents and flags and, evoking the rural past, little wooden *casitas*, acted in a physical way to link people to the island while framing direct action in terms of Puerto Rican culture.[1] The symbolic framework opened a space for the emergence of new actors, most significantly women and the church, who have been vital in broadening and sustaining the movement.

The movement's framework and organization allowed it to expand from a locally based effort to a broader mobilization involving numerous and often divergent sectors of civil society that shaped mainstream political debate within Puerto Rico and the United States as a whole.

The Organization of Discontent

Vieques had long lived under the threat of a navy mishap. Mayor Antonio Rivera Rodríguez complained about the vulnerability of Vieques back in the 1950s after a series of accidents on Culebra demonstrated the real risks of living on a military target range (Mélendez López 1989: 107). The forties, fifties, and sixties saw a string of civilian casualties in Vieques. In 1940, a man and his son were killed when they walked down a path and their horse stepped on a grenade. In the mid-sixties the navy lost a "test bomb with nuclear characteristics" off the coast of Vieques. In the nineties there were a series of incidents. In 1993, the navy dropped five bombs on the border of the civilian sector. In 1996, bombs exploded in the coastal waters by a group of fishermen, seriously injuring one. In 1997, the National Guard riddled a parked police car and town school bus with bullets.

But popular outrage over accidental firings never crystallized into a sustained movement in Vieques, nor did protest in the late 1970s highlight this aspect of Vieques's woes. Charges that the navy was bombing an island that was simultaneously a civilian residential community took a back seat to other issues. Governor Romero, for example, focused his case on a set of environmental claims rather than on the notion of a human population under siege. The Crusade, under the influence of the fishermen, focused attention on the restriction of the seas and the destruction of traps, and connected these grievances to broader claims about the right to live and work on Vieques. Activists wrote tomes about the naval expropriations in the 1940s, highlighting the abuse residents suffered and the navy's intransigence. It wasn't until David Sanes's death, however, that Viequenses articulated the most dramatic element of their story—indeed, to the outsider, what often seems the most salient and defining feature of the conflict—that the navy's weapons testing range is an island inhabited by people. There can be no real buffer zone on a twenty-one-mile-long island when planes travel between 500 and 1,300 miles per hour; there can be no barrier to prevent dust and residues from explosives from traveling downwind or contaminating the civilian water supply. Sanes's death focused the movement on the singular issue of the bombing, and gave rise to the movement's slogan: *Ni una bomba más*, not one more bomb.

"In the beginning, the struggle the Committee faced was to challenge the navy's characterization of the death as just like any other workplace-related accident," noted Mario Martínez. "If this incident had occurred and we didn't do all the work we did, it would have passed as just another death, as just another accident. It is normal that an event, a tragedy like this one, would provoke a reaction. What is not normal is that it should be so prolonged."

The Committee's ability to effectively challenge the navy's credibility was the direct result of the ROTHR struggle. In the course of the four-year fight against the radar, the Committee had continually challenged the ROTHR installation as a health threat and tapped into fears of surrounding cancer rates. The group's nonpartisan and diverse internal structure built and mobilized a strong coalition of supporters. Through countless peace marches, pickets, and candlelight prayer vigils the group established its moral authority. As noted, the projection of Dr. Rivera as the group's spokesperson was crucial to strengthening the group's legitimacy.

Notwithstanding popular opposition, the navy erected its ROTHR towers in 1998. To raise the radar antennae the military razed 100 acres of the mahogany trees it once claimed as its major contribution to the environmental rehabilitation of the island. On the most obvious level, the navy had won the battle. But in the long run, the ROTHR eroded the military's hegemony. The erection of the radar in the face of widespread public opposition stirred a groundswell of resentment and confirmed suspicions that the navy was not only indifferent to islanders' health concerns but was actually contributing to the perceived genocide of islanders.

David Sanes Rodríguez: Vieques's Martyr

It seems ironic that it was the death of a navy employee that brought civilian grievances to a head in Vieques. David Sanes Rodríguez was at work patrolling the observation post when he met his demise. How was it that a navy employee killed on base during routine training maneuvers became such a catalyst to popular mobilization? Was there validity in the navy's defense that Sanes's unfortunate death was just a work-related accident?

For most Viequenses, the defining characteristic of Sanes was not that he wore a navy uniform but that he was an ordinary Viequense, who worked and struggled to live on the island. He was not seen as a sell-out or traitor because

he worked for the navy. This perception connects to the broader political realities of Puerto Rican life: people are generally supportive of continued political and economic association with the United States, have often served in the
military, and regard the armed forces as a legitimate venue for economic
advancement.

The perception of Sanes as an ordinary working man, as opposed to a symbol of the naval presence, also speaks to the pragmatism of the local populace.
Despite the long history of tensions between the navy and the community,
Viequenses express virtually no hostility toward residents who work on the
base. This is particularly striking because the navy started hiring locals as security guards in the midst of the protest in the seventies, to create a loyal bloc
of support, and has mobilized the security guards to attend pronavy rallies.
Still, even the most fervent antinavy activists express no animosity toward residents employed by the base.

Jorge Rodríguez Beruff (2001) interprets the symbolism surrounding David
Sanes's death differently. The military uniform, Rodríguez argues, was vital in
establishing Sanes's innocence and legitimacy, and made it possible to translate Vieques's message to broad sectors of Puerto Rican society. "The fact that
the victim was a Viequense above suspicion of opposition to the navy, whose
image was in uniform and in a military salute, politically broadened the impact of the tragedy. He was not a 'radical troublemaker,' but a faithful servant.
How many Puerto Ricans who had served in the Armed Forces could see themselves in his image? How many Viequenses who still believed there was a future with the navy or who had served it felt that tragedy as an intimate event?"
(Rodríguez Beruff 2001: 12).

On a local level, however, the vehement response to Sanes's death ultimately
expresses the intensity of local identity. More important than wearing a uniform was the fact that Sanes was a working man, endeavoring to live and raise
a family on the island. He was seen as a native son. His death connected symbolically to charges of genocide. "David Sanes was one of us!" exclaimed an
activist at a rally. "The navy killed one of us!" Although there had been countless quiet deaths to cancer that residents attributed to the navy, Sanes was the
clear, indisputable victim of navy activity. He provided the movement its martyr.

The Embodiment of Protest

Sanes's death sparked a new movement to remove the navy. In subsequent days, demonstrators entered the heart of the base, erecting tents on
the live-impact range. They built settlements to fortify their claims to the land
and to block bombing exercises.

The protestors who positioned themselves as human shields on the navy's impact zone drew on an established legacy of civil disobedience. Protestors constructed a *casita*, a church, and a schoolhouse, echoing the work of antinavy demonstrators in Culebra. Like the fishermen's interruptions of naval maneuvers, the encampments on the bombing range were symbolic challenges to military authority and power. Protest, however, shifted from the seas to the land: from clashes over restrictions on the water to incursions into the heart of military territory. "We have gone from *pescadores* [fishermen] to *rescatores* [land rescuers]," said one activist. The form of protest, rescuing the land, was more provocative, more directly confrontational. Viequenses, who had long demanded access to the island and return of the land, seized control of the most strategically significant part of the base.

The encampments halted naval bombing exercises and military maneuvers on Vieques Island for over a year. Moreover, they kept Vieques in the spotlight of the international media. They provided a concrete way for people to become involved in Vieques's struggle. The encampments elicited a complex network of support, maintained by thousands of people from Vieques, Puerto Rico, and the United States.

Although the encampments had important links to past expressions of civil disobedience, they were a new development in the organization and expression of protest. Those in the encampments had autonomous networks of support. In the 1970s it had been the PIP that sponsored the construction of a chapel on Culebra; in 1999 the encampments in Vieques represented a diverse coalition of groups, including local Viequenses, students, independence activists, teachers, church members and members of the Committee to Rescue and Develop Vieques.

The logistics of maintaining the encampments were quite complex, requiring the organization of people, transportation, funds, and supplies. The preexistence of the Committee, with its extensive links in Puerto Rico and the United States, was crucial to sustaining this more spontaneous and creative expression. The Committee had an established financial structure and managed the stream of contributions. In the first year alone, the Committee accounted for and distributed over $100,000 worth of donations. Although some money paid for activists to travel on speaking tours, most of it went directly to the camps.

To live on this barren, pockmarked bombing range for over a year, people required shelter, fresh water, and food. Because it was so difficult to live there, and because of the risk of arrests, activists kept a minimal number of people on the bombing range, constantly rotating personnel. One of the major expenses was gasoline to fuel the fishing boats that shuttled back and forth. Every day for over a year fishing boats traveled through restricted waters to ferry people, food, water, and supplies.

To Monte David: September 1999

We gathered early Saturday morning by the fishermen's dock on the north of the island, just past the ferry and the fleet of small boats belonging to Vieques's fishermen. There were fourteen of us: several middle-aged men and women from Vieques, a renowned Puerto Rican folk singer, several members of the Committee, environmental activists from Lajas, Puerto Rico, their teenage daughters, and our fisherman guide. We carried tanks of water and coolers of fresh fish, sandwiches, and dough to make *arepas*. We piled onto a twelve-foot boat rigged with two motors. With some effort, both engines were revved up, rumbling, stalling, belching out black clouds of smoke and diesel fumes before finally roaring forward. We headed to the bombing range.

The familiar coastline of Vieques receded. We passed the faded blue lighthouse, the closely settled houses. We reached the limits of the civilian sector, passed the wooden houses squatting on the hills of the no-man's land. Ahead of us we saw only miles of rocky cliffs. There was a feeling of giddiness aboard our small vessel as we entered restricted waters.

After an hour, we saw the first signs that we had entered the impact zone. The eerie shell of a battered, rusting tank sat on a cliff. We saw the observation post, the red-checkered tower where David Sanes was killed. Then the graffitio, Vive Vieques Libre (Long Live Free Vieques), defiantly scrawled on the rock.

Finally we started to see the encampments. First we saw Cayo Yayi, situated on a tiny islet offshore the tip of Vieques. A Puerto Rican flag waved on a tall pole by tents on the beach. On the opposite shore was a second set of camps: one formed by local schoolteachers, another associated with Congreso Nacional Hostosiano, representing a coalition of pro-independence groups. Again the encampments were composed of a series of flags and tents, and several projects under construction. One would never expect to see people swimming in these waters, but about a dozen young boys were tumbling in the waves ahead of us. We were greeted by a flurry of raised fists as our boat approached the shore.

The beauty in the impact zone was stunning. The clouds looked like puffs of white powder, sitting low in the brilliant blue sky. The water was liquid turquoise, clear as glass. The scalloped shores of Punta Salinas, Vieques's easternmost tip, had white sand beaches so thick and soft our feet sank six inches deep as we stepped from the boat. Vieques, the island of pristine beaches, had no more beautiful shore. But as our gaze shifted from the beach to the scrub edging the white sand, we started to see bombs tangled in the vines. The contrast of natural glory and human destruction was surreal. We approached the teachers' and Hostosiano camps.

In the months after the encampments were founded, hundreds of visitors had poured onto the bombing range, shuttled by an organized circuit of fishing boats. On this day there were already about thirty people across the water at Cayo Yayi, and twenty people here at the teachers' and Hostosiano camps. Practically speaking, the boundaries between the latter two camps blurred into an overlapping series of tents and members. Schoolteachers in Vieques had long backed the antinavy movement, and a number of teachers were members of the Committee. Still, the Committee officially associated itself with the pro-independence Hostosiano camp, although the links to the teachers' camp were obvious. We did not visit the camp at Cayo Yayi. This was partly a matter of logistics. Our fisherman guide would return to town, so we would have no way to get across to the other camp, and in any case, we wanted to visit the camps in the inner range. Cayo Yayi was isolated across the water. But there seemed to be an unspoken conflict here. One activist said that Cayo Yayi was the fishermen's camp, and indeed it featured a shrine devoted to the Virgen del Carmen, the patron saint of local fishers. But another activist dismissed this characterization. The camp was one of local businesspeople, she asserted, not fishermen, and she rattled off the names of local merchants who were fixtures there. Underneath these differing accounts seemed to be unresolved questions about the leadership of the camp, a problem connected to broader questions about the leadership of the antinavy movement and the strength of the coalition that supported it.

Because the primary purpose of our visit was to bring the supporters from Lajas to the bombing range, we went to the teachers' camp and the Hostosiano camp, which were associated with the Committee. The Committee's links to Lajas in the common struggle to block the navy from erecting its radar antennae continued. On this visit, activists from Lajas arrived with a check for the Committee for $10,000 that they had raised at a recent Vieques solidarity concert, "An Urgent Song for Peace" (Canción Urgente por la Paz), featuring folk music and salsa bands. The Committee planned to distribute the money equally among each of the encampments. Money was flowing into the camps, in the form of $50 and $100 contributions from individuals who had been to the camps or had read about Vieques on the Internet as well as from T-shirt sales and fund-raising concerts and activities like the one in Lajas.

We unloaded our coolers and tanks of water at the teachers' camp, next to a makeshift stove. Creating a working kitchen had been one of the demonstrators' first priorities. With that accomplished, the teachers' campsite became a center of hospitality, where solidarity was forged over meals on the beach. Metal poles supported wide tarps sheltering visitors from the searing tropical sun. Out back, visiting environmentalists constructed a latrine, a practical necessity given the hundreds of visitors who rotated through the camp. The activists were determined to keep the camps continually occupied with the minimum number of people, keeping a larger reserve pool of demonstrators on hand to fill the camps in the event of arrests.

We inspected a chapel and a wooden schoolhouse under construction, projects of the Hostosiano camp. The construction of simple, wooden structures, like the *casita*, schoolhouse, and chapel, which assert human need in the face of broader inhospitable forces, is a particularly Puerto Rican form of protest.[2] Protestors had ferried lumber, sheets of corrugated zinc, ladders, and other construction material out here on small fishing boats. Men were hammering the roof on the four-hundred-square-foot schoolhouse. The design was that of a simple wooden *casita*, built on stilts with a zinc roof and a front porch. Banners proclaiming "No to Militarism: Navy out of Vieques" were pegged on the front of this work in progress.

The chapel was a smaller, open structure. A Puerto Rican flag and a white flag of peace flew on either side of a huge cross on its roof. The chapel sat in line with the docking point of amphibious tanks on the shore. To one side of it there was a circle of stones and a cross erected during a recent ecumenical service. On the other side there were rows of palm saplings planted on this denuded land. Activists hoped to create both centers for activities and living symbols of peace and humanity on the target range.

These construction projects echoed the work of the demonstrators in Culebra who in the 1970s had built a schoolhouse and chapel on Flamenco Beach, then the navy's target range. Indeed, the history of Vieques seems inexorably linked to that of Culebra. As we have seen, in the seventies a fiery direct action movement championed by the PIP succeeded in evicting the navy from Culebra, only to have the military intensify its activities in Vieques. Although the PIP was at the forefront of the Culebra effort—some say the PIP directed the movement there—the party was noticeably absent in Vieques in the late seventies. Rubén Berríos, the president of the PIP, was jailed for his role in leading the civil disobedience campaign, yet he never showed up in Vieques as activists struggled against the navy in 1978. His absence was at least in part due to PSP involvement in the antinavy struggle in Vieques. Although fractious political infighting is the norm in Puerto Rico, it is perhaps a sign of unity at this juncture that Berríos, now a Puerto Rican senator and still head of the PIP, was in Vieques on this day. We loaded our backpacks with water, ate cheese sandwiches and apples from one of the coolers we carried in the boat, and headed toward the PIP camp and Monte David in the inner range.

We followed the roads normally traveled only by military vehicles into the heart of the bombing range. The scrub had grown back after a four-month hiatus from bombing, but the land was hot and silent. There were no birds; we saw few insects. Decades of bombing had blown away the topsoil. All over the dusty land were craters and shell casings. We passed a stark sandy field spotted with puddles, all that remained of a mangrove swamp, the cradle of marine life. Bombs stuck out of the hills like needles from a cactus. A plane, pulverized by weapons fire, sat in an empty field. The navy often emphasizes how small the impact zone is, only 3 percent of its landholdings in Vieques, but the 980 acres constituted an area larger than New York's Central Park. We felt the size of the area as we traipsed across land with little vegetation and no respite from the intensity of the tropical sun.

Finally we saw the PIP camp emerge like a mirage in the distance. Berríos had set up camp on the inner shores of the impact zone. Tents and the green-and-white flags of the independence party were staked between the checkered target boards the navy used for firing practice. The *pípiolos* had scraped together enough sea grass to scrawl large graffitio across the beach: Fuera Marina Vieques PIP (Navy out of Vieques, PIP). The encampment was extremely orderly, with long rectangular tents and tables and chairs set up along the beach. They had brought in a generator, computers, and fax machines. A yacht was anchored off shore. About fifteen people milled about. Berríos himself came out to greet us, looking like he had stepped off of a golf course. His white beard was carefully trimmed; he wore a dapper white hat and black sunglasses, a crisp, white polo shirt with its collar turned upward, and plaid bermuda shorts. One would never guess from his appearance that he had been camped out here for over one hundred days. Whatever Berríos's political objectives were in coming to Vieques, and whatever skepticism existed when he first arrived, he had earned widespread respect among activists and Viequenses in general for his endurance. He welcomed us, shook our hands, and chatted with us for fifteen minutes or so.

The *pípiolos* pointed us on the path to our ultimate destination, Monte David. To avoid stepping on live ordnance, we walked along the edges of the shore. The shimmering sea offered psychological relief from the heat, but the waters were littered with bombs, which we could see clearly beneath the surface. We stuck close to the path. One of the Lajas activists had a video camera and filmed missiles, unexploded bombs, the shells of abandoned tanks. The teenagers were cavalier, collecting handfuls of bullets, posing for photos in front of bombs. We came to a barren field, roped off with yellow tape. There, in the midst of twisted metal and scorched earth, waved a solitary Puerto Rican flag. We had reached the foot of Monte David.

The encampment at Monte David could only be described as a stunning act of defiance. The hill was the bull's eye of the impact zone, and on its summit sat a little wooden *casita* emblazoned with a Puerto Rican flag. Next to the *casita* sat a charred tank, covered with flags. The *casita* evoked Puerto Rican rural traditions. It was probably no more than 150 square feet, built of plywood with a corrugated metal roof. Yet its construction here on this hill in the heart of the bombing range, directly opposite the observation post, was a brazen act. The hill was aflutter with Puerto Rican flags, white flags of peace, and raised highest on a burned-out tank, the blue-and-white flag of Vieques, bleached by the sun and tattered by the wind. A large white cross leaned against the tank, and a series of little white crosses formed a fence around the perimeter of the hill. We carefully climbed a narrow path littered with live ordnance toward the summit, watching every footstep. We met a horse on the path halfway up and could only speculate how it got there.

The Monte David encampment was in many ways the heart and soul of the movement. The image of this humble *casita*, flanked by a battered tank in the middle of a no-man's land of missiles and muddy craters, had inspired an outpouring of songs, photographs, and paintings by Puerto Rican artists. Monte David was the destination of every visiting supporter, including celebrities such as Jesse Jackson, who vowed to camp here himself if the demonstrators were evicted.[3]

The camp was a collective effort. Puerto Rican activists from Utuado helped build the *casita*, and supporters from Adjuntas equipped it with solar panels, so there was light. The various flags on the tank were from different Puerto Rican municipalities, left by visitors as a sign of their solidarity. Like the other encampments, Monte David received cash infusions from a solidarity network organized by the Committee. But the daily maintenance of Monte David was the work of the Zenón family: Carlos Zenón, the sixty-two-year-old fisherman renowned for leading the fishermen's campaign against the navy in the late seventies; his wife, Leidi, a longtime activist in her own right; and their sons, Carlos, Cacimar, and Yaureibo, university students. The Zenóns took turns sleeping in the camp. They strung a hammock from the barrel of the tank and took in the night air on that desolate hill. Doña Leidi maintained a calendar back home in Montesanto that outlined the schedule of who would be staying at Monte David. On this day there were about half a dozen people at the camp when we arrived, including don Carlos and one of his sons.

Don Carlos greeted us and gave us a tour. He is a slight man with bronze, leathery skin, and he wore an old baseball jersey and cap and faded blue jeans. His gritty appearance contrasted with the more polished image of Berríos down the hill; so too did the two camps differ. Although both were in the bombing range, the PIP camp sat by the beach with rows of chairs, fax machines, and access to a yacht; Monte David planted itself in the marked desolation of the impact range. Rather than anchoring itself in party politics and the status question, Monte David resonated on the cultural level. The working symbol at Monte David was the *casita*. Zenón himself is a fisherman, an occupation imbued with great cultural nostalgia and, like the *casita*, links to Puerto Rican rural traditions.

The hilltop surveyed an apocalyptic scene of destruction, a lagoon decimated by bombing. Don Carlos's father fished here in the 1930s, he told us; now the lagoon was little more than a pitted stew of miry water. Don Carlos became quite animated as he described how the grass had grown back in the four months he had been here. He showed us his collection of ordnance. His time in the U.S. Army had enabled him to distinguish various types of bombs and grenades and determine which were live and which were inert. He plucked a blue orb from a pile at his feet and demonstrated how to throw a grenade. Don Carlos's greatest find, however, was not this colorful pile of bombs but an abandoned military truck he and his sons recovered and, with Viequense mechanical ingenuity, resurrected. The Zenóns stuck a Puerto Rican flag in this black rusty vehicle and now had convenient transportation within the bombing zone.

What linked the defiant, confrontational character of Monte David to the more moderate and often ambivalent sentiment of the wider community of Vieques were the white crosses that lined the summit, framing the view of the desolate lagoon and Atlantic Coast. The crosses were in many ways central to the encampment, key symbols that enabled activists to translate their message to a diverse audience. Although the crosses came to signal to an international audience the involvement of the religious sector and the legitimacy this lent to the movement, they also had more locally based meanings attached to them.

The first cross had been erected in honor of David Sanes at the founding of the camp. Activists then decided to put up crosses to symbolize the lives of everyone in Vieques who had died as a result of the military presence, such as Julián Felipe Francis, the elderly bartender murdered by drunken sailors in the fifties, and Angel Rodríguez Cristóbal, the independence activist killed in federal prison in Tallahassee after he was arrested for trespassing on a navy beach in the seventies. But the crosses on Monte David took hold of the Viequense consciousness once activists forged links between this religious symbol and the widespread fears about rising cancer rates on the island. Activists decided to include crosses for all Viequenses who have died of cancer, poisoned, people here believe, by air, land, and water contaminated by bombing. The line of crosses grew, and Viequenses started to make pilgrimages to erect crosses for their own loved ones who had died of cancer. The line of white crosses stood silently on this hill at the center of the U.S. bombing range.

We left Monte David to return to the teachers' camp to swim and eat a festive meal of *arepas* and fried fish served on the beach. A heavy-set, unassuming Viequense woman in her sixties took a position of authority in the kneading of *arepas* dough. The teenage girls among our group were suddenly transformed from carefree children into adult women, working and pinching balls of dough in their hands. With plates of fish and *arepas* dished out from the little makeshift stove, the teachers' camp was converted into a large kitchen on the beach. We ate our fill; there was enough food for ten more people. Several women rinsed the pots and pans in the foamy surf.

Food has been a central part of the movement, and indeed, as Nancy Morris (1995) notes, a key element of Puerto Rican cultural identity. Like the *casita* and the schoolhouse, the kitchen and meals of rice and beans, fried fish and *arepas*, have been a way of forging ties to Puerto Rican cultural traditions and redefining the use of land from bombing and maneuvers to nurturing and sustaining life. Significant energy was devoted to the planning and preparation of meals, shuttling coolers of food and water back and forth to sustain demonstrators and feed visitors. Two women in particular worked in the kitchen on a regular basis, preparing home-cooked meals that became an institutionalized part of the movement.

This focus on food, though, drew attention to one irony of the encampments: women were out on the frontline of the struggle and yet they were still in the kitchen. Like Florence Nightingale on the battlefields nursing the warriors, the women here were supporting, sustaining, and tending to the men. This work was crucial to the maintenance of the campsite. Indeed, it was the resolve of two women activists to support and continue de Jesus's individual act of defiance that led to the founding of the first encampment. Now Leidi Zenón organized the schedule of personnel at Monte David. Julia Ramos planned the rotation of staff at the Hostosiano camp and organized and distributed the food. It was Carlos Zenón, however, who was interviewed by the press, who traveled to Okinawa on a speaking tour. It was Mario Martínez who lectured the visitors from Lajas on the history of the military presence in Vieques while Ramos distributed sandwiches. Rubén Berríos appeared on nightly newscasts. Many writers have noted that while women take political action and perform important political roles, the nature of their participation is often different from that of men (Bookman and Morgen 1988; Kaplan 1982; Susser 1982, 1992). Here we see the way in which their participation was filtered into the organizational and "domestic" chores, while men were in the spotlight. In this sense, the current movement seemed much like the mobilization of the seventies.

The encampments on the bombing range continued to spread in subsequent months. In November 1999 an ecumenical coalition of Methodists, Baptists, Presbyterians, and evangelical Protestants set up a camp they called the Christian Camp in Evangelical Obedience. In February the Catholic diocese of Caguas, Puerto Rico, set up a camp with the blessings of its bishop, Alvaro Corrado del Río, and christened it with a mass celebrated by the local priest. Students from the University of Puerto Rico set up an encampment called Friends of Vieques. By the time federal authorities removed demonstrators from the range in May 2000, there were between eleven and fourteen camps.

Writers have noted a frequent tendency to portray social movements as monolithic (Burdick 1992; Edelman 1999), but the physical manifestation of this movement in a variety of different camps reveals its diverse membership and interests. The Campamento Hostosiano and PIP were avowedly *independentista* in orientation, and supported the movement in Vieques as part of a broader anticolonial effort. Monte David, the work of longtime antinavy activists from Vieques, signaled the local working-class roots of the movement, and the historical depth of the conflict. The church camps were newcomers to the Vieques cause and supported the movement as one founded on respect for basic human rights and as a struggle for peace and social justice.

Cultural Framing of Protest

Vieques's revitalized movement of 1999 had a much broader base than the mobilization of the 1970s, with a symbolic framework broader in scope. Although the fishermen had succeeded in unifying the populace in the 1970s, they at the same time narrowly focused their movement on claims of livelihood and local grievances that may have inhibited the expansion of the struggle. The white crosses that spread across the hill of Monte David signaled a reformulation of the case.

The crosses fused two key themes of the movement. First, they identified the struggle as one of life and health. This was the crux of the movement slogan, *Ni una bomba más* (not one more bomb). The crosses, by memorializing the martyrdom of a Viequense at the hands of the navy, demonstrated people's worries about accidents and contamination by bombing. When the crosses' symbolism was expanded to represent those Viequenses who had died of cancer, they drew attention to the health effects of the military presence and Viequenses' feelings of victimization by the navy. The cross, the Christian symbol of martyrdom, merged the tragic death of David Sanes with the plight of Viequenses who had died of cancer.

Second, the crosses expanded the significance of the movement from one based predominantly on local claims to one with a broader message of pacifism and human rights. This was the basis of the movement's other main slogan: Paz para Vieques (Peace for Vieques). The crosses allowed activists to signal that the struggle in Vieques was about peace, about resisting military use and destruction of land, because Viequenses were a peaceful people who wanted to live without conflict. While the fishermen had emphasized the local and material, the crosses provided a framework with transcendent and universalistic claims. This framework proved crucial in dispelling navy allegations that Vieques was just another "not in my backyard" movement.

Like Vieques's fishermen-led movement of the seventies, which carefully crafted a symbolic framework to communicate a controversial message, the movement of the late nineties fused its defiant tactics with a message of pacifism and religious devotion. The play of religious symbols became a key feature of the new movement. Activists staked white crosses in the bombing range, in front of the gates of Camp García, and carried them in marches and pickets. The emphasis on martyrdom and sacrifice, on the *rescatores* blocking bombs with their bodies, drew on the same kind of David and Goliath imagery as the fishermen's battle. The cross, however, in unanticipated and important ways, created the framework for the growth of the new movement and opened the terrain for the emergence of new actors.

Because Vieques Is Our Home: Women's Changing Participation in Protest

Researchers have noted that women's participation in protest frequently centers on community issues such as health, education, food, and the environment. Temma Kaplan (1982) has argued that women's responsibility for "social reproduction," those conditions necessary for the reproduction and sustenance of life, nurtures a particular "female consciousness" that can spur them to political action.

In Vieques's long struggle with the navy, women have played an integral role in organizing and demonstrating against the military. In the 1970s women formed a crucial presence in pickets, served meals that sustained demonstrators, and helped write pamphlets and organize demonstrations. The focus on fishermen's claims, however, shaped a framework that defined the leadership as male. In the 1990s, by explicitly defining the struggle in terms of social reproduction as opposed to livelihood, activists opened the door for the greater involvement and leadership of women. Women continued to play the important but auxiliary roles that they had in the past, but the Vieques Women's Alliance (Alianza de Mujeres de Vieques) gave them a new voice and stronger presence that proved crucial to the struggle's continuity.

The Birth of the Vieques Women's Alliance

The chain-link fence of Camp García has long stood as a stark symbol of the military presence in Vieques, cutting across the hills, demarcating a vast, empty swath of military-controlled land. On this day the fence looked more like a clothesline. To each honeycomb of wire was tied a small white ribbon, a petition for peace and an end to the bombing. There were so many ribbons the fence appeared as a tattered white sheet, dancing in the wind. The white-ribbon campaign was a project of the newly formed Vieques Women's Alliance. It was an outgrowth of the group's first public action: a demonstration in front of the gates of Camp García in June 1999.

"The navy said it would resume bombing in June," explained Dora Vargas, one of the founders of the Women's Alliance. "We called for a caravan—over a hundred cars came." The caravan traveled all over the island before stopping in front of the camp gates. The protestors, mostly women and children, blocked traffic and banged on pots and pans. They sang antinavy songs and attached white ribbons to the fence. Vargas announced that the group would continue to attach white ribbons to the fence until it was completely covered, as a testament to Viequenses' desire for peace. "It was a great success," she said. "We were newly formed and didn't expect that many people would come. We saw that we had the power to convoke a meeting and involve people who would never have participated in the struggle before." The response was so great that the Women's Alliance started distributing white ribbons and encouraging supporters to wear them as a symbol that "Vieques wants peace."

The women's campaign emerged on Vieques's political landscape a month after the death of David Sanes. Two local women, Dora Vargas, a home economist at the agricultural extension in her early thirties, and Amelia Mulero, a forty-two-year-old social worker, decided to found a group that would support the burgeoning movement and provide a space for women to articulate their concerns. Both Vargas and Mulero worked with women in Vieques at the grassroots level and were concerned that their voices and experiences were not being represented in the antinavy movement. They wanted to both support the movement and project a "women's" perspective: "The men tend to emphasize the economic and political aspects [of the military presence]. We [emphasize] the emotional and psychological aspects. How we are affected on an individual level as wives and as mothers trying to raise families. It's a more sentimental, emotional approach," Vargas explained. Mulero remarked that her own work in the community had demonstrated to her the profound emotional damage the military had inflicted upon children and adults. She described the pictures children drew of navy boats and fighter jets over images of Vieques dripping with blood. Mulero and Vargas wanted both to create a forum in which women could express how the military presence affected them on an individual level, as wives and mothers trying to raise families on Vieques, and to mobilize women from that shared experience. They organized a meeting one evening in mid-May. Twenty-five women attended.

"The women were interested in expressing themselves and were looking for an opportunity to speak," remembered Mulero. Although Mulero and Vargas were able to reach new sectors of populace, they also drew together a number of veteran women activists in a specifically female forum. Some of these women were the wives of leading male activists and had participated in rallies and pickets, written letters, helped produce leaflets, boarded visitors in their homes, and provided demonstrators with food and drink, but had never risen to positions of leadership in the movement themselves. The overriding concern the women expressed was cancer and the menace it represented to their children and families. Mulero and Vargas's grassroots work in the community and knowledge of the sensibilities of Vieques women helped them craft a framework for mobilizing the women. "We presented to them that just as we want our homes clean and safe to raise our children, so we want Vieques. We, the women, have to be concerned because this is our home and we have to take care of it. Obviously, the navy has to go since they are causing damage."

The success of the framework was demonstrated at the group's first demonstration in June; over one hundred women participated. The idea of situating protest within the context of the defense of the domestic resonated with Viequense women. Yet as much as Mulero and Vargas struggled to find appropriate symbols and rhetoric to connect to the women, they also consciously manipulated symbols and maintained a somewhat ironic perspective on their import. Despite the initial meeting in which women expressed concern about issues of cancer and health, Mulero and Vargas elected to emphasize women's concerns for peace in their rhetoric and imagery. It was harder to prove that the navy caused cancer on the island, Mulero explained, while peace was a universally recognized basic human right. The white-ribbon campaign reflected this strategy, and emerged as one of the group's most successful contributions to the antinavy movement.

"Everyone *loves* the ribbons," noted Norma Jiménez, a thirty-nine-year-old elementary schoolteacher and one of the spokespersons for the Alliance. There was sarcasm in her voice, and she shrugged her shoulders and rolled her eyes for emphasis. "We in Puerto Rico operate on symbols," she explained. "On the surface, the white ribbon seems innocent, feminine, and nice. It's appealing. Everyone says, 'Give me a ribbon. I'll wear that.' But the more people see the ribbons, the more they think of Vieques. It raises consciousness."

The imagery of pretty white ribbons, of women as the defenders of the domestic, as emotional, sentimental protectors of peace seemed to emanate from conservative, even essentialist notions of women's roles and potential. Indeed, the Women's Alliance rejected any association with feminism, emphasizing instead the therapeutic aspects of the group. The awareness that these activists demonstrated of the conservatism of their rhetoric and symbols suggested that their strategies were more tactical than ideological in motivation. Paradoxically, the group's organization and symbolic framework allowed room for the expression of fiery sentiment and provided space for the emergence of women's leadership in a way the Committee, with male and female membership, did not.

While the Alliance's rhetoric, on the surface, seemed conservative, celebrating women's links to the domestic, it tapped into the reservoir of passion and attachment that many Viequenses feel for the island. When Jiménez traveled to San Juan to speak at a conference at the Metropolitan University, she breathed passion into the group's motto. She spoke with anger about the legacy of the military occupation of the island, how women in the fifties and sixties were confined to their homes by the presence of drunken sailors on the street. "How would you like to be pushed into the corner of your house and told that this is your house?" she raged. "This house is mine! I will defend it!" she exclaimed to a rousing ovation. The rhetoric of women as guardians of the home and keepers of children sparked the same kind of emotion that gave strength, courage, and a sense of legitimacy to the fishermen of the 1970s.

Vargas noted that the Alliance's work was difficult. Women were often fearful to become involved because they thought they might lose their food stamps or jeopardize their own or their husband's work. She recounted one story about a woman who was thrown out of the house by her father for wearing a white ribbon. But Vargas was heartened by the transformation of a number of women who told her earlier that they would never get involved in protest. On July 4, 1999, the Women's Alliance sent a contingent to demonstrate in front of the gates of Roosevelt Roads in Puerto Rico."The reality is that they are at the front lines," Vargas commented. "I feel so happy. Women who told me they didn't want to get involved are picketing in front of the base at Ceiba. They say, 'I'm raising my child in Vieques, so all of this affects me.' Now they say they are going to the target range, that they are prepared to be arrested. (Laughing) I have created a monster!"

Not only were women on the front lines, but the Alliance gave them room to ascend the ranks. Ana Rosaldo is a fifty-nine-year-old retired schoolteacher who is active in the Alliance. She has long participated in the movement to evict the navy, but admitted that in past the role she played was largely supportive. She cooked for demonstrations. She took care of the leading activist Mario Martínez's children. But now she was in the limelight. In February 2000 Rosaldo traveled to Washington to take part in a Capitol Hill press conference followed by a noisy demonstration outside of the White House. In March she traveled to Springfield, Massachusetts, to meet with a support group and promote solidarity for Vieques's struggle for peace. In May, during the arrests, she was in the office of Vermont senator Patrick Leahy in an effort to promote links with a senator who had "played a role in fighting for world peace." She had speaking engagements at Dartmouth College, public forums in Burlington and Montpelier, Vermont.

The Alliance's focus on the personal and emotional consequences of the military presence translated into a speaking style much more engaging than that of a number of leading male activists. While the men frequently chronicled the history of the navy's abuse or gave statistics about cancer rates, Rosaldo riveted crowds with stories from her childhood. She recalled her mother sleeping at night with a machete under her pillow to defend her family in case carousing sailors broke into the house. Rosaldo carried with her photos of a little girl who was dying of brain cancer to dramatize islanders' concerns about rising cancer rates. She clutched a tissue when she spoke, her voice breaking with emotion.

In this way Rosaldo demonstrated the Alliance's emphasis on the personal, individual story, the struggle women faced to raise their children on the island and the health risks the navy caused. She also attracted a great deal of media attention because her stories translated well into sound bites and feature articles. Her photo appeared on the front page of regional newspapers and she was quoted extensively by the press. So while "defending her house" Rosaldo traveled far from home to advance the cause, away from the kitchen and into the limelight.

The work of the Alliance rippled throughout the varying groups that made up Vieques's movement. Although the ribbon campaign was well received, Vargas noted that a number of men had problems with women's leadership. Still the Alliance forced other groups, like the Committee to Rescue and Develop Vieques, to focus on the role of women within the movement. The Committee started shifting public attention away from leading male activists, like Dr. Rivera, to emphasize the voice of Julia Ramos in press conferences and press releases. It also began to highlight women's leadership in various demonstrations and activities. Women had previously often formed a slight majority in pickets and demonstrations, but now the Alliance gave them greater voice.

One of the most significant, if unplanned, contributions of the Alliance was developing a presence at the gates to Camp García. With its pot and pan protest and ribbon campaign at the entrance to the base, the Alliance effectively opened another front of the battle and broadened Vieques's struggle. "Not everyone can be so macho, not everyone can be out at the bombing range," Vargas noted. The leadership at the bold, confrontational encampments on the bombing range was almost entirely male. In the same way, the highly confrontational Fishermen's War was also male. The Alliance focused attention on another space where protest could develop, a site that was more accessible to a broader range of people.

This presence was institutionalized in December 1999 when demonstrators locked the gates to Camp García and planted themselves squarely in front of them. They built an encampment they christened the Peace and Justice Camp. The camp "became like the center of town for those of us who couldn't be on the bombing range," reflected Zoraída López. Many elderly people, who could not handle the arduous journey and terrain on the bombing range, took up regular positions at the gates. Women with small children, residents who could not leave their jobs or family passed through the encampment. Significantly, the Catholic church shared with the Alliance a common vision of Vieques's movement as a grassroots struggle for peace. The church moved pews in front of the gates and started holding Saturday night prayer vigils there. Activists rented a house across the street and tapped into electric and water lines to maintain the camp.

After protestors were evicted from the bombing range in May 2000 and the Peace and Justice Camp was dismantled by the navy, protest simply shifted across the street from Camp García. The house that had provided electricity and water became the command center, with computers, phone lines, and fax machines broadcasting Vieques's struggle to the world. New structures were erected, banners strung from fences, tents staked on the hill. The prayer vigils, the meals of rice and beans, the domino games, the music and pickets continued in the face of a wall of riot police. The Peace and Justice Camp allowed Vieques's movement to continue even after protestors lost the encampments that had focused and defined the movement for over a year.

The Peace and Justice encampment was not specifically the project of the Women's Alliance, although its members participated in activities and prayer vigils held outside the gates to Camp García. Rather, the camp demonstrated the way in which the work of the Alliance contributed to the expansion and continuity of Vieques's struggle.

The Church

"There is not a bomb sufficiently small to be morally acceptable," writes Alvaro Corrado del Río, Catholic bishop of Caguas, Puerto Rico. One of the most striking transformations of Vieques's struggle has been the active participation and crucial leadership of major religious institutions. Although in the past individual clergymen, like Catholic bishop Antulio Parrilla in the 1970s and Methodist minister John Vincent in the 1960s, supported Vieques's cause, the institutional presence of the church was notably absent on the level of both Vieques and Puerto Rico. Although the American Friends Service Committee played an important role in Culebra and Vieques, especially through the Puerto Rican office of the Caribbean Justice and Peace Project (Proyecto Caribeño de Justicia y Paz), this did not represent the position of the mainstream religious establishment. In the seventies, García Martínez (1978) noted the overwhelming conservatism of both the Catholic and the Protestant churches in Puerto Rico, and their lack of involvement in social struggles. This situation changed fundamentally in 1999.

From the earliest days of the late nineties movement, mainstream religious institutions supported Vieques's cause as a struggle against militarism, war, and violence. Bishop Alvaro Corrado del Río, in whose diocese Vieques falls, traveled there to officiate at David Sanes's funeral mass, signaling concern for the case at the very highest level of the Catholic church in Puerto Rico. Corrado called for the immediate exit of the navy, the liberation of Puerto Rico from U.S. military domination, and the practice of civil disobedience to stop the bombing.[4] He was backed by the archbishop of San Juan, Roberto González Nieves, who traveled to New York preaching the cause of peace and justice for Vieques.

Navy efforts to gain support from Protestant religious establishments failed. In the early weeks of the movement, the Methodist bishop of Puerto Rico, Juan Vera Méndez, denounced the navy for pressuring its religious chaplains to serve as intermediaries and encourage protestors to abandon their campsite at Monte David. According to Vera, the navy asked its military chaplains in Puerto Rico and the United States to contact various clergy in Vieques and ask them to assist the navy. The bishop was outraged. "The navy has taken audacious and censurable measures," he exclaimed. "We will not permit the Army or Navy of the United States to use chaplains to silence the outcry of a people demanding an end to war."[5]

The Methodist church soon joined with other Protestant denominations to form the Pro-Vieques Ecumenical Coalition (La Coalición Ecuménica por Vieques), which coordinated religious activities and support for the Vieques movement. Although Protestant and Catholic activities tended to be separate—

for instance, the Catholic church and the Ecumenical Coalition sponsored separate encampments on the bombing range—the Methodist and Catholic bishops joined together to travel to Washington and meet with President Clinton, demanding the navy's immediate exit.

The religious sector provided sustenance and support to the movement on a grassroots level. Local ministers and priests attended conferences, pickets, marches, leading attendees in prayer for the peace of Vieques. The Catholic church celebrated mass at the Peace and Justice encampment and held nightly prayer vigils in the church pews before the gates to Camp García. The churches sent dozens of clergy and laypeople to fill the encampments on the bombing range, offering people in Vieques, in the words of one Carmelite nun, "a space to breathe." The nun explained, "They feel understood and supported. As a result they feel more interior peace in the middle of so much struggle. When you feel accompanied, although you have so many problems, you experience new strength and peace."[6]

The moral support and ideological influence of the religious actors played an important role in defining and directing the struggle. The religious sector strengthened the movement's commitment to nonviolence. It did this not only through sermons and prayers but through training programs in civil disobedience. All of the participants in the Catholic camp on the bombing range, for example, received training in nonviolence and relevant church catechism. The emphasis on nonviolence became increasingly important when the governor called in the Puerto Rican riot squad to defend the base. Conditions were volatile, and the police were quick to pepper spray demonstrators. "If weren't for the church," declared one activist, "there would be blood in the street. Thanks to the church things haven't turned ugly."

The solid backing of the religious sector gave Vieques's struggle a new legitimacy and moral authority. Church involvement helped change the cold war framework that depicted opposition to the naval installation in Vieques as anti-American or communist-inspired. With priests and ministers in congregations throughout Vieques and Puerto Rico celebrating Vieques's work for peace, the movement expanded. Conservative denominations, such as the Baptist church in Vieques, spoke out against "sinful" naval bombing exercises. Individuals who had never felt comfortable participating in pickets or demonstrations joined prayer vigils for peace.

One of the most striking indications of changing sentiment was seen in the federal court. The federal court in Puerto Rico has long been a bastion of zealous support for Puerto Rican statehood and the U.S. military. Thus it was unprecedented when U.S. district judge Carmen Consuelo Vargas de Cerezo refused to preside over the trial of PIP president Rubén Berríos, who was arrested for trespassing on the bombing range. Judge Vargas de Cerezo used strikingly religious language to express her support for Vieques's struggle: "Vieques is a silent prayer for peace and renewal before the Holy Sacrament," she wrote. "So it has been, will be, and will continue to be. The undersigned recuses herself from any participation in this case."[7] Although the judge's faith-based withdrawal from the case did not typify the attitude of the court in general, it did suggest the way religious ideology penetrated civil society.

That the involvement of the church was a crucial factor in explaining the unity and continuity of the movement became clear in late winter 2000, when Puerto Rican governor Pedro Rosselló reached an agreement with the White House that would allow the resumption of naval training exercises on the island. Despite forceful earlier declarations that "not one more bomb" would fall on Vieques Island, Rosselló capitulated and signed an agreement that allowed limited bombing in exchange for a referendum. The referendum would allow residents to vote in a year on whether they wanted continued bombing indefinitely or limited further bombing for three years. The plan included a cash incentive. Vieques would immediately receive a $40 million aid package and would receive an additional $50 million if residents voted to let the navy stay. The Clinton-Rosselló pact broke the rare consensus among Puerto Rican political parties that bombing must end in Vieques. It had the potential to fracture and derail the movement, much in the way Romero's 1983 accord with the navy diffused protest.

The religious sector roundly rejected the agreement. Leaders were upset that the pact did not include an option to immediately halt all bombing, and that the navy would be allowed to resume bombing exercises in the months before the referendum. They denounced the cash incentives as immoral. Religious leaders called on all Puerto Ricans to march in a parade that would publicly reject the Clinton-Rosselló agreement. The governor was furious.

In face of angry denunciations by the governor, religious leaders organized the largest mass mobilization in Puerto Rican history. On February 21, 2000, thousands of demonstrators marched silently down the streets of San Juan carrying Puerto Rican flags and portraits of Jesus, calling for peace for Vieques. Commonwealth police superintendent Pedro Toledo called the march the largest demonstration in Puerto Rican history and estimated the crowd at 85,000. San Juan municipal police officials estimated the turnout to be 150,000.[8] "We are showing the consensus in Puerto Rico's heart in favor of peace and justice," declared San Juan archbishop González. "It's a signal of hope and confidence."[9]

Conclusion

At dawn on May 4, 2000, heavily armed federal agents arrived by helicopter to remove hundreds of protestors from the bombing range. Local community leaders, artists, elected officials from Puerto Rico and the United States (including two members of the U.S. House of Representatives), church leaders, the heads of the Puerto Rican Independence Party, and ordinary citizens were cuffed with plastic bands and hauled off the range in trucks. To pave the way for bombing, federal marshals cleared chapels, *casitas,* tents, kitchens, church pews, and pots and pans from the range. The arrests put an end to a sit-down strike that had extended for over a year. Over two hundred people were arrested in Vieques that morning.

The dismantling of the civil disobedience camps ended months of speculation over whether violence might erupt if the navy moved forcibly against demonstrators. Instead, protestors sang religious hymns as they were carried away. Demonstrators' peaceful retreat from the range, however, did not signal their surrender. In the following months, protestors continued to defy military authority and cross military borders. On one day, a handful of protestors would scale a fence; on another dozens would arrive by fishing boat and march across the range. Political celebrities such as Robert Kennedy, Jr., and the Reverend Al Sharpton traveled to Vieques to support these acts of civil disobedience. They were arrested and jailed for trespassing on military property.

In the aftermath of the May arrests tensions heightened between residents and the navy. A wall of Puerto Rican riot police, clubs in hand, walled the entrance to Camp García. This show of force was one manifestation of Governor Rosselló's controversial "resolution" to the Vieques conflict. Rather than bringing an end to tensions, however, the Rosselló-Clinton accord only intensified the discord.

With the encampments on the bombing range destroyed, only two camps remained on Vieques, and they faced each other at Camp García. One, the Peace and Justice Camp, sat on a hillside under the shade of mango trees across the street from the base. The other, a police encampment at Camp García, defended the entrance to the base. The Peace and Justice encampment was really a festive shantytown, sprouted around a small rental house, festooned with white flags and banners, always pulsing with music and chanting. Camp García was a sober wall of force. Twelve police cordoned the gates to the base; another twelve sat to the rear in reserve. The officers looked perpetually bored. They plugged the holes of the chain-link fence with empty water bottles while they baked in the tropical sun.

"I'm worried about what will happen," admitted Janice Pabón, a local clergy member. Doña Janice had been very active in the mobilization, speaking out against the military presence from her pulpit. She was arrested that May morning when the navy dismantled the camps. "The people are really angry, really indignant. The riot squad barricade provokes them. The police are tired, they have an attitude. This bothers the people. Someone threw bottles at the navy. This dynamic could become violent. Not everyone has the capacity to be tolerant. Not everyone has training in pacifism. I'm worried about maintaining the passive resistance."

Several days earlier the navy had resumed bombing the island. According to the terms of the Rosselló-Clinton agreement, these were dummy bombs, containing no explosives, only inert materials. Residents would have a chance to vote later to determine whether they wanted live-fire exercises to continue. Few people in Vieques, if any, were satisfied by this agreement.

"I'll never forget the bombing," said doña Janice, with tears in her eyes. "I'll never forget it," she continued.

> When they bombed several weeks back, I was in my house alone. And I heard it because I'm on that little hill near the fort. I started to hear it. I felt that they were violating my right to live in peace. And that they were damaging me. It was as if they were hitting me directly. It was as if they were saying, "You don't matter at all." Simply as if it didn't matter what we were saying. If they wanted to bomb here, they would bomb here. This was the attitude of the navy: that it doesn't matter if the people die, if they suffer, that the people here want human rights. This always bothers me because the United States is a country that talks about human rights. One of the most important concerns in the United States is the violation of human rights. It's a contradiction.

Clashes increasingly occurred between residents and the riot squad. There were reports of rock-throwing skirmishes between adolescent boys and police who were stationed at a perimeter fence in a residential neighborhood. Riot police were quick to use pepper spray and tear gas to disperse any movement or activity they perceived as threatening.

Yet what centered the movement and allowed it to continue was a widespread commitment to nonviolence. The focus on peace and civil disobedience transformed the current mobilization from the charged and volatile mobilization of the seventies. When leading activist Samuel Rivera was jumped and beaten by a group of riot police, he publicly announced his commitment to pacifism. When demonstrators were pepper sprayed and tear gassed by the riot squad, activists took bullhorns and reminded people to stay calm. Even Lolita Lebrun, the Nationalist Party member who had been jailed for twenty-five years for opening fire on Congress, was on the front lines of Vieques's struggle, pronouncing her new commitment to nonviolent resistance. Nonviolence sustained the movement. "Without a doubt, peace is the worst enemy of the navy and the entire military apparatus," noted Archbishop Corrado del Río. "The natural strategy of the navy is to provoke violence, and in this manner annul our moral superiority."[10] Protestors remained focused on the struggle as one of human rights, peace, and human dignity.

The resilience of protestors and their refusal to accept the terms of the Rosselló-Clinton agreement shifted the political terrain in Vieques, Puerto Rico, and the United States as a whole. In the Puerto Rican general elections, the *populares* unseated the governing PNP to take control of the governor's seat and the residential commissioner's post in Washington. The victors, Sila Calderón and Anibal Acevedo Vila, supported the immediate and permanent cessation of all military activities on Vieques in their campaigns, while the losing candidates declared the situation resolved. In Vieques, *popular* Damaso Serrano soundly defeated his PNP rival, marking the first victory in Vieques by a mayoral candidate who openly campaigned for the navy's departure.

In the United States, New York's Republican governor George Pataki surprisingly emerged as Vieques's champion, traveling to the island to back its struggle. While his Democratic opponents derided him for pandering to the state's substantial Hispanic vote, Pataki's visit to Vieques suggested that the political fortunes of this once seemingly remote Caribbean island were now of central importance to politics in the metropolis. Vieques had moved from margin to center.

Seven

The Battle of Vieques

In June 2001, over a year after federal marshals evicted protestors from the Vieques bombing range, U.S. president George W. Bush announced his plan to halt all military exercises on Vieques Island in 2003. His decision appeared to reverse the navy's long-running insistence that Vieques was the irreplaceable "crown jewel" of military weapons testing and battle simulation. After decades of conflict and more than two years of sustained protest, the decision appeared to be a victory for opponents of the base. Presidential political advisors were concerned that continued protest and arrests on the island were costing the president crucial political support from Latinos in the United States. Bush yielded to mounting pressure, while offering a timeline that allowed the navy to continue to use the range as it searched for an alternate training location.[1] Bush's plan, however, seemed to please no one.

Conservative legislators denounced the plan as a politically motivated decision that jeopardized the training of troops and national security. They predicted that bowing to pressure in Vieques would have a domino effect, leading to the closure of other military facilities, such as those on the Japanese island of Okinawa. Critics of the navy, however, insisted that the exit was not soon enough. The Bush plan, they argued, offered no more than the unpopular resolution already reached by Governor Rosselló and President Clinton, allowing for continued bombing until a referendum was held to offer Vieques residents the end of bombing in 2003 or continued bombing with an economic aid package.[2] After the Catholic diocese of Caguas, Puerto Rico, conducted its own survey in June 2000 that determined that 88.5 percent of the population favored

173

the immediate exit of the navy, there was little doubt that residents would vote for a cessation of bombing.[3] Thus opponents of naval training exercises argued that Bush's statement was really a mirage that rationalized continued assault of the island. The battle of Vieques continued.

At this writing, naval training exercises continue on Vieques; protest continues as well. Although the Bush decision appeared to shift the terms of debate from "if" to "when" the Vieques bombing range would close, the terrorist attacks on the United States on September 11, 2001, dramatically changed the political terrain. Bush's decision to close the Vieques installation, to date, has not been translated into a legally binding executive order. With national security suddenly paramount and U.S. forces waging combat in Afghanistan, it is possible that Bush could abandon his commitment to Vieques. Furthermore, the surge of patriotism and widespread support in the United States and Puerto Rico for the war against terrorism have made challenging the U.S. military much more difficult. It is a measure of this changed climate that protestors in Vieques declared a temporary moratorium on civil disobedience in the weeks following September 11.

Despite the United States' shift to a war footing, however, the fundamental conflict in Vieques remains. The grassroots movement is still strong, and widespread opposition to military training endures. The navy's exit may come in a year or a decade, but its departure seems inevitable in light of irreconcilable tensions. What are the implications of Vieques's struggle thus far, and what struggles lie ahead?

Shifting Balance of Power

Vieques's struggle suggests a change in Puerto Rico's colonial relationship with the United States. For six decades Vieques has stood as a dramatic illustration of Puerto Rico's lack of sovereignty and political power. Bush's decision to halt military training exercises on Vieques speaks to shifting political realities in both Puerto Rico and the United States.

In Puerto Rico, the Vieques effort has represented a new convergence of popular forces that has mobilized broad sectors of civil society. The success of the Vieques movement stemmed from activists' ability to move debate outside the realm of existing political parties and stifling debates about Puerto Rican status. The focus on health, the environment, peace, and social justice drew together a wide coalition that gave not only Viequenses but Puerto Ricans in general space to voice a say about their own destiny. Vieques, Juan García Passalacqua suggests, has emerged as a symbol of national affirmation. "The people have found a way to express their rejection of colonialism without having to choose between the options for political status."[4]

After more than one hundred years of domination by the U.S. military, Puerto Ricans, as Jorge Rodríguez Beruff (2001) argues, have for the first time exercised "veto" power over their fate. By mobilizing to stop naval bombing exercises on Vieques, Puerto Ricans have challenged the structures of power that have long controlled their island. Victor Rodríguez Domínguez (2000) notes that in the history of U.S.–Puerto Rico relations, all of the major milestones, whether the conferral of U.S. citizenship or of Commonwealth status, have been set by the United States. The Vieques mobilization stands as the first instance in which Puerto Ricans have made their own history.

It is sobering to note, however, that it has required the mass mobilization of Puerto Rican civil society and its allies in the United States and overseas, the pressure of the Puerto Rican and U.S. political and religious establishment, and constant media scrutiny and international condemnation to shake the structures of military power that have gripped Puerto Rico for over a century. Through hundreds of arrests, daily incursions onto the bombing range, mass marches, constant pickets, and thousands of people putting their bodies on the line for over two years, the navy has been forced from a training facility that several prominent defense analysts have concluded is obsolete.[5] That it should take such a tremendous effort to challenge such an apparently egregious abuse of power indicates the struggle Puerto Rico still faces to control its own destiny.

In the United States, one of the intriguing developments of the Vieques case has been its shift from the margins to the center of mainstream political discourse. Vieques has long been on the "radar screen" in the United States. In the late 1970s, Puerto Ricans and sectors of the U.S. left championed the struggle. A number of city councils in the U.S. Northeast adopted municipal resolutions in solidarity with the Vieques struggle to reclaim its land from the navy. The U.S. Congress held hearings in response to protests. But Vieques's struggle has now emerged as pivotal to mainstream political debate. The New York's Republican governor George Pataki saw it as necessary to his political base to travel to the island to shore up votes in the upcoming New York gubernatorial election. As George W. Bush recognized, Vieques illuminates the growing importance of Latinos as a political bloc. Vieques is not just a "Puerto Rican issue" but a struggle with salience for Latino voters in the United States. Vieques suddenly expanded in political significance by millions of votes.

But Vieques's significance is much broader than these specific political developments. It speaks to the much larger issue of the relationship between the military and civil society. In a world increasingly dominated by military power and defined by the flagrant trampling of basic human rights (Glover 2000), Vieques's struggle asserts the values of civil society over military encroachment.

Military Power and Civil Society

The navy's arrogance and intransigence have created and perpetuated conflict in Vieques throughout the sixty years of the island's relationship with the military. Even the New Deal governor of Puerto Rico, Rexford Tugwell (1976), who had little else to say about Vieques in his memoirs, commented on the navy's sorry treatment of the islanders. Two different congressional panels concluded that "insensitivity has been the hallmark of the navy's approach" to community relations on the island (U.S. House 1981; quoted in U.S. Senate 1999). What is striking is that the response of the civilian population has been so moderate, given the incendiary nature of the relationship.

While protest leaders condemned the 1983 Fortín Accord, the civilian community at large was willing to put aside its grievances and settle for a good-neighbor agreement with the navy, all in the belief that the navy would bring several hundred jobs to the island. The navy repeatedly failed to meet its promises. In 1994 a compromise that proposed returning empty land in the western part of the island, while allowing continued bombing and military control over land in the east, received widespread support among Viequenses. The navy quashed this effort.

The navy has remained adamant that Vieques is both crucial and irreplaceable to U.S. defense. Shifting geopolitical realities and the changing nature of warfare, however, raised questions about how essential Vieques was, even before Bush declared his intention to close the range. Two prominent retired navy admirals, John Shanahan and Eugene Carroll, have argued that the training the navy conducts in Vieques is neither unique nor necessary for contemporary amphibious warfare. Shanahan argues that the amphibious landings the navy rehearses in Vieques are akin to the "Army's practicing cavalry charges" (Shanahan 2001: 3). They are not viable in the face of modern weaponry. "Proof that we are not capable of opposed amphibious assaults today," notes Carroll, "is that we had major amphibious forces in the Persian Gulf in 1991 and did not put one troop ashore because of the certainty of unacceptable casualties."[6]

Air-to-ground bombing and ship-to-shore firing can be conducted elsewhere, Shanahan argues, as indeed they were in the year demonstrators occupied the Vieques range. Shanahan further points out that the kind of short-range gunfire support and close-in bombing the navy rehearses in Vieques is in itself becoming obsolete as the military shifts to cruise missiles and more powerful weapons fired from long ranges (Shanahan 2001).

This analysis raises important questions. Has the navy's uncompromising defense of the Vieques range reflected not national security needs but rather institutional rigidity and an inability to shift course? Was Vieques not irreplaceable but rather extremely convenient and cost effective, indeed a revenue producer? The navy and its supporters in Congress contend that the closure of the Vieques range will compromise training. If this is the case, why has the navy invested so little in shoring up public support, even when under intense public scrutiny? How is it that the navy has allowed public relations to deteriorate so irreversibly at a site it deemed so crucial?

The current political uprising is the result of sixty years of military missteps. The navy has been unwilling to acknowledge the material harm it has caused the community and compensate in any meaningful way for the negative effects of its presence. That this community of politically moderate American citizens should rally against the navy is the result of misguided military policy rather than the handiwork of outside extremists, as the navy commonly asserts.

The Vieques conflict dovetails with a growing sense of concern that the U.S. military is becoming polarized from the public it is supposed to serve, and is characterized by a "combat" mindset no longer suitable to contemporary political realities (Foster 1998; Kohn 1994). Recent controversy surrounding allegations that the navy physically abused and systematically mistreated Vieques demonstrators raises troubling signals. Reports that the navy kept protestors in dog kennels and denied them water, kicked a congressman on the ground and stepped on his neck, groped women and subjected them to humiliating cavity searches, tear-gassed a Catholic priest and shot him with nonlethal bullets, and engaged in other degrading and punitive treatment stand as a disturbing breach of public trust.[7]

The clashes between demonstrators and the U.S. Navy in Vieques thus speak to broader issues of the relationship between the military and civil society. Significant challenges lie ahead. If Bush does indeed close the Vieques base, the struggle will center on Puerto Rico's ability to secure a commitment from the military to remove the colossal mess it will leave in its wake. The animosity between Vieques and the navy will make negotiations difficult during the conversion process.

Conversion and Cleanup

A number of long-term studies have concluded that military base closures have a largely positive economic impact on surrounding communities (Bradshaw 1999; U.S. Department of Defense 1986, 1994). The closure of military facilities in Vieques will undoubtedly have a positive effect on the island's economy, which has been almost completely stifled by the military. The exit of the navy, in and of itself, has the potential to allow for tremendous change. The economic life of the civilian sector may improve immeasurably, for example, just by lifting the military restrictions on transportation that have long crippled the island.

A central issue facing Vieques is the return of the majority of its land. One of the main problems in base closures in the United States in general has been the slow pace of federal property transfer and the commitment of funds for cleanup. Without a commitment of cleanup funds, land can languish under federal jurisdiction indefinitely. In Culebra, more than two decades lapsed before funds were allocated to clean up ordnance. This limbo period saw widespread land speculation, gentrification, and economic marginalization of the local community (Iranzo Berrocal 1994; Rivera Torres and Torres 1996).

An additional problem with conversion has been a lack of financial resources for planning and development. In Vieques, an awareness of Culebra's plight has prompted considerable work on planning over the past ten years. There exist at least three economic conversion studies and development plans and an organized group of university professors and professionals in Puerto Rico (the Multidisciplinary Professional and Technical Group for the Sustainable Development of Vieques) ready to assist in the island's sustainable development (GATP 2000; McIntyre and Dupuy 1996; Rivera Torres and Torres 1996). The fear of land speculation and gentrification is quite real, given current patterns of land ownership on the island.

There should be no doubt that the scope of the cleanup in Vieques will be tremendous and the struggle will be intense. Several recent base shutdowns raise warning signals for Vieques.

When the navy left its live-impact range in Kaho'olawe, Hawaii, Congress agreed to finance a ten-year $400 million cleanup for the forty-five-square-mile island. In 2001, eight years into the project, the navy had cleaned up one-tenth of Kaho'olawe and had scrapped plans to clean the entire island.[8] The failure of cleanup efforts in Hawaii is particularly troubling, because Puerto Rico, a U.S. territory, presumably lacks the political leverage of a U.S. state.

The U.S. military track record overseas is also disconcerting. While acknowledging pollution abroad, the Pentagon has devoted significantly fewer resources to cleanup overseas than in the States.[9] In a number of countries, like Panama and the Philippines, the military has contributed nothing in spite of significant environmental contamination. For example, when the United States left Clark Air Base in the Philippines, it removed waste containers, but refused to release to the Philippine government data on toxic dumping. Twenty thousand Filipino families, left homeless by the eruption of Mt. Pinatubo, were relocated onto the grounds of the former installation, only to discover that the land and water were dangerously contaminated by heavy metals, pesticides, acids, degreasing solvents, and old munitions. Residents have suffered from rising rates of serious health conditions and premature deaths that experts now believe are the result of military pollution (Satchell 2000).

Vieques is in a better political situation than the Philippines because it exists within the purview of U.S. law.[10] Nevertheless even within the United States it has proved difficult to make the military comply with environmental laws, both because the Environmental Protection Agency often lacks enforcement power and because the military presses for exemptions under the rubric of national security.[11] New efforts are under way to remove these exemptions.[12]

Even when the federal government has agreed to take responsibility for base cleanup, there have been considerable problems with funding and allocation of resources. In California, for example, the state environmental protection agency estimated that the cleanup of bases shut in the first three rounds of closures by the Federal Base Realignment and Closure Committee (BRAC) would cost $3.4 billion, but only $2.3 billion had been allocated nationally for cleanup. Federal funds allocated to BRAC were used not only for toxic cleanup but for new military construction to accommodate realigned units. The Department of Defense, more concerned with the future than with the past, gave higher priority to construction than to cleanup (California Defense Conversion Council 1996).

Puerto Rico's lack of representation in the federal government will compound difficulties in ensuring that the navy meets its obligations. Specific issues now confront the island in both the west and the east.

Western Land

As we have seen, navy land in western Vieques was used principally for ammunition storage and was also the site of a small operational base. President Clinton issued an executive directive in January 2000 that instructed the navy to return all eight thousand acres of the former Naval Ammunition Facility (NAF) on the western side of Vieques to the government of Puerto Rico. Clinton's executive order essentially achieved the objectives of the Vieques Land Transfer Act of 1994, submitted by then Puerto Rican resident commissioner Carlos Romero Barceló. It was not until the height of the protest, however, that Viequenses appeared to win the return of the western land. The western part of the island is particularly valuable, because it represents the closest transportation point between Vieques and Puerto Rico.

Political developments, however, soon eroded the islanders' apparent victory. Congress altered the Clinton directive when it translated the order into law. Rather than returning land to the municipality, Congress ordered 4,000 acres returned to the municipality, 3,100 acres to the federal Department of the Interior, and 700 acres to the Puerto Rican Department of Natural Resources, with the remaining 200 (the site of the ROTHR installation) to remain under the control of the navy. By the terms of the law passed by Congress, the navy is responsible for cleaning up contaminated land according to future plans for its use.

Although land in the west has not suffered the severe ecological destruction of constant bombing, the navy used multiple sites there as dumping grounds for a variety of hazardous materials. Nearly two million pounds of military and industrial waste—oil, solvents, lubricants, lead paint, acid, and other refuse—were disposed of in different sites in mangrove swamps and sensitive wetland areas. A portion of this waste contained extremely hazardous chemicals. The extent to which this waste has leached into the groundwater and coastal water is unknown. Of particular concern is a site used for disposing left-over and defective munitions. Old munitions, bomb components, and flares were burned in an open pit. The site was closed in the 1970s after three youths accidently detonated a bomb when they lit a bonfire. Unexploded ordnance may still exist there (Márquez and Fernández Porto 2000; UMET et al. 2000).

The evolving struggle in the west now centers on the designated land use of this territory. The Puerto Rican government has proposed designating territory returned to Vieques as "conservation land." The Department of the Interior has not stated its intentions, but in numerous other cases it has transferred polluted former base land to the Fish and Wildlife Service for use, paradoxically, as "wildlife preserves."[13]

The main problem with identifying the land for conservation purposes is that not only does it continue to estrange islanders from the majority of their land, but it avoids cleanup. Land designated for "conservation use" would require only a superficial cleanup, since presumably no humans would inhabit it (Márquez and Fernández Porto 2000). If these toxic sites are not adequately cleaned, they will not only impede the recovery of a sensitive wetland environment but threaten the health of residents and the economic recovery of the island as a whole.

Eastern Land

The cleanup of the eastern side of Vieques is much more dramatic in scope than the west. The eastern area has been used for naval bombing exercises and maneuvers since the 1940s. In the military base conversion process, the cleanup of firing ranges has proved one of the most dangerous, expensive, and challenging tasks (Sorenson 1998). According to the navy, Vieques has been bombed an average of 180 days per year. In 1998, the last year before protest interrupted maneuvers, the navy dropped twenty-three thousand bombs on the island, the majority of which contained live explosives (U.S. Navy 1999). The point of the most intense destruction is the live-impact range, which constitutes 980 acres on the island's eastern tip. Yet all 14,000 acres and surrounding waters in eastern Vieques have been used as shooting ranges, amphibious landing sites, and toxic waste dumps. Coral reefs and sea grass beds have sustained significant damage from bombing, sedimentation, and chemical contamination (Márquez and Fernández Porto 2000; Rogers, Cintron, and Goenaga 1978). The groundwater has been contaminated by nitrates and explosives (Márquez and Fernández Porto 2000). Recently two sunken barges were found in offshore waters, with 1,200 barrels (55-gallon drums) leaking unknown contents into the sea. This alone could constitute its own Superfund site.[14]

The cleanup of unexploded ordnance on land is a clear safety issue and will be a top priority. Of particular concern are revelations that the navy has fired depleted uranium munitions on the range and the particular dangers and risks that poses for the civilian population.[15] Despite the existence of numerous bombs off the shores of Vieques, cleaning the water is outside the purview of military cleanup requirements.

The live-impact range is seriously contaminated by heavy metals, and studies have documented that those metals have entered the food chain (Massol Deya and Diaz 2000a,b). An important question is the extent to which this severe contamination in the eastern tip has fanned outward and what immediate and long-term risks it poses for residents. One study (Cruz Pérez 1988) found the contamination of the civilian water supply with explosives to be at the same level as in lagoons in the impact zone. This investigation suggests serious contamination by airborne explosives at significant distances from the impact range.

The cleanup of the eastern land will be expensive and time consuming. Over time live ordnance sinks beneath the surface of the land, requiring cleanup crews to remove both surface and subsurface soil. It is unclear how much depleted uranium was fired on the range, but cleaning up these munitions has its own unique problems. Depleted uranium, because of its mass and the size of the guns that fire it, can penetrate the earth to depths of hundreds of feet, requiring the removal of enormous amounts of soil to recover lost rounds (Sorenson 1998: 83n174). Cleaning groundwater is also difficult and expensive. Subterranean water must first be located under thousands of acres of land, which is in itself a difficult process, then pumped to the surface, cleaned with scrubbing devices, and returned to the ground (Sorenson 1998: 81).

The worst-case scenario, but a real possibility, is that the government might decide that the live-impact range is too contaminated to clean and declare the 980-acre bombing area uninhabitable.[16] Although the live-impact range constitutes only a fraction of the total land mass currently controlled by the navy, it seems crucial to clean up this area to guarantee the health and safety of the neighboring civilian population.

Environmental Justice

These issues of environmental contamination increasingly cut to questions of civilian authority over the military. After decades of secrecy surrounding its activities, the military is emerging as the largest polluter in the United States, having single-handedly created twenty-seven thousand toxic waste sites in this country.[17] The military, cloaked by the protective cover of national security interests, has not been held accountable for its toxic legacy.[18] It has acted well outside the purview of law, with seeming indifference to the will of civil society. Internationally, the struggle is even more profound.

The emerging evidence of environmental catastrophe at former base sites in the United States and in the battlefields of the Persian Gulf and Yugoslavia has sparked a growing consciousness of the environmental devastation caused by the military. Increasingly, the military that was once celebrated as an economic provider is becoming challenged and unwelcome in numerous areas by citizens concerned by its threat to the environment and health.[19] Already this changed consciousness is making it difficult for the navy to locate a replacement range for Vieques. Two sites under preliminary consideration have responded with fierce opposition.[20]

Vieques's struggle is not over. September 11's acts of terrorism have presented the Vieques movement with its most serious political setback in the post–cold war era. Protest lost significant momentum immediately after the attacks as activists retreated from confrontation with the navy at a time of national crisis. Now protestors must struggle to reassert their claims in a political climate dominated by military concerns.

The terror attacks, in fact, are an argument for a new type of military training to suit the challenges of nontraditional warfare. As U.S. covert forces enter caves in the Afghan desert, a training facility devoted to a 1940s-era amphibious warfare seems obsolete. Undoubtedly, though, conservative proponents of the Vieques base will use this political opportunity to struggle for control of this piece of contested real estate. Since World War II, Vieques's interests have been sacrificed to the ever-shifting demands of national security. Crises in Korea, Vietnam, Cuba, Iraq, and Haiti all necessitated the subjugation of civilian interests in Vieques to military concerns. In this sense there is little new about this last chapter of global conflict.

The grassroots mobilization faces new challenges, but it is clear that local opposition to the naval installation will persist despite changing geopolitical realities. Washington will need to address the health and environmental concerns that surfaced in the late 1990s. In order to regain control over the land, activists will need to rely on the broad network of support they have cultivated since

1999. They will need to maintain a focus on the same health and environmental concerns that have proved key in mobilizing and uniting Puerto Ricans across class and partisan affiliation. This powerful coalition and this focus on health and the environment will be crucial to ongoing efforts to achieve true peace and justice for the people of Vieques.

Notes

Introduction

1. For a summary of the U.S. Navy's interest in Vieques, see U.S. House (1981, 1994) and U.S. Navy (1999).
2. For a detailed analysis of Vieques in comparison to other live-firing ranges, see Giusti Cordero (1999).
3. International power relations and U.S. strategic interests determine who is paid and how much. The United States has paid European allies like Greece, Turkey, and Spain billions in access fees, while it has paid former colonies like the Philippines nothing. When a less powerful ally, Indonesia, balked at the presence of foreign bases on its territory, the United States agreed to provide security assistance in lieu of access payments (Cottrell and Moorer 1977; Harkavay 1982). The United States pays no fees to Puerto Rico, a U.S. territory, asserting that Puerto Rico benefits from the presence of the U.S. military, which provides a "common defense" for the island.
4. The $80 million figure appeared on the navy's now inaccessible Vieques website, which advertised the availability of the range under a blinking, banner headline: "One-Stop Shopping: Yields High Return on Investment." See *www.viequeslibre.addr.com/articles/onestop.htm* for a discussion of this inflammatory site.
5. *CBS News*, "60 Minutes," August 15, 2000.
6. *Boston Globe*, May 18, 1997. See also *Vieques Times*, May 1999.
7. In the early 1980s, the Puerto Rico Environmental Quality Board announced its intention to deny the navy a water-quality certificate required by the Environmental Protection Agency (EPA) to allow the continued firing of shells and dropping of bombs off the coast of Vieques. The U.S. District Court for the District of Puerto Rico ordered the navy to cease target practice until it obtained a National Pollution Discharge Elimination System permit from the EPA. The case was dropped when Puerto Rico signed an accord with the navy in 1983, but the pollution continued. Later, a well-circulated study (Cruz Pérez 1988) documented high concentrations of explosives in Vieques's drinking water. To date no action has been taken as result of these findings.

8. Heightening local anxieties, a long-term investigative report by a Puerto Rican television station (Noticentro 4-WAPA TV), aired August 9–11, 2000, confirmed that the navy lost a nuclear bomb off the coast of Vieques in the mid-1960s and covered up the incident.

9. For a discussion of nuclear testing in the U.S. Southwest and its impact on surrounding populations and environment, see Fradkin (1989); Gallagher (1993); and Kuletz (1998).

10. For a discussion of U.S. nuclear testing in the Pacific and its impact on resident islanders, see Delgado (1996); Dibblin (1988); Kiste (1974); and Weisgall (1994).

11. For example, U.S. analysts have typically interpreted conflict in the Philippines as stemming from the emotional affront of a foreign presence on its soil, and understood that most people who objected to the bases did so on ideological and symbolic grounds. These observers attributed anti-U.S. sentiment to the association of the U.S. military with the unpopular dictator Ferdinando Marcos (Colbert 1987; Cottrell and Hanks 1980; Gregor and Aganon 1987). For an example of this perspective in the popular media, see *U.S. News and World Report*, November 23, 1987. Although Filipino nationalists indeed viewed the bases as an insult to national dignity, the base controversy was grounded in concrete issues of sovereignty, neutrality, and social cost. See García and Nemenzo (1988); and Ramos-Jimenez and Chiong-Javier (1988).

12. Citizens of Comiso, Sicily, for example, protested the central Italian government's unilateral decision to establish a NATO cruise missile base in their town (Simich 1991). The national government in Japan signed a security agreement with the United States over opposition in Okinawa to the continued U.S. military presence on that island (Johnson 1999).

13. For example, in response to an islandwide antinavy mobilization on October 1, 2000, navy spokesman Jeff Gordon stated, "These people are not part of the democratic process. It is not the people of Vieques who are rejecting the navy, but people from outside of Vieques. These are the same groups that are making false declarations about the navy" (*El Nuevo Día*, October 2, 2000).

14. According to Carmen Ortíz Roque of the Puerto Rico Surgeons and Doctors Association, the infant mortality rate in Vieques has climbed in the past twenty years while decreasing in Puerto Rico as a whole. Between 1990 and 1995 Vieques infant mortality rates were 50 percent higher than in Puerto Rico as a whole (*El Nuevo Día*, February 23, 2000). Puerto Rican governor Sila Calderón publicized a study that suggested that residents suffer from vibroacoustic disease, an unusual heart disorder associated with exposure to loud noises like jet engines or deep explosions (*New York Times*, January 14, 2001). The study was later challenged by Johns Hopkins researchers (*New York Times*, July 15, 2001).

15. Throughout the text the term "North American" is used to refer to U.S. citizens from the continental United States.

16. Of course there are a number of exceptions, such as Chicago, where Mayor Richard Daley pushed the government to close two Air National Guard units at O'Hare to expand the commercial part of the airport. The mayor of Bayonne, New Jersey, also welcomed the closure of the Military Ocean Terminal on prime riverfront property (Sorenson 1998: 57).

17. In 1978 chemical engineer Rafael Cruz Pérez, the former director of the Puerto

Rican Environmental Quality Board's air division, carried out a study of airborne particulate matter as part of the lawsuit filed by the Romero administration that culminated in the memorandum of understanding between Puerto Rico and the United States signed in 1983. Cruz determined that dust and contaminants from the bombing range could travel through the air to the civilian population. Later that year the navy conducted a study that determined that there were similar levels of HMX and RDX (high-power explosives) in the drinking water of Vieques and the lagoons in the live-impact area. This finding was a surprise, since Vieques water is piped in from Puerto Rico. Cruz (1988) theorized that high concentrations of explosives in the air must be entering the local drinking-water supply through the tanks' air vents (Márquez and Fernández Porto 2000).

18. Analysis of the island's cancer rates has been mired in politics. The latest statistics available from the Puerto Rican Department of Health show that between 1985 and 1989, the incidence of cancer in Vieques was 26.7 percent higher than in Puerto Rico (Márquez and Fernández Porto 2000). The navy refutes the statistics. The Rosselló administration commissioned a study on cancer rates on the island, but after signing a compromise agreement with the Clinton administration in December 2000, refused to release the data. Dr. Rafael Rivera Castaño, a retired epidemiologist and leading antinavy activist, estimates the incidence of cancer in Vieques has increased to 52 percent higher than in Puerto Rico.

19. There have been preliminary studies on samples of residents' hair and stools that suggest high concentrations of heavy metals (GATP 2000).

20. The U.S. press has been consistently critical of the navy bombing of Vieques. See, for example, *New York Times* editorial coverage and op-ed pieces on May 3, 2000; and June 14 and 16, 2001. See also the *Washington Post*, July 1, 2001. Mainstream politicians like New York Republican governor George Pataki have spoken in opposition to the Vieques bombing exercises.

21. It should be noted that Nixon ordered the end of live-bombing exercises in Culebra in 1974, and Bush ordered a halt to the bombing of Kaho'olawe in 1990.

22. Clinton's difficulties with the issue of gays in the military were of course emblematic (Kohn 1994).

23. One of the most inflammatory moments of the 1995 Okinawa scandal came when the commander of American forces in the Pacific, Admiral Richard C. Macke, commented: "For the price they [the confessed rapists] paid to rent the car, they could have had a girl [that is, a prostitute]" (quoted in Johnson 1999: 116). Chalmers Johnson makes a strong case for understanding the rape incident as part of a generalized pattern of U.S. military conduct on the island, an argument strengthened by another high-profile rape case that has threatened the U.S.–Japan security alliance (*New York Times*, July 19, 2001). See also Francis (1999) and Enloe (2000). In both the Italian ski lift incident and the Japanese fishing boat debacle, there were serious breaches of protocol and delays in admitting responsibility, heightening international tensions (*New York Times*, February 18, 1998, and February 23, 2001).

24. Fishel (1997) discusses the military's role in ending war and in postwar restructuring and reconstruction. For an interesting interchange on clashing military and civilian perspectives, see Lange (1998) and the letters to the editor in the subsequent issue.

25. Although a U.S. Army commander claimed that misconduct by peacekeepers was isolated and in no way reflective of flaws in army training, he acknowledged that some soldiers went to Kosovo with the mistaken impression that they were there to engage in combat rather than to keep a fragile peace. *Yahoo News Headline*, Associated Press, November 30, 2000.

One   A Strategic Colony on the Margins of the Empire

1. The Vieques Cultural Center has adopted the name of these two Taino chieftains, Cacimar and Yaureibo. The resistance of these two chiefs against the Spanish has led local antinavy activists to assert that Vieques has a five hundred-year-old legacy of resistance to colonialism.
2. Quintero (1976, 1980) argues that the assimilationist tendencies of the working classes were really a shield in their class struggle against Puerto Rican plantation owners, given that independence implied the ascendancy of this class.
3. In 1943 a report commented: "When the physical background of the cane industry in Vieques Island is appraised first hand, it seems very strange that this crop be considered the most dependable enterprise for that Island by all those fully acquainted with its problems and conditions. The extraordinarily scanty and poorly distributed rainfall, the existence of extensive areas of relatively unproductive soils, and the backwardness of the production technique, all seem to point to the inability of sugar cane to stand as a competitive enterprise" (UPR 1943).
4. United Porto Rico initially milled its cane at Vieques's remaining Central Playa Grande, which was owned by an independent Puerto Rican grower. By the late 1930s, however, after United Porto Rico reorganized and changed its name to Eastern Sugar Associates, it shipped its Vieques cane harvest to the Central Pasto Viejo in Humacao to be milled (Ayala 2001).
5. The only other municipality that comes anywhere near Vieques's rate of unemployment is Rincón, with 60.3 percent of its male labor force unemployed. The average percentage of unemployed for Puerto Rico as a whole was 23.1 percent in 1935. Still, these official statistics conceal the fact that only a small portion of the adult population was actually in the labor force. Sidney Mintz (1974) illustrates how formal rates of unemployment do not indicate more pervasive patterns of underemployment, since cane is seasonal work.
6. Rabin's (1993) study of St. Croix also suggests historical links between Vieques and St. Croix, noting that in the early twentieth century, workers from the Virgin Islands represented an important part of Vieques's population.
7. *El Mundo*, June 6, 1939, cited in Rabin (1993).
8. *New York Times*, February 16, 1941.
9. See Berman Santana (1996: 39–40) for a brief discussion of Camp Santiago in Salinas, Puerto Rico, and Rodríguez Beruff (1988: 205) for general comments on the social cost of the military presence in Puerto Rico, which has included the physical displacement of a number of communities.
10. In 1961 Vieques mayor Antonio Rivera Rodríguez denounced the Puerto Rican government: "In 1941, the Republican-Socialist administration turned over Vieques to the United States navy without protest, without demanding any responsibility, just to win the friendship of generals and admirals, even though it was to the detriment of the people of Vieques" (*El Mundo*, August 30, 1961).

11. *San Juan Star*, October 9, 1988.
12. Another particularly visible symbol of this conflict was Fort Brooke army base, located on the grounds of El Morro, an eighteenth-century Spanish fortification on the coast of San Juan. To the Puerto Rican government, El Morro stood as an important historical landmark that represented the island's struggle to repel invading forces. Taken over by the U.S. Army, it was converted into a military golf course and home base for high-ranking army forces. The U.S. Army insisted Fort Brooke was essential to national defense, despite its obvious lack of strategic importance. *San Juan Star,* May 2, 1964.
13. *El Mundo*, June 6, 1947.
14. *El Mundo*, October 16, 1947.
15. *El Mundo*, June 30, 1961.
16. *San Juan Star*, March 29, 1964.
17. *El Mundo*, June 30, 1961.
18. *San Juan Review*, June 1964.
19. *El Mundo*, July 24, 1961.
20. *El Mundo*, July 6, 1961.
21. *El Mundo*, June 30, 1961.
22. The U.S. public reacted with a greater outcry to plans to put animals on ships that would be targeted than to the eviction of one hundred people from their homeland (Delgado 1996).
23. The text of Muñoz's letter appears in the appendix of Meléndez López (1989).
24. *San Juan Star*, April 29, 1964.
25. *El Mundo*, May 1, 1964.
26. *San Juan Star*, April 29, 1964.
27. *El Imparcial*, April 23, 1964, and *El Nuevo Día*, April 23, 1964.
28. *El Imparcial*, April 23, 1964.
29. Quoted in *San Juan Star*, April 29, 1964.
30. *San Juan Star*, May 7, 1964.
31. *El Imparcial*, April 28, 1964.
32. This consternation was apparent in an *El Imparcial* editorial that criticized Muñoz for his apparent indifference to Vieques's plight, but worried about the implications of the struggle: "They are getting ready to start pickets in front of the Pentagon and UN declaring the savage assassination of a Puerto Rican community, the intent to annihilate a people, they use provocative phrases like 'put an end to this intolerance that is an indignation to our race.' It is expressions like these that can be exploited by communists and enemies of America. It is the obligation of *El Imparcial* to define the line between the defense of a community and the carcass of demagoguery. But it is up to the authorities here and there to respond to a situation that gives nourishment to this propaganda" (*El Imparcial*, April 23, 1964).

Two   Cultural Identity in Vieques

1. *El Imparcial*, January 12, 1948.
2. See, for example, U.S. House (1994): 126.
3. This context contrasts with that of Okinawa, Japan, where property expropriated from landowners during World War II created a set of class and colonial antagonisms

that underlies all contemporary discussion of the military installations on that island (see Johnson 1999).

4. The *libreta* system, enacted in 1849, required *jornaleros* (defined as men sixteen years or older who worked for wages or goods for all or part of the year) to carry a passbook to indicate their employment, their work behavior, and the debts they accrued while employed. Those who were found without a passbook were subject to eight days of public labor at half pay (Dietz 1986: 45).

5. In his very definition of *agregado*, Mintz (1974: 281) notes that between 1900 and 1944 *agregados* were subject to political repression and control. The memory of one ninety-one-year-old Vieques resident offers a window on the political climate on the island. The elderly resident worked as an election observer in 1924 in Vieques for the Socialist Party. While most working people were in favor of the socialists, he felt, few dared to vote for the socialist ticket. "Pepe Benitez controlled the election," he remembered. (Benitez owned the Central Playa Grande.) Elections were held at the *central*. Benitez hired twelve men (*jefes*) on horseback who were armed with revolvers and whips with hooks at the end. If the horsemen saw someone wearing a Santiago Inglesias (head of the Socialist Party) button, they would whip the person.

6. The federal food stamp program was introduced to Puerto Rico in the mid-seventies, and Richard Weisskoff (1985) argues that the program served as a rescue operation for the entire Commonwealth economy. For a discussion of the significance of federal transfer payments to Puerto Rico, see Weisskoff (1985) and Dietz (1986).

7. For example, *El Mundo* (September 29, 1951) reported that ninety thousand sailors and marines would converge on the island of Vieques for large-scale maneuvers.

8. Although prostitution is commonly associated with military bases, Enloe (1990, 2000) argues that brothels should not be seen as an inevitable consequence of military installations. Deliberate policies structure the interaction between women and soldiers. She notes, for example, that the U.S.-Saudi base negotiations specifically prohibited the establishment of brothels in Saudia Arabia (2000: 72).

9. A July 2000 art exhibit, sponsored by the Fuerte Conde de Mirasol in Vieques, featured paintings by the prominent Puerto Rican artist Antonio Martorell. His depictions of Vieques in the 1960s were characterized by images of prostitution and illicit sex between sailors and Puerto Rican women, which for him characterized the island during this period.

10. *El Mundo,* April 8, 1953.

11. See *El Mundo,* April 8, 13, 14, and May 25, 1953.

12. *El Mundo,* February 10, 1959.

13. *El Mundo,* May 16, 1960.

14. *San Juan Star,* August 29, 1967; *New York Times,* August 29, 1967.

15. It is interesting to note that the only municipality in Puerto Rico with a greater loss of population was Culebra, which also was in the grip of the navy.

16. *El Mundo,* March 6, 1964.

17. *El Imparcial,* May 1, 1964.

18. In May 1960, *El Mundo* sent a reporter to Vieques to cover the island's mounting social and economic crisis. The reporter described conditions of widespread poverty, with people living in dirt-floored shacks with no title to their land. The re-

porter noted that many families turned to the seas to meet their subsistence needs. *El Mundo*, May 20, 1960.

Three The Fishermen's War

1. In 1960, concerned about the influence of the Cuban Revolution on the Puerto Rican left, J. Edgar Hoover expanded his undercover counterintelligence program COINTELPRO against the Puerto Rican independence movement. Federal efforts to subvert the movement were extensive. They included efforts to influence the 1967 plebiscite, planting federal agents in the press, and infiltrating left organizations. In addition, the Puerto Rican government maintained its own surveillance program on tens of thousands of Puerto Rican "subversives." The government kept dossiers on perceived leftists and independence activists, intimidated individuals, and blackballed "subversives" from work. See Bosque Pérez and Colón Morera (1997); and Comisión de Derechos Civiles de Puerto Rico (1989).
2. For a discussion of the struggle over the mines, see Hermida and Morera (1969) and García Martínez (1972).
3. *El Imparcial*, March 5, 1970; *El Mundo*, March 5, 1970; *New York Times*, March 5, 1970; *San Juan Star*, March 5, 1970.
4. *El Mundo*, March 12, 1971; *New York Times*, March 12, 15, 1971; *San Juan Star*, March 12, 1971.
5. These were not the first instances of right-wing vigilante violence. In 1965 and 1969, the national headquarters of the MPI (Puerto Rican Independence Movement) were firebombed and destroyed. In 1970 the main offices of *Claridad*, a leftist newspaper, were destroyed (Center for Constitutional Rights 1971). The Center for Constitutional Rights appointed a commission to examine political repression in Puerto Rico after the beating of attorney Roberto José Maldonado by police on March 11, 1971. Maldonado, a senior staff attorney of the Legal Institute of Puerto Rico, arrived at a police station to confer with a client who had been arrested during the riots at UPR. Maldonado was denied access to his client and was severely beaten by the police, leaving him with a fractured skull (Center for Constitutional Rights 1971).
6. *San Juan Star Sunday Magazine*, March 6, 1988.
7. *New York Times*, May 3, 1970.
8. *San Juan Star*, June 27, 1970.
9. *San Juan Star Sunday Magazine*, March 6, 1988.
10. *New York Times*, February 21, 1971.
11. While the local PIP was active in Vieques, the PIP on a national level did not demonstrate a sustained interest in Vieques, nor did the party connect the antimilitary struggles on the two islands.
12. *San Juan Star*, October 9, 1978.
13. Charles Menzies letter to author, July 24, 1994. Charles Menzies, assistant professor of anthropology at the University of British Columbia, was raised in a fishing family and has written and researched extensively on fisheries management and issues of sustainability. See *www.anso.ubc.ca/menzies*.
14. The Cerro Maravilla incident sparked immediate indignation from pro-independence sectors of Puerto Rican society. Governor Romero, however, declared the

shooting the "triumph of forces of law and order over illegal forces of terror and subversion" (April 1978), and a U.S. Justice Department investigation absolved officers of any wrongdoing. Nonetheless, serious doubts were soon raised about the accuracy of the government's description of events. Ultimately an investigation conducted by the Puerto Rican Senate confirmed that the youths had been set up and murdered by members of the Special Intelligence Division of the police. For further discussion, see Aponte Pérez (1995); O'Sullivan (1992); Steif (1992); and Suárez (1987).

15. *El Mundo,* February 4, 1979.
16. *Pensamiento Crítico* (1980b, 1980c) describe these tensions.
17. In 1868, coffee growers and small merchants joined together in a brief revolt against Spanish colonial rule. In the 1930s, Nationalist Party founders declared the Grito de Lares, as this rebellion came to be known, a symbol of Puerto Rican identity and nationhood. Since the 1930s, thousands of islanders travel to Lares on September 23 to pay tribute to these revolutionary patriots (Jiménez de Wagenheim 1993).
18. See for example *San Juan Star,* January 18, 1980.
19. Rear Admiral William O'Connor stated: "With Guantánamo, there's always uncertainty in the long term, it could always be subject to some discounting. Even in Panama there's an agreement that at some time has to be renegotiated. But the one unqualified American military presence in the Caribbean is Puerto Rico, the one certain place" (quoted in García Muñiz 1991).
20. Ida Susser (1985) describes a similar process in Yabucoa, Puerto Rico, where Union Carbide assigned a Spanish-speaking official to suppress a protest movement.
21. A number of defendants appealed their cases, and their convictions were reversed on appeal. Others, like Ismael Guadalupe and Angel Rodríguez Cristóbal, refused to acknowledge the jurisdiction of U.S. federal courts in Puerto Rico and participate in the appeals process.
22. A drama within the drama unfolded when the Puerto Rican Socialist Party's Central Committee member Pedro Baíges Chapel, who was detained on May 19, missed the hearing on trespassing charges in order to attend a conference of non-aligned countries in Havana, Cuba. Judge Torruella ordered Baíges arrested and held in contempt of court, and ordered the arrest as well of his lawyer, Juan Marí Bras, the general secretary of the Puerto Rican Socialist Party, who had also gone to Havana. Federal bailiffs tried to arrest Marí Bras during the bar association annual meeting, but the lawyers, who believed the judge was persecuting Marí Bras for traveling to Havana, formed a human chain and prevented his arrest. Marí Bras was arrested two days later. The FBI sparked outrage when it delivered subpoenas to all newspapers and television stations in Puerto Rico to present all material related to the incident at the bar association to a federal grand jury. The subpoenas were dropped after public outrage was stirred over this apparent challenge to freedom of the press (*San Juan Star,* October 30, 1979; Berkan 1979).
23. It is a measure of how disconnected the Puerto Rican left became from the local movement in Vieques that an editorial in the leftist journal *Pensamiento Crítico* (1980a) not only defended the slayings in Sebana Seca but argued that local Viequenses largely supported this act of violence.
24. *San Juan Star,* January 16, 1980.

25. Bishop Antulio Parrilla-Bonilla reports turning away FBI agents from his home shortly after the Sabana Seca killings (*Claridad*, January 11, 1980). Eleida Encarnación, wife of the fishermen's leader Carlos Zenón, describes being harassed by federal marshals at her home (PRISA 1984: 34–35).
26. *San Juan Star*, July 10, 1980.
27. On November 3, 1977, the Romero administration disclosed a memo of November 13, 1973, written by Richard Copaken, the attorney for the Hernández Colón administration. In this memo Copaken, acting on behalf of the Puerto Rican governor, offered the navy unconditional use of the southern shores of Vieques for military maneuvers. See *San Juan Star*, February 1, 1980. This incident was not the first time that a Puerto Rican governor was accused of colluding with the navy. In the 1972 Puerto Rican gubernatorial elections controversy raged over allegations that former governor Roberto Sanchez Vilella and then governor Luis A. Ferré had capitulated to navy demands to remove and resettle residents from Culebra. Beneath these controversies are real questions about how much political power the Puerto Rican government truly wielded in the face of navy demands.
28. This was a clearly stated, essential part of the navy's "Community Action Plan" (U.S. Navy 1978).
29. *San Juan Star*, January 20, 1980.
30. Administration of the land passed from one bankrupt Commonwealth agency to another until a highly politicized and bitter conflict erupted in which government officials sought to charge residents market value for land that they had occupied for decades. See *Vieques Times*, July 1989, September 1994, and March 1995.

Four The Aftermath of the Fishermen's Crusade

1. Sara Grusky (1992) offers an excellent analysis of the economic limitations of the 1983 accord. For an overview of the economic theory behind Puerto Rico's Operation Bootstrap, see Baver (1993) and Dietz (1986).
2. Residents founded Villa Borinquén in 1976 on approximately five hundred acres on the eastern limits of the base. The organized takeover of land as an act of political defiance is an established form of protest in Puerto Rico See Cotto (1993) on the *rescate* movement in Puerto Rico.
3. Vieques's bioluminescent bay is a remarkable natural phenomenon, one of only twenty-one such ecosystems in the world. At night, high concentrations of light-emitting microorganisms produce flashes of blue-green light when water is agitated. Fish darting through the water look like shooting stars.
4. By 2000 the politics of the VCHT had shifted dramatically. The group made a conscious effort to incorporate more Viequenses and became actively involved in the effort to stop the bombing of the island.
5. *Vieques Times*, June 1994.
6. Jorge Duany (2000) argues persuasively that territorially based definitions of identity are exclusionary and elitist and mask the reality of the Puerto Rican experience that moves fluidly between Puerto Rico and the United States. Without disputing his conclusions, I suggest that the case of Vieques presents an alternate way of thinking about Puerto Rican cultural identity, in particular the regional differences within the Commonwealth and the ways in which territorial criteria weigh differently in definitions of identity.

Five   Organizing for Change

1. *Vieques Times*, November 1993.
2. In May 1997 fishermen clashed with navy battleships anchored off the island during international maneuvers on Mother's Day. Fishermen claimed navy boats were destroying fishing gear. A melee erupted and a Dutch sailor lost an eye in the fracas (*San Juan Star*, May 21, 1997).
3. Arlene Dávila discusses the history and character of the Institute for Puerto Rican Culture and the cultural centers it sponsors throughout Puerto Rico. She notes that many *independentistas* have found refuge for their political convictions and work in these centers throughout the island (1997: 81).
4. *Vieques Times*, January 1994.
5. *San Juan Star*, November 24, 1995.
6. *Vieques Times*, June 1994.
7. *Vieques Times*, August 1994.
8. *San Juan Star*, November 10, 1995.
9. *San Juan Star*, December 3, 1995.
10. *San Juan Star*, December 3, 1995.

Six   From Pescadores to Rescatores

1. Luis Aponte Parés describes the *casita* as belonging to a family of "balloon-frame wooden structures—shacks, bungalows and cottages—generally identified with Third World vernacular architecture" (1995: 10). *Casitas* are often brightly colored, with corrugated metal roofs, front porches, and shutters. Sometimes they are built on stilts.
2. Throughout the 1970s and 1980s, Puerto Rican community activists in New York City seized abandoned lots and built playgrounds and *casitas*, creating community gardens and public spaces out of squalor (Aponte Parés 1995; Serrano 1998).
3. Jesse Jackson never did come back after the evictions and arrests of May 2000, but his wife was arrested in Vieques in June 2001 for trespassing on navy land.
4. *El Nuevo Día*, May 23, 1999.
5. *El Nuevo Día*, May 4, 1999.
6. *National Catholic Reporter*, March 21, 2000.
7. *El Nuevo Día*, May 13, 2000.
8. *Washington Post*, February 22, 2000.
9. *Associated Press*, February 22, 2000.
10. *Voz de Vieques*, June 30, 2000.

Seven   The Battle of Vieques

1. *New York Times*, June 14, 2001.
2. *New York Times*, June 15, 16, 2001.
3. The Diocese sent 100 volunteers to the homes of 2,214 Viequenses. "Consulta a Vieques," Diócesis de Caguas, June 2000.
4. *New York Times*, July 29, 2001.
5. Retired navy admirals Eugene Carroll and John Shanahan are among the most high-profile commentators.

6. Retired navy admiral Eugene Carroll, personal communication.
7. *Orlando Sentinel,* June 6, 2001; *El Vocero,* June 6, 2001; *El Nuevo Día,* June 6, 2001; *New York Times,* June 14, 2001; *Vieques Times,* June 2001.
8. *New York Times,* June 16, 2001.
9. For example, in 1998 the U.S. Department of Defense spent $2 billion cleaning up installations in the United States and its territories, but only a total of $18.6 million in its bases in Great Britain, Germany, Belgium, Italy, Japan, and South Korea. No money was allocated to the Philippines or Panama (Satchell 2000).
10. A number of lawsuits are currently pending against the navy, including one filed by the Puerto Rican government in the U.S. District Court for the District of Columbia and another by Robert Kennedy, Jr., in the District Court for the District of Puerto Rico. The Mississippi-based law firm of John Arthur Eaves intends to sue the navy over charges of cancer.
11. In fact, the case Puerto Rican governor Carlos Romero Barceló brought against the navy, which focused on environmental damage, was denied largely on the grounds that granting injunctive relief would compromise national defense. See Carlos Romero Barceló et al. v. Harold Brown et al., U.S. District Court for Puerto Rico, September 17, 1979.
12. In June 2001 California congressman Bob Fimer introduced a bill, "Military Environmental Responsibility Act," which seeks to remove military exemptions from existing environmental, worker, and public safety laws and regulations (Environmental News Service, June 26, 2001).
13. David Sorenson (1998: 82n168) notes that most of the fifty thousand acres of the most contaminated firing ranges have been transferred to the Department of Fish and Wildlife Service to be designated, ironically, as conservation areas.
14. *El Nuevo Día,* December 30,1999.
15. For a discussion of the depleted uranium controversy, see links to depleted uranium on *viequeselibre.org* and visit the website of the Military Toxics Project at *miltoxproj.org.*
16. Sorenson (1998: 82) notes that fifty-five thousand acres of former base property was so contaminated by unexploded ordnance that it will remain controlled by the government in perpetuity.
17. *Environmental News Service,* June 26, 2001, and Sorenson 1998: 78.
18. One extreme example surrounds allegations by former employees and their surviving family members that the U.S. military and its contractors regularly and illegally burned large volumes of toxic waste at a secret military base in central Nevada. Efforts by plaintiffs to recover damages were met with the air force's invocation of military and state-secret privilege to block the inquiry (Howard 1997).
19. For example, in Hawaii a coalition of residents and environmentalists are waging a fierce battle to halt U.S. Army combat training in the Makua Valley, arguing that the military is destroying the valley's environment and cultural and historical legacy (*New York Times,* April 1, 2001).
20. Citizens in Kingsville, Texas, rallied against the relocation of firing practices there, after a group of local officials initially invited the navy to turn the area into an "expeditionary warfare training center" (*New York Times,* June 27, 2001). Citizen groups in Nevada opposed relocating the bombing exercises to Fallon Naval Air Station sixty miles east of Reno (*Las Vegas Review-Journal,* July 8, 2001).

References

Abril, Santos. 1978. "Cerro Maravilla: El Entrampamiento Represivo." *Pensamiento Crítico* 1 (8): 2–6.

Acosta, Ivonne. 1989. *La Mordaza: Puerto Rico, 1948–1957.* Río Piedras, Puerto Rico: Editorial Edil.

Alland, Alexander, with Sonia Alland. 1994. *Crisis and Commitment: The Life History of a French Social Movement.* Yverdon, Switzerland: Gordon and Breach.

Aponte Parés, Luis. 1995. "What's Yellow and White and Has Land All around It? Appropriating Place in Puerto Rican *Barrios.*" *Centro* 7 (1): 8–19.

Aponte Pérez, Francisco. 1995. *Las Víctimas del Cerro Maravilla.* San Juan, Puerto Rico: Centro de Estudios Legales y Sociales.

Avant, Deborah. 1998. "Conflicting Indicators of 'Crisis' in American Civil-Military Relations." *Armed Forces and Society* 24 (3): 375–387.

Ayala, César J. 1999. *American Sugar Kingdom: The Plantation Economy of the Spanish Caribbean, 1898–1934.* Chapel Hill: University of North Carolina Press.

———. 2001. "Del Latifundio Azucarero al Latifundio Militar: Las Expropiaciones de la Marina de Guerra de los Estados Unidos en Vieques, Puerto Rico, 1940–45." *Revista de Ciencias Sociales* (Universidad de Puerto Rico), n.s., 10 (January): 1–33.

Baver, Sherrie L. 1993. *The Political Economy of Colonialism.* Westport, Conn.: Praeger.

Bergad, Laird W. 1983. "Coffee and Rural Proletarianization in Puerto Rico, 1840–1898." *Journal of Latin American Studies* 15 (1): 83–100.

Berkan, Judith. 1979. "Points for a Chronology of the Struggle in Vieques from 1978 to 1979." Luchas Contra el Militarismo (2). Archivo Histórico, Fuerte Conde de Mirasol, Vieques, Puerto Rico.

Berman Santana, Déborah. 1996. *Kicking off the Bootstraps: Environment, Development, and Community Power in Puerto Rico.* Tucson: University of Arizona Press.

Blaker, James R. 1990. *United States Overseas Basing: An Anatomy of a Dilemma.* New York: Praeger.

Blaustein, Susan. 1991. "Steamrollered One More Time." *Nation* 253 (7): 258–260.

Bookman, Ann, and Sandra Morgen, eds. 1988. *Women and the Politics of Empowerment.* Philadelphia: Temple University Press.

Bosque Pérez, Ramón, and José Javier Colón Morera, eds. 1997. *Las Carpetas: Persecución Política y Derechos Civiles en Puerto Rico.* Río Piedras, Puerto Rico: Centro para la Investigación y Promoción de los Derechos Civiles.

Bradshaw, Ted K. 1999. "Communities Not Fazed: Why Military Base Closures May Not Be Catastrophic." *Journal of the American Planning Association* 65 (2): 193–206.

Brau, Salvador. 1912. *La Isla de Vieques.* San Juan, Puerto Rico: Gráfico.

Burdick, John. 1992. "Rethinking the Study of Social Movements: The Case of Christian Base Communities in Urban Brazil." In *The Making of Social Movements in Latin America: Identity, Strategy, and Democracy,* edited by Arturo Escobar and Sonia E. Alvarez. Boulder, Colo.: Westview Press.

Burk, James. 1998. "The Logic of Crisis and Civil-Military Relations Theory: A Comment on Desch, Feaver, and Dauber." *Armed Forces and Society* 24 (3): 455–462.

Cabán, Pedro A. 1999. *Constructing a Colonial People: Puerto Rico and the United States, 1898–1932.* Boulder, Colo.: Westview Press.

California Defense Conversion Council. 1996. "Defense Conversion in California: Economics in Transition."

Carr, Raymond. 1984. *Puerto Rico: A Colonial Experiment.* New York: Vintage Books.

Caute, David. 1978. *The Great Fear: The Anti-Communist Purge under Truman and Eisenhower.* New York: Simon and Schuster.

Center for Constitutional Rights. 1971. "Report from Commission of Inquiry into Political Repression in Puerto Rico." Ruth Reynolds Collection, Centro de Estudios Puertorriqueños, Hunter College, New York.

Clark, Victor S. 1930. *Porto Rico and Its Problems.* Washington, D.C: Brookings Institution.

Colbert, Evelyn. 1987. "The United States and the Philippines Bases." Foreign Policy Institute, School of Advanced International Studies, Johns Hopkins University, Washington, D.C.

Colón, Awilda. 1984. "The Militarization of Puerto Rico and North American Intervention in Central America and the Caribbean." Proyecto Caribeño de Justicia y Paz, Hato Rey, Puerto Rico, Dossier no. 1.

Colón Morera, José Javier. 1997. "Consenso, Represión y Descolonización." In *Las Carpetas: Persecución Política y Derechos Civiles en Puerto Rico,* edited by Ramon Bosque Pérez and José Javier Colón Morera. Río Piedras, Puerto Rico: Centro para la Investigación y Promoción de los Derechos Civiles.

Comisión de Derechos Civiles de Puerto Rico. 1989. "Informe Sobre Discrimen y Persecución por Razones Políticas: la Práctica Gubernamental de Mantener Listas, Ficheros, y Expedientes de Ciudadanos por Razón de Su Ideología Política." San Juan, Puerto Rico.

Cotto, Liliana. 1993. "The *Rescate* Movement: An Alternative Way of Doing Politics." In *Colonial Dilemma: Critical Perspectives on Contemporary Puerto Rico,* edited by Edwin Meléndez and Edgardo Meléndez. Boston: South End Press.

Cottrell, Alvin, and Robert J. Hanks. 1980. "Military Utility of the U.S. Facilities in the Philippines." Center for Strategic and International Studies, Georgetown University, Washington, D.C.

Cottrell, Alvin, and Thomas H. Moorer. 1977. *U.S. Overseas Bases: Problems of Projecting American Military Power Abroad*. Center for Strategic and International Studies, Georgetown University. Washington, D.C.: Sage Publications.

Cruz Pérez, Rafael. 1988. "Contaminación Producida por Explosivos y Residuous de Explosivos en Vieques, Puerto Rico." *Dimensión* 8 (2): 37–42.

Dardia, Michael et al. 1996. "The Effects of Military Base Closures on Local Communities: A Short-Term Perspective." National Defense Research Institute, Rand, Santa Monica, Calif.

Dávila, Arlene. 1997. *Sponsored Identities: Cultural Politics in Puerto Rico*. Philadelphia: Temple University Press.

Delgado, James. 1996. *Ghost Fleet: The Sunken Ships of the Bikini Atoll*. Honolulu: University of Hawaii Press.

Delgado Cintrón, Carmelo. 1989. *Culebra y la Marina de Estados Unidos*. Río Piedras, Puerto Rico: Editorial Edil.

Desch, Michael C. 1998. "Soldiers, States, and Structures: The End of the Cold War and Weakening U.S. Civilian Control." *Armed Forces and Society* 24 (3): 389–406.

Dibblin, Jane. 1988. *Day of Two Suns: U.S. Nuclear Testing and the Pacific Islanders*. New York: New Amsterdam.

Dietz, James.1986. *Economic History of Puerto Rico: Institutional Change and Capitalist Development*. Princeton: Princeton University Press.

Dookhan, Isaac. 1973. "Vieques or Crab Island: Source of Anglo-Spanish Colonial Conflict." *Journal of Caribbean History* 7: 1–22.

Duany, Jorge. 2000. "Nation on the Move: The Construction of Cultural Identities in Puerto Rico and the Diaspora." *American Ethnologist* 27 (1): 5–30.

Dunlap, Charles. 1992. "The Origins of the Military Coup of 2012." *Parameters* 22 (4): 2–22.

Edelman, Marc. 1999. *Peasants against Globalization: Rural Social Movements in Costa Rica*. Stanford: Stanford University Press.

Enloe, Cynthia. 1990. *Bananas, Beaches, and Bases: Making Feminist Sense out of International Politics*. Berkeley: University of California Press.

———. 2000. *Maneuvers: The International Politics of Militarizing Women's Lives*. Berkeley: University of California Press.

Estades Font, María Eugenia. 1988. *La Presencia Militar de Estados Unidos en Puerto Rico, 1898–1918*. Río Piedras, Puerto Rico: Ediciones Huracán.

Feliciano, María Luisa. 1980. "Vieques: Dos Concepciones de Lucha" Archivo Histórico, Fuerte Conde de Mirasol, Vieques, Puerto Rico.

Fernández, Ronald. 1996. *The Disenchanted Island: Puerto Rico and the United States in the Twentieth Century*. New York: Praeger.

Fishel, John T. 1997. *Civil Military Operations in the New World*. Westport, Conn.: Praeger Press.

Foner, Philip S. 1972. *The Spanish-Cuban-American War and the Birth of American Imperialism*. New York: Monthly Review Press.

Foster, Gregory. 1998. "Combating the Crisis in Civil-Military Relations." *Humanist* 58 (1): 6–11.

Fradkin, Philip.1989. *Fallout: An American Nuclear Tragedy*. Tucson: University of Arizona Press.

Francis, Carolyn Bowen. 1999. "Women and Military Violence. In *Okinawa: Cold War Island*, edited by Chalmers Johnson. Cardiff, Calif.: Japan Policy Research Institute.

Fried, Richard. 1990. *Nightmare in Red: The McCarthy Era in Perspective*. New York: Oxford University Press.

Gallagher, Carole. 1993. *American Ground Zero: The Secret Nuclear War*. Cambridge: MIT Press.

Garcia, Ed, and Francisco Nemenzo. 1988. *The Sovereign Quest: Freedom from Foreign Military Bases*. Quezon City, Philippines: Claretian Publications.

García Martínez, Neftalí. 1972. *Puerto Rico y la Minería*. San Juan, Puerto Rico: Ediciones Librería Internacional.

———. 1978. "Puerto Rico Siglo XX: Lo Histórico y lo Natural en la Ideología Colonialista." *Pensamiento Crítico* 1 (8): 1–28.

———. 1979. "Consecuencias Histórico-Naturales de la Presencia de la Marina en Vieques." Hato Rey, Puerto Rico: Comité Nacional pro Defensa de Vieques.

García Muñiz, Humberto. 1987. "Boots, Boots, Boots: Intervention, Regional Security, and Militarization in the Caribbean, 1979–1986." Militarism Series 2. Proyecto Caribeño de Justicia y Paz, Hato Rey, Puerto Rico.

———. 1991. "U.S. Military Installations in Puerto Rico: An Essay on Their Role and Purpose." *Caribbean Studies* 24 (3–4): 79–97.

Gaspar, David B. 1985. *Bondmen and Rebels: A Study of Master-Slave Relations in Antigua*. Baltimore: Johns Hopkins University Press.

GATP (Grupo de Apoyo Técnico y Profesional para El Desarrollo Sustenatable de Vieques). 2000. "Guidelines for the Sustainable Development of Vieques."

Geertz, Clifford. 1977. "Centers, Kings, and Charisma." In *Culture and Its Creators: Essays in Honor of Edward Shils*, edited by Raymond Aron, Edward Shils, Joseph Ben-David, and Terry Clark. Chicago: University of Chicago Press.

Giusti Cordero, Juan. 1996. "Labour, Ecology, and History in a Puerto Rican Plantation Region: 'Classic' Rural Proletarians Revisited." *International Review of Social History* 41: 53–82.

———. 1999. "La Marina en la Mirilla: Una Comparación de Vieques con los Campos de Bombardeo y Adiestramiento en los Estados Unidos." In *Fronteras en Conflicto: Guerra contra las Drogas, Militarización y Democracia en el Caribe, Puerto Rico y Vieques*, edited by Humberto García Muñiz and Jorge Rodríguez Beruff. San Juan, Puerto Rico: Red Caribeña de Geopolítica.

Glover, Jonathan. 2000. *Humanity: A Moral History of the Twentieth Century*. New Haven: Yale University Press.

Goodno, J. B. 1997. "Converting Subic Bay." *Technology Review* 95 (2): 18–19.

Gregor, A. James, and Virgilio Aganon. 1987. "The Philippine Bases: U.S. Security at Risk." Washington, D.C.: Ethics and Public Policy Center.

Grosfogel, Ramón. 1997. "The Divorce of Nationalist Discourses from the Puerto Rican People: A Socio-Historic Perspective." In *Puerto Rican Jam: Essays on Culture and Politics*, edited by Frances Negrón-Muntaner and Ramón Grosfogel. Minneapolis: University of Minnesota Press.

Grusky, Sara. 1992. "The Navy as Social Provider in Vieques, Puerto Rico." *Armed Forces and Society* 18: 215–230.

Harkavay, Robert E. 1982. *Great Power Competition for Overseas Bases: The Geopolitics of Access Diplomacy*. New York: Pergamon Press.

Harris, W. W. 1980. *Puerto Rico's Fighting 65th Infantry: From San Juan to Chorwan.* San Rafael, Calif.: Presidio Press.

Hermida, Angel G., and Luis Morera, eds. 1969. *La Explotación Minera del Cobre en Puerto Rico: Factores Legales, Económicos y de Contaminación.* Río Piedras, Puerto Rico: Universidad de Puerto Rico.

History Task Force, Centro de Estudios Puertorriqueños. 1979. *Labor Migration under Capitalism: The Puerto Rican Experience.* New York: Monthly Review Press.

Howard, Malcom. 1997. "Environmental Secrecy: A Lawsuit Alleges Environmental Crimes at the Country's Most Secret Military Base." *Amicus Journal* 19 (Spring): 34–36.

Hunt, Lynn. 1984. *Politics, Culture, and Class in the French Revolution.* Berkeley: University of California Press.

Iranzo Berrocal, Guillermo. 1994. "Aproximación Antropológica al Turismo y la Gentrifacación de la Tierra en Culebra, Puerto Rico." Paper delivered at a conference in Cancún, México. Archivo Histórico, Fuerte Conde de Mirasol, Vieques, Puerto Rico.

Jesús de Castro, Tomás. 1937. "La Agonia Industrial de Vieques." *Puerto Rico Ilustrado,* 14, 15, 52. Archivo Histórico, Fuerte Conde de Mirasol, Vieques, Puerto Rico.

Jiménez de Wagenheim, Olga. 1993. *Puerto Rico's Revolt for Independence: El Grito de Lares.* Princeton: Markus Wiener Publishers.

———. 1998. *Puerto Rico: An Interpretive History from Pre-Columbian Times to 1900.* Princeton: Markus Wiener Publishers.

Johnson, Chalmers. 1999. *Okinawa: Cold War Island.* Cardiff, Calif.: Japan Policy Research Institute.

Kaplan, Temma. 1982. "Female Consciousness and Collective Action: The Case of Barcelona, 1910–1918." *Signs* 7 (3): 545–566.

———. 1992. *Red City, Blue Period: Social Movements in Picasso's Barcelona.* Berkeley: University of California Press.

Kertzer, David. 1988. *Ritual, Politics, and Power.* New Haven: Yale University Press.

Kiste, Robert. 1974. *The Bikinians: A Study in Forced Migration.* Menlo Park, Calif.: Cummings Publishing Company.

Knight, Franklin. 1990. *The Caribbean: The Genesis of a Fragmented Nationalism.* New York: Oxford University Press.

Kohn, Richard. 1994. "Out of Control: The Crisis in Civil-Military Relations." *National Interest* 35: 3–17.

Kuletz, Valerie. 1998. *The Tainted Desert: Environmental Ruin in the American West,* New York: Routledge Press.

Lange, John. 1998. "Civil-Military Cooperation and Humanitarian Assistance: Lessons from Rwanda." *Parameters* 28 (2).

Langley, Lester. 1985a. "Roosevelt Roads, Puerto Rico, U.S. Naval Base 1941–." *In United States Navy and Marine Corps Bases, Overseas,* edited by Paolo E. Coletta with K. Jack Bauer. Westport, Conn.: Greenwood Press.

———. 1985b. "San Juan, Puerto Rico, U.S. Naval Station, 1898–1950." In *United States Navy and Marine Corps Bases, Overseas,* edited by Paolo E. Coletta with K. Jack Bauer. Westport, Conn.: Greenwood Press.

———. 1989. *The United States in the Caribbean in the Twentieth Century.* Athens: University of Georgia Press.

Linnekin, Jocelyn. 1983. "Defining Tradition: Variations on the Hawaiian Identity." *American Ethnologist.* 10 (2): 241–252.

Lotchin, Roger. 1984. *The Martial Metropolis: U.S. Cities in War and Peace.* New York: Praeger.

Markusen, Ann, Peter Hall, Scott Campbell, and Sabina Deitrick. 1991. *The Rise of the Gun Belt: The Military Remapping of Industrial America.* New York: Oxford University Press.

Márquez, Lirio, and Jorge Fernández Porto. 2000. "Environmental and Ecological Damage to the Island of Vieques Due to the Presence and Activities of the United States Navy." Special International Tribunal on the Situation of Puerto Rico and the Island Municipality of Vieques.

Massol Deya, Arturo, and Elba Díaz. 2000a. "Biomagnificación de Metales Carcinógenos en el Tejido de Cangrejos de Vieques, Puerto Rico." Casa Pueblo de Adjuntas y Departamento de Biología del Recinto de Mayagüez, Universidad de Puerto Rico.

———. 2000b. "Metales Pesados en la Vegetación Dominante del Area de Impacto de Vieques, Puerto Rico." Casa Pueblo de Adjuntas y Departamento de Biología del Recinto de Mayagüez, Universidad de Puerto Rico.

McCaffrey, Katherine. 1998. "Forging Solidarity: Politics, Protest, and the Vieques Solidarity Network." In *The Puerto Rican Movement: Voices from the Diaspora,* edited by Andrés Torres and José Velázquez. Philadelphia: Temple University Press.

McIntyre, Lionel, and Rudy Dupuy. 1996. "Vieques Island, Puerto Rico: A Development Strategy for the Naval Ammunitions Facility." Vieques Studio Urban Planning Program, Columbia University.

Meléndez, Edgardo. 1993. "Colonialism, Citizenship, and Contemporary Statehood." In *Colonial Dilemma: Critical Perspectives on Contemporary Puerto Rico,* edited by Edwin Meléndez and Edgardo Meléndez. Boston: South End Press.

Meléndez López, Arturo. 1989. *La Batalla de Vieques.* Río Piedras, Puerto Rico: Editorial Edil.

Merrill, Christopher. 1994. "A Little Justice in Hawaii." *Nation* 259 (7): 235–236.

Mintz, Sidney. 1956. "Cañamelar: The Subculture of a Rural Sugar Plantation Proletariat." In *The People of Puerto Rico,* edited by Julian Steward et al. Urbana: University of Illinois Press.

———. 1974. *Worker in the Cane.* New York: W. W. Norton and Company.

———. 1985. "From Plantations into Peasantries in the Caribbean." In *Caribbean Contours,* edited by Sidney W. Mintz and Sally Price. Baltimore: Johns Hopkins University Press.

———. 1989. *Caribbean Transformations.* New York: Columbia University Press.

Moon, Katharine H. S. 1997. *Sex among Allies.* New York: Columbia University Press.

Morales Carrión, Arturo. 1971. *Puerto Rico and the Non-Hispanic Caribbean: A Study in the Decline of Spanish Exclusivism.* Río Piedras, Puerto Rico: University of Puerto Rico.

———. 1983. *Puerto Rico: A Political and Cultural History.* New York: W. W. Norton and Company.

Morris, Nancy. 1995. *Puerto Rico: Culture, Politics, and Identity.* Westport, Conn.: Praeger.

Nash, June. 1979. *We Eat the Mines and the Mines Eat Us: Dependency and Exploitation in Bolivian Tin Mines.* New York: Columbia University Press.

Nazario, Zydnia. 1986. *The Battle of Vieques*. Videorecording. Zemi Productions, Puerto Rico.

Nieves Falcón, Luis, Pablo García Rodríguez, and Félix Ojeda Reyes. 1971. *Puerto Rico: Grito y Mordaza*. Río Piedras, Puerto Rico: Ediciones Libreria Internacional.

O'Sullivan, Gerry. 1992. "Terror/Counter Terror: Reopening Case of 1978 Police Shooting of Two Independence Activists in Puerto Rico." *Humanist* 52 (May/June): 47–48.

Pantojas-García, Emilio. 1990. *Development Strategies as Ideology: Puerto Rico's Export-Led Industrialization Experience*. Boulder, Colo.: Lynne Rienner Publishers.

Pensamiento Crítico. 1980a. "Sabana Seca." 3 (17): 1.

———. 1980b. "Vieques es Puerto Rico." 3 (19): 5–7.

———. 1980c. "Vieques y Nuestro Movimiento Revolucionario." 3 (19): 1.

Picó, Fernando. 1987. *La Guerra Despues de la Guerra*. Río Piedras, Puerto Rico: Ediciones Huracán.

Picó, Rafael. 1950. *The Geographic Regions of Puerto Rico*. Río Piedras, Puerto Rico: University of Puerto Rico Press.

PRISA. 1984. "Ni Pa' Cojer Impulso: Testimonios de Mujeres Viequenses." Los Triunfos del Pueblo 1. Bayamon, Puerto Rico.

Quintero Rivera, Angel. 1976. *Workers' Struggle in Puerto Rico: A Documentary History*. New York: Monthly Review Press.

———. 1980. "The Development of Social Classes and Political Conflicts in Puerto Rico." In *Puerto Ricans: Their History, Culture, and Society*, edited by Adalberto López. Cambridge, Mass.: Schenkman Publishing Company.

———. 1991. "Culture-Oriented Social Movements: Ethnicity and Symbolic Action in Latin America and the Caribbean." *Centro* (Spring): 97–104.

Rabin, Robert. 1993. "Historic Relations between St. Croix and Vieques." Virgin Islands Humanities Council.

Ramos-Jimenez, Pilar, and Ma. Elena Chiong-Javier. 1988. *Social Benefits and Costs: People's Perceptions of the U.S. Military Bases in the Philippines*. Manila, Philippines: Research Center, De La Salle University.

Ramos Mattei, Andrés A. 1985. "Technical Innovations and Social Change in the Sugar Industry of Puerto Rico, 1870–1880." In *Between Slavery and Free Labor: The Spanish-Speaking Caribbean in the Nineteenth Century*, edited by Manuel Moreno Fraginals, Frank Moya Pons, and Stanley L. Engerman. Baltimore: Johns Hopkins University Press.

———. 1989. "La Importación de Trabajadores Contratados para la Industria Azucarera Puertorriqueña, 1860–1880." In *Inmigración y Clases Sociales en el Puerto Rico del Siglo XIX*, edited by Francisco A. Scarano. Río Piedras, Puerto Rico: Ediciones Huracán.

Rivera Martínez, Antonio. 1963. *Así Empezó Vieques*. Río Piedras, Puerto Rico: Centro de Investigaciones Históricas, Universidad de Puerto Rico.

Rivera Torres, Leticia, and Antonio J. Torres. 1996. "Vieques, Puerto Rico: Economic Conversion and Sustainable Development." Archivo Histórico, Fuerte Conde de Mirasol, Vieques, Puerto Rico.

Robson, Martha. 1980. "The Church Woman Magazine." Church Women United. Ruth Reynolds Collection, Centro de Estudios Puertorriqueño, Hunter College, New York City.

Rodríguez Beruff, Jorge. 1986. "La Nueva Política Militar de los Estados Unidos Hacia el Caribe: Orígenes y Consecuencias." *Revista de Ciencias Sociales* 25 (3–4): 445–483.

———. 1988. *Política Militar y Dominación: Puerto Rico en el Contexto Latinoamericano.* Río Piedras, Puerto Rico: Ediciones Huracán.

———. 1999. "Guerra contra las Drogas, Militarización y Democracia: Políticas y Fuerzas de Seguridad en Puerto Rico." In *Fronteras en Conflicto: Guerra contra las Drogas, Militarización y Democracia en el Caribe, Puerto Rico y Vieques*, edited by Humberto García Muñiz and Jorge Rodríguez Beruff. San Juan, Puerto Rico: Red Caribeña de Geopolítica.

———. 2001. "Vieques and Puerto Rican Politics." Paper delivered at the symposium "None of the Above: Puerto Rican Politics and Culture in the New Millennium," Rutgers University, New Brunswick, N.J.

Rodríguez Domínguez, Victor M. 2000. "Vieques Movement Redefines U.S./Puerto Rico Relations." *Politico Magazine* 3 (22).

Rogers, Caroline S., Gilberto Cintron, and Carlos Goenaga. 1978. "The Impact of Military Operations on the Coral Reefs of Vieques and Culebra." Report submitted to the Department of Natural Resources, San Juan, Puerto Rico.

Rouse, Irving. 1952. "Porto Rico Prehistory: Excavations in the Interior, South and East; Chronological Implications." Scientific Survey of Puerto Rico and the Virgin Islands. Volume 18 (4). New York: New York Academy of the Sciences.

Ruíz, Justo Pastor. 1947. *Vieques Antiguo y Moderno, 1493–1946.* Yacuo, Puerto Rico: Tipografía Rodríguez Lugo.

Satchell, Michael. 2000. "What the Military Left Behind." *U.S. News and World Report* 128 (3): 30.

Scarano, Francisco A. 1984. *Sugar and Slavery in Puerto Rico: The Plantation Economy of Ponce, 1800–1850.* Madison: University of Wisconsin Press.

———. 1993. *Puerto Rico: Cinco Siglos de Historia.* San Juan, Puerto Rico: McGraw-Hill Interamericana.

Schemmer, Ben, and Bruce Cossaboom. 1970. "Culebra Act II: House Panel Reschedules Hearings." *Armed Forces Journal* (June 6): 16–20.

Schemmer, Ben, Clare Lewis et al. 1970. "Culebra: Navy Focus on Cinclant's Bull's-Eye Is Way Off Target, But May Be Coming into Range." *Armed Forces Journal* (May 23): 28–39.

Schrecker, Ellen. 1994. *The Age of McCarthyism: A Brief History with Documents.* Boston: Bedford Books.

Senior, Clarence. 1947. "The Puerto Rican Migrant in St. Croix." Río Piedras, Puerto Rico: Social Science Research Center, University of Puerto Rico.

Serrano, Basilio. 1998. "'Rifle, Cañón y Escopeta!' A Chronicle of the Puerto Rican Student Union." In *The Puerto Rican Movement: Voices from the Diaspora*, edited by Andrés Torres and José E. Velázquez. Philadelphia: Temple University Press.

Shanahan, John J. 2001. Declaration of John J. Shanahan. The Commonwealth of Puerto Rico v. Hon. Donald Rumsfeld et al. United States District Court for the District of Columbia.

Simbulan, Roland. 1983. *The Bases of Our Insecurity: A Study of the U.S. Military Bases in the Philippines.* Quezon City, Philippines: BALAI Fellowship.

Simich, Laura. 1991. "The Corruption of a Community's Economic and Political Life:

The Cruise Missile Base in Comiso." In *The Sun Never Sets: Confronting the Network of Foreign U.S. Military Bases*, edited by Joseph Gerson and Bruce Birchard. Boston: South End Press.

Smith, Daniel. 2000. "The Disappearing Welcome Mat." *Weekly Defense Monitor* (Center for Defense Information) 4 (38).

Sorenson, David. 1998. *Shutting Down the Cold War: The Politics of Military Base Closure*. New York: St. Martin's Press.

Sprout, Harold, and Margaret Sprout. 1939. *The Rise of American Naval Power, 1776–1918*. Princeton: Princeton University Press.

Steif, William. 1992. "Puerto Rico's Watergate." *Progressive* 56 (October): 28–31.

Stetson, Conn, and Byron Fairchild. 1960. *The Framework of Hemispheric Defense*. Washington, D.C.: Office of the Chief of Military History, Department of the Army.

Suárez, Manuel. 1987. *Requiem on Cerro Maravilla: The Police Murders in Puerto Rico and the U.S. Government Cover-Up*. Maplewood, N.J.: Waterfront Press.

Susser, Ida. 1982. *Norman Street: Poverty and Politics in an Urban Neighborhood*. New York: Oxford University Press.

———. 1985. "Union Carbide and the Community Surrounding It: The Case of a Community in Puerto Rico." *International Journal of Health Services* 15 (4): 561–583.

———. 1992. "Women as Political Actors in Rural Puerto Rico: Continuity and Change." In *Anthropology and the Global Factory*, edited by Frances A. Rothstein and Michael Blim. New York: Bergin and Garvey.

Tarrow, Sidney. 1994. *Power in Movement: Social Movements, Collective Action, and Mass Politics in the Modern State*. New York: Cambridge University Press.

Torres, Analisa. 1981. "The U.S. Naval Presence in Vieques, Puerto Rico and the Rise of the Political Opposition, 1940–1980." B.A. thesis. Department of Romance Language and Literature. Harvard University, Cambridge, Mass.

Trías Monge, José. 1997. *Puerto Rico: The Trials of the Oldest Colony in the World*. New Haven: Yale University Press.

Tugwell, Rexford G. 1976. *The Stricken Land: The Story of Puerto Rico*. New York: Greenwood Press.

UMET (Universidad Metropolitana), New Jersey Institute of Technology y el Centro de Acción Ambiental. 2000. Resumen de Estudios y Datos Ambientales en Vieques.

UPR (University of Puerto Rico). 1943. "Report on the Possibilities of Utilizing Navy Lands in Vieques Island for a Resettlement Project." Agricultural Experiment Station, Department of Agricultural Economics, Puerto Rico.

U.S. Department of Defense. 1981. Summary of Completed Military Base Economic Adjustment Projects, 1961–1981. November.

———. 1986. "Twenty-five Years of Civilian Reuse: Summary of Completed Military Base Economic Adjustment Projects." Pentagon, Washington, D.C.

———. 1994. "The Relationship between Base Closures/Realignments and Non–Department of Defense Federal Costs." Pentagon, Washington, D.C.

U.S. House. 1973. Congressional Record. Proceedings and Debates. 93d Congress, 1st session. No. 16.

———. 1981. Committee on Armed Services. Report of the Panel to Review the Status of Navy Training Activities on the Island of Vieques, Puerto Rico. 96th Congress, 2d session. No. 31.

———. 1994. Subcommittee on Insular and International Affairs of the Committee on

Natural Resources. Vieques Land Transfer Act of 1994: Hearings on H.R. 3831. 103d Congress, 2d session.

U.S. Navy. 1978. "Vieques Community Action Plan." Archivo Histórico, Vieques, Puerto Rico.

———. 1999. "The National Security Need for Vieques."

U.S. Senate. 1999. Committee on Armed Services. Report of the Special Panel on Military Operations on Vieques: Hearing before the Committee on Armed Services. 106th Congress, 1st session.

Wagenheim, Kal. 1964. "Vieques: Tragic Island." *San Juan Review* (June): 7–46.

Wagenheim, Kal, and Olga Jiménez de Wagenheim. 1994. *The Puerto Ricans: A Documentary History*. Princeton and New York: Markus Wiener Publishers.

Weigley, Russell. 1993. "The American Military and the Principle of Civilian Control from McClellan to Powell." *Journal of Military History* 57 (5): 27–58.

Weisgall, Jonathan.1994. *Operation Crossroads: The Atomic Tests at Bikini Atoll*. Annapolis, Md.: Naval Institute Press.

Weisskoff, Richard. 1985. *Factories and Food Stamps: The Puerto Rican Model of Development*. Baltimore: Johns Hopkins University Press.

Wolf, Charlotte. 1969. *Garrison Community: A Study of an Overseas American Military Colony*. Westport, Conn.: Greenwood Press.

Young, Alma H., and Dion E. Phillips. 1986. *Militarization in the Non-Hispanic Caribbean*. Boulder, Colo.: Lynne Rienner Publishers.

Zeimet, Roger T. 1985. "Vieques Island, Puerto Rico, U.S. Marine Corps Camp García, 1959–1978." In *United States Navy and Marine Corps Bases, Overseas*, edited by Paolo Coletta with K. Jack Bauer. Westport, Conn.: Greenwood Press.

Zenón, Carlos. 1979. "The Fight for Vieques." *Puerto Rico Libre*, May/June. Ruth Reynolds Collection, Centro de Estudios Puertorriqueños, Hunter College, New York.

———. 1982. Interview by Proyecto Caribeño de Justicia y Paz Research Team. Archivo Histórico, Fuerte Conde de Mirasol, Vieques, Puerto Rico.

Index

About the Author

Katherine T. McCaffrey is an assistant professor of anthropology at Montclair State University.